LOOKING LIKE THE ENEMY

Looking Like the Enemy

Japanese Mexicans, the Mexican State, and US Hegemony, 1897–1945

JERRY GARCÍA

THE UNIVERSITY OF ARIZONA PRESS
TUCSON

Para mis padres,

Gloria Torres y Ruben D. García

The University of Arizona Press
www.uapress.arizona.edu

First paperback edition 2018

ISBN-13: 978-0-8165-3025-0 (cloth)
ISBN-13: 978-0-8165-3809-6 (paper)

Cover design by David Drummond
Cover image courtesy of Archivo General de la Nación, Fondo Hermanos Mayo, concentrados sobre 363

Publication of this book is made possible in part by funding from the Eastern Washington University College of Social and Behavioral Sciences and Social Work and the Eastern Washington University Chicano Education Program.

Library of Congress Cataloging-in-Publication Data
García, Jerry, 1963–
Looking like the enemy : Japanese Mexicans, the Mexican state, and US hegemony, 1897–1945 / Jerry García.
pages cm
Includes bibliographical references and index.
ISBN 978-0-8165-3025-0 (hardback)
1. Japanese—Mexico—History—20th century. 2. Japanese—Mexico—Ethnic identity. 3. Japanese—Mexico—Evacuation and relocation, 1942–1945. 4. World War, 1939–1945—Social aspects—Mexico. 5. Mexico—Foreign relations—United States. 6. United States—Foreign relations—Mexico. I. Title.
F1392.J3G37 2014
327.7207309'04—dc23

2013034400

Printed in the United States of America
⊗ This paper meets the requirements of ANSI/NISO Z39.48-1992 (Permanence of Paper).

Contents

Illustrations

Figures

Tables

Acknowledgments

Many individuals helped bring this book to its final conclusion that I wish to acknowledge. From inception to completion, this has been a long and interesting journey. The genesis of this book began when I was eighteen years of age as I spent three years at Camp Zama, Japan, serving in the US Army—it seems like a lifetime ago. It was during my time in Japan that I first learned of the movement of Japanese to Mexico. My interest in Japanese immigration to Mexico was piqued in graduate school during a seminar course I took with my adviser at Washington State University, Professor John Kicza, as I read Frederick Katz's *Secret War in Mexico*. I owe a great deal to John Kicza, the Department of History, and Washington State University for their generous financial support. John grounded me well in the historiography of Latin America and especially Mexico. His support and encouragement during the ebb and flow of graduate school were instrumental in keeping me focused. I also thank Noriko Kawamura, who grounded me in Japanese history, and Paul Hirt (now at Arizona State University), for his advice and friendship. Other members of the department that I wish to acknowledge include Thomas Kennedy, Richard Hume, Leroy Ashby, Sue Armitage, David Coon, and David Stratton. I also wish to thank Linda Trinh Vo (now at UC Irvine), for her encouragement and advice as I completed graduate school. Lastly, Peter Utgaard, fellow graduate student and friend, now at Cuyamaca College.

I was fortunate to have started my academic career at Iowa State University. The time that I spent in Iowa and Iowa State University will always remain important, especially regarding my intellectual development. The history department at Iowa State welcomed me with open arms. I would like to acknowledge the financial support I received from the Department of History at Iowa State, which allowed me to continue my research on the Japanese diaspora in Mexico. I wish to acknowledge my first chair, George McJimsey, for helping me settle into my first academic job. The following individuals provided strong emotional support and friendship that sustained me during my stay at Iowa State University: Sidner Larson, Devery

Fairbanks, Caskey Russell, Larry Gross, and Ed Munoz. I also wish to acknowledge Bernhard Rieger and a friendship that began as newly minted assistant professors at Iowa State University, and Elizabeth Buettner at the University of York for her hospitality and friendship. Also, for their friendship and collegiality, I thank Sharon Bird, James Andrews, Michael Bailey, John Monroe, David Hollander, Xiaoyuan Liu, David Wilson, Hamilton Cravens, Pamela Riney-Kehrberg, Brian Behnken, Amy Bix, Charles Dobbs, and Wayne Osborn. A special acknowledgment goes to Andrejs Plakans, my last chair at Iowa State University. Andrejs became friend, mentor, and racquetball partner, and his counsel I will always carry with me.

In the years leading up to the publication of this book I have used a number of sources in Mexico City, Oaxaca, and Chiapas. I wish to extend a tremendous amount of gratitude and thanks to the staff at the Archivo General de la Nación (AGN). A special thanks goes to Joel Zúniga and the staff in Galería 2 of the AGN, which holds the archive of the Dirreción General de Investigaciones Políticas y Sociales, where the secret intelligence police files are. Also special thanks to Erika Ive Gutierrez Mosqueda at the AGN, who made every effort to accommodate my requests, no matter how bizarre or absurd they sounded. I also thank El Colegio de México and the late Profesora María Elena Ota Mishima, whose path-breaking work on the Japanese in Mexico echoes throughout my book. Maria Elena also shared with me original documents from the first Japanese immigrants to Mexico who landed in Chiapas. She remains the first and only professor who greeted me with a shot of tequila as I entered her office! I also thank the staff at the US National Archives and Records Administration II at College Park, Maryland, for their help in finding important US and Mexican documents pertaining to Japanese in Mexico and for their patience. A thank you goes to Lorraine Orlandi, a freelance journalist based in Mexico who conducted very important interviews with descendants of the original Japanese immigrants who came to Mexico. Lorraine generously shared those interviews with me. Thanks to Yuya Kiuchi for translating important Japanese documents. I wish to acknowledge Julia Taylor for images she provided. Also, thanks to Sean O'Brien-Hickey, who worked many hours compiling and organizing the data sets on Japanese immigrants in Mexico. A special thanks goes to Evelyn Hu-Dehart, who provided critical feedback on parts of the manuscript and encouraged me to complete this study. And, to the late James L. Tigner, whose work on the Japanese in Latin America and Mexico guided a new generation of scholars.

At Michigan State University I found my intellectual community and extended family, which provided the support and guidance to keep this project alive. The history department granted crucial financial support to complete the research for this book. I especially thank my chair while at Michigan State University, Mark Kornbluh, for his support. The following individuals became not only an extended *familia* but also colleagues who provided a vibrancy that is rare in academia: Estrella Torrez, Javier Pescador, and LaShawn D. Harris. Theresa Melendez and Dionicio Valdes, co-founders of the second doctorate program in chicana/o studies in the nation (Michigan State University), provided important mentorship and guidance. My experience at MSU was enriched by Theresa and Dionicio's friendship and mentoring. I owe deep gratitude to the following individuals: Benjamin T. Smith, whose love for Mexico and its archives we share, but more important, for challenging me on many fronts regarding the Japanese experience in Mexico and pushing me to complete this book; Pedro G. Dagbovie, whose inner spirit is much like a Motor City prizefighter that both inspires and humbles at the same time; and Dylan Miner, a true scholar-activist-artist who provided important feedback on my discussion on popular culture and art in this book. I also want to thank the following individuals for their friendship and support while at Michigan State University: Nwando Achebe, David Bailey, Kirsten Fermaglich, Leslie Moch, John Waller, Peter Alegi, Peter Beattie, Walter Hawthorne, Edward Murphy, Ethan Segal, Sayuri Shimizu, Michael Stamm, Gordon Stewart, Thomas Summerhill, Samuel T. Thomas, Lisa Fine, Lewis Siegelbaum, Erica Windler, Susan Sleeper-Smith, Anna Pegler-Gordon, Scott Michaelsen, Diana Rivera, and Luis A. García. I also was fortunate to work with a number of students at Michigan State University whom I wish to acknowledge for teaching me a few things along the way: Luis Moreno, Jose Moreno, Todd Mireles, Antonio Vasquez, Marshanda Smith, Nora Salas, Elizabeth O'Brien, Sierra Lopes, Claudia Gonzalez, Micalee Sullivan, Aaron Van Oousterhout, Jose Villagran, and Oscar Vega.

I also wish to thank Eastern Washington University (EWU) for their support and allowing me some time away from my director's duties to complete this book especially Rodolfo Arvealo and Vickie Shields. Thank you to Stacy Warren at EWU who helped with maps and introduced me to Tom Wickesser, a student at EWU, who created the maps in the introduction and chapter 6. The following individuals provided support and friendship at Eastern Washington University: Edward Slack Jr., Liping Zhu, Larry Cebula, Sarah Lee Monroe, Raphael Guilory, Erika Enciso-Castillo, Eric

Palomino, Robert Bartlett, Deirdre Almeida, Aurelia Murguia, and Jennifer Nunez. A special acknowledgement to Ivan José Martinez, my research assistant since I arrived at Eastern and wise beyond his years.

Through the years, a number of people were willing to listen to my stories of Japanese in Mexico, some very politely, that I wish to acknowledge: my long-time mentor, friend, and colleague Gilberto García, Rogelio Riojas, Linda Heidenreich, Jorge Madrazo, Erasmo Gamboa, Betty Kumiko Samulitis, Esperanca Camara, Yola Habif, Cynthia Vila, and the late Juan Gabriel Ibarra. As a first-generation college graduate, I have always had the support of my family, especially my siblings, Ruben "Mosquito" García, Yolanda García, Juan García, Patricío García, and Casey García. I also want to thank all of my *sobrinas* and *sobrinos*, too many to list here, for their inspiration. Lastly, I dedicate this book to Ruben D. García and Gloria Torres, my parents. A special thanks goes to Kristen A. Buckles, acquisition editor at the University of Arizona Press, and to Nicholle Lutz, production editor for this book. I wish to convey my thanks to the University of Arizona Press anonymous reviewers.

Abbreviations

AGN	Archivo General de la Nación (General Archives of the Nation)
CJAM	Comité Japonés de Ayuda Mutua (Japanese Mutual Aid Committee)
CPI	Committee of Public Information
FBI	Federal Bureau of Investigation
IPS	Investigaciones Políticas y Sociales (Social and Political Investigations)
LEAR	Liga de Escritores y Artistas Revolucionarios (League of Revolutionary Writers and Artists)
NARA	National Archives and Records Administration
OIAA	Office of Inter-American Affairs
PAU	Pan American Union
PCM	Partida Comunista Mexicanos (Mexican Communist Party)
SRE	Secretaría Relaciones Exteriores (Secretariat of Foreign Relations)
TGP	Taller de Gráfica Popular (People's Graphic Workshop)

LOOKING LIKE THE ENEMY

Introduction

The Japanese Experiment in Mexico

Hemos nacido en México, trabajamos en México, vivimos en México.
(*We were born in Mexico, we work in Mexico, we live in Mexico.*)
—Ernesto González Gálvez, "Mexico-Japón: a un siglo del primer encuentro" (1997)

On the morning of August 18, 1897, Mexican police awakened the Japanese consul general in Mexico City, Murota Toshibumi. Murota was informed that eight Japanese from the Enomoto Colony in Chiapas journeyed nearly thirty days through mountains and were in the capital waiting to see him. Five of the Japanese staggered into the capital together, and over the course of several days three additional Japanese appeared. What barely resembled clothing clung raggedly on the disheveled and malnourished bodies, with their faces so sunburned and swollen that the immigrants were unrecognizable as they stood there before Murota. Consul Murota immediately sent a telegram to the foreign minister, Shigenobu Okuma, saying:

> The police took five emigrants from Chiapas who had walked a great distance into custody. They are seeking the cancellation of the contract with the company and wish to return to Japan. I was able to reason with them and convinced them to return to the colony. I urgently request that funds be sent for their maintenance immediately.[1]

The eight Japanese immigrants that appeared in Mexico City at the doorsteps of the Japanese legation, along with the other Enomoto colonists, represented the ambitious endeavor to create the first Japanese colony in Mexico, which was intertwined with the expansionist platform of the Japanese government of the late nineteenth and early twentieth centuries and Porfirio Díaz's attempt to modernize Mexico with immigrant labor and

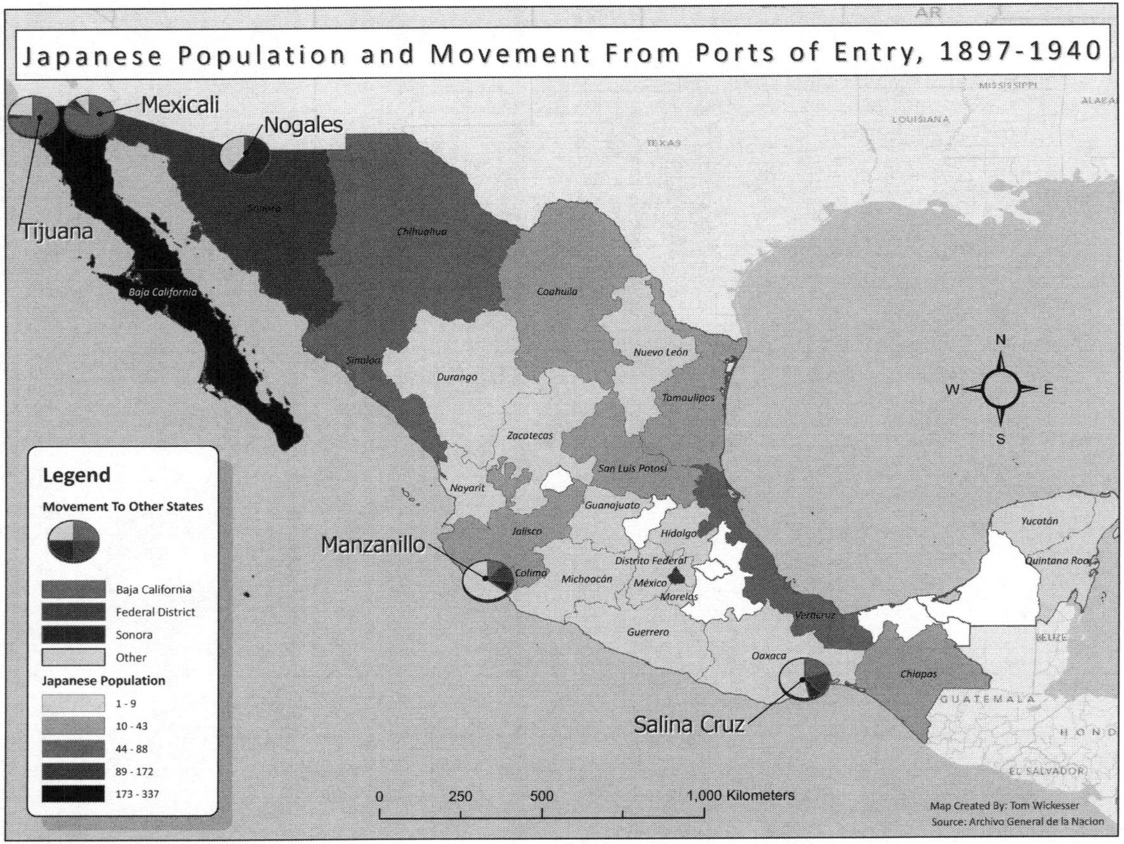

Figure 0.1. Japanese population and movement from ports of entry, 1897–1940. Although the beginning of Japanese immigration to Mexico began in Chiapas, by the early twentieth century the majority of Japanese migrated to the northern region of Mexico, with the largest enclave in Baja, California.

entrepreneurs. Over the next five decades the ebb and flow of Japanese immigration to Mexico mirrored the turbulent and vacillating trilateral relations between Mexico, Japan, and the United States.

Although World War II exacerbated Mexican relations with Japanese immigrants, ambivalent attitudes toward the Japanese had existed since they had arrived during the late nineteenth century. To understand wartime relations, it is necessary to trace the experience of Japanese Mexicans back over the fifty years before their persecution, which is the aim of this book. The treatment of Japanese in Mexico during these periods was predicated on several intersecting positions, which are traced through important historical periods that coincided with profound change in Mexico and Japan. The advent of Japanese emigration to Mexico developed during the late *Porfiriato* and coincided with the Mexican Revolution, the postrevolutionary period and reconstruction of the 1920s, and the tumultuous 1930s that included the rise of Mexican nationalism. Consequently, Japanese immigration is placed along the contours of Mexican history of the late nineteenth and early twentieth centuries and is discussed within the broader context of Mexican modernity, revolution, and reconstruction. At the same time, Japanese emigration occurred during rapid change in Japanese society that began with the Meiji Restoration of 1868, Japanese industrialization, militarization, and the rise of an expansionist empire that utilized conquest, occupation, and emigration as a means to colonize and settle outside of its national domain. However, in such places as Mexico, Japan deployed a settlement process, rather than forced occupation.

The history of the Japanese in Mexico would not be complete without a discussion on United States, Japanese, and Mexican relations. The challenging relationships that developed between these nations placed Mexico in a diplomatic quandary as it enjoyed cordial relations with both countries. Simultaneously, during the first half of the twentieth century, US-Japanese relations spiraled in a downward trajectory, with Mexico constantly maneuvering to deflect US imposition on its sovereignty that often challenged its relationship with Japan. The 2,000-mile border the United States and Mexico shared meant that US domestic and foreign policy initiatives impacted Mexico, especially regarding the Japanese diaspora. The rise of US imperialism and hegemony in Latin America affected the Japanese diaspora throughout the Western hemisphere. Finally, the entrance of the United States and Mexico into World War II terminated Japanese emigration to Mexico until the postwar period.

Mexico received immigrants at a much lower rate than other countries in the Americas, and the Japanese in Mexico, compared with Chinese or

US citizens, were one of the smaller immigrant groups to Mexico. Yet, the presence of Japanese in Mexico justifies study for a number of reasons. There is an obvious gap of scholarship and literature on Japanese immigration to Mexico. Most of the English language scholarship on the Japanese in the Americas tends to focus on regions outside of Mexico and largely on the Japanese American, Brazilian, and Peruvian experience. Studies on the Japanese beyond the United States are few. There are approximately 100 volumes that explore Japanese emigration to various regions of Latin America.[2] The pioneers of these specific fields include C. Harvey Gardiner, James L. Tigner, Iyo Kunimoto, and María Elena Ota Mishima. With the exception of Ota Mishima, what the other authors have in common are English language publications that examine individual countries or are sweeping studies of the Japanese in Latin America. These early pioneers focused primarily on the movement and settlement of Japanese throughout the Americas, leaving the more nuanced studies to later generations. This book builds upon the foundational work listed above, in addition to the next generation of scholars.

The last decade has seen an increasing body of literature examining the Asian experience, more specifically, the Japanese experience in Latin America. For example, Jeffrey Lesser's, *Negotiating National Identity: Immigrants, Minorities, and the Struggle for Ethnicity in Brazil* charts new territory by attempting to break through Brazil's bifurcated notions of race and ethnicity that is largely based on the black/white paradigm. *Negotiating National Identity* brings in the experiences of Japanese, Chinese, Middle Eastern, and African groups in Brazil, arguing that Brazil's national identity is partially attributed to the various groups that immigrated to Brazil in the early twentieth century. Lesser's study examines how the Japanese, Chinese, and others challenged Brazil's construction of whiteness and, in the process, brought out the specifics of the individual ethnic experience in Brazil. A more recent publication that examines mixed identity is Rudy P. Guevarra's *Becoming Mexipino: Multiethnic Identities and Communities in San Diego*. Although not specifically about Japanese, Guevarra's study provides important scholarship on the complex nature of multiethnic groups within the confines of traditional communities and enclaves. Like the Japanese Mexicans in my study, Mexipinos negotiated a delicate space that required the formation of important relations with various organizations and groups and created lasting ties through intermarriages.[3]

New Worlds, New Lives: Globalization and the People of Japanese Descent in the Americas and from Latin America in Japan is an anthology edited by Lane Ryo Hirabayashi, Akemi Kikumura-Yano, and James Aikira Hirabayashi that examines the Japanese experience in Latin America, especially from the *Nikkei* perspective.[4] This anthology provides excellent scholarship on a number of different Latin American countries, including Brazil, Bolivia, Peru, Paraguay, and Chile, as well as the United States. Although no chapter is devoted to Mexico, *New Worlds, New Lives* nevertheless contributes to the important historiography of Japanese in Latin America and examines the movement of Latin Americans of Japanese ancestry back to Japan. More important, this anthology delves into ideas of identity, gender, place, and culture.

Studies by Lane Ryo Hirabayashi examine not only the Japanese American experience but also the Japanese diaspora in Latin America, particularly regarding Japanese internment in the hemisphere during World War II.[5] The study by Daniel M. Masterson with Sayaka Funada-Classen, *The Japanese in Latin America*, is a broad examination of the general Japanese experience in Latin America that includes chapters on Brazil, Peru, and Mexico. Masterson's attempt at synthesis takes away from the subtleties of the Japanese experience in the various Latin American countries. Nevertheless, Masterson's book helps fill the gulf of scholarship on the Japanese in Latin America.[6]

Regarding the scholarship on Japanese in Mexico, the gap widens. Only a handful of books published on the Japanese in Mexico exist, and all in a language other than English (Japanese and Spanish). The late María Elena Ota Mishima's *Siete Migraciones Japoneses, 1890–1970*, and Enrique Cortés's *Relaciones entre Mexico y Japón durante el Porfiriato*, are the only two books in the Spanish language that discuss at length Japanese emigration to Mexico.[7] More important, Ota Mishima is the only scholar to recognize the importance of the Enomoto Colony, the first official settlement of Japanese in Mexico and Latin America in general. To say that a significant void of scholarship exists on Japanese in Mexico is an understatement.[8] In fact, *Looking Like the Enemy* is the first full-length study of the Japanese in Mexico in English. Japanese sources are more numerous.[9] For example, Yukihiro Tsunoyama's *Enomoto Buyo (Takeaki) to Mekishiko Shokumin Iju* (*Takeaki Enomoto and Migration to Mexican Settlements*) provides an excellent biography of the Enomoto Colony's benefactor, Enomoto Takeaki. Another influential and useful Japanese source is Masaaki Kodama's *Nihon imin-shi Kenkyu josetsu* (*An Introduction to the Study of Japanese Immigration History*). Kodama's study provides an overview of the various immigration companies responsible for taking Japanese people overseas. This source richly details the causes for the emigration out of Japan in the late nineteenth century by examining internal and external factors. Lastly, a committee of Japanese scholars compiled the *Nihon Mekishiko Imin* (*Japanese Emigration to Mexico*), an extensive overview of the movement of Japanese to Mexico.[10]

It is fair to say that most scholarly material on immigration and colonization in Mexico generally fails to mention the first Japanese arrivals in Mexico or their attempts at settlement in Chiapas. By and large, scholars have concentrated their considerations of Japanese immigration to the northern regions of Mexico, and while these studies contribute to the scholarship on Japanese in Mexico, there is no clear contextualization of the Japanese experience within the formative period of Mexican history during the first half of the twentieth century. And, unlike some recent scholarship such as Jeffrey Lesser's work on the Japanese in Brazil, studies on Mexican Japanese remain general and focused heavily on statistical data, leaving out the rich narrative of the Japanese lived experience. Consequently, most studies on the Japanese in Mexico simply relegate them to victims that lacked a voice or agency in relations with the state. My book makes important distinctions. First, it brings the Japanese voice to the forefront and, by uncovering previously unseen documents, demonstrates how the Japanese displayed forms of agency and utilized their talents to protect themselves during trying times. This study builds on the earlier work of Mexican historian María Elena Ota Mishima and takes into consideration the larger context of Mexican history during the first half of the twentieth century.[11]

Second, one scholar concluded that, between 1868 and 1941, 42 percent of all Japanese immigrants went to some place in Latin America. Yet, most of the scholarship on Japanese has focused on the east-west dynamic or the movement from Asia to the United States. My book situates the Japanese experience beyond the east-west paradigm and broadens our understanding of the hemispheric experience of Asians.[12] Along these same lines, this study provides interconnected threads of Western hemispheric Orientalism as defined by historian Erika Lee, using Edward W. Said's seminal discussion on Orientalism as a place not only in Asia but also in the imagination of Western European powers and the United States. Said states that Britain and France became so obsessed with the Orient that it came to define them as colonial powers. Just as important is how Western powers "orientalized" the Orient through images, academic discourse, colonialism; in short, Orientalism became a Western style of thought that juxtaposed the West and the East while simultaneously creating the foundation for the reconfiguration of the East as seen through Western eyes.[13] Similar to Lee, I argue that Asian groups in the Americas such as the Chinese, Japanese, Koreans, and Southeast Asians were homogenized, configured as inferior groups, and made to feel outside the orbit of the United States and other nations in the Western hemisphere. Regardless of location, the Chinese and Japanese in the Western hemisphere faced similar circumstances of racialism or an unequal treatment compared with the native population that transcended national boundaries.[14]

Third, the Japanese movement to Mexico can also be compared and contrasted with the Chinese experience, the largest Asian diaspora in Mexico.[15] Indeed, each group had distinct experiences that are explored while probing why the Japanese were viewed differently from the Chinese by Mexican society. For example, unlike the Japanese, no national or international celebrations have commemorated the arrival of the Chinese to Mexico, despite their great numbers. This book argues that the Japanese negotiated a distinct space within Mexican culture where their identity and ethnicity was maintained and was rarely challenged or was ignored due to a perception that the Japanese displayed markers of whiteness that were associated with Western imperialism and power. These perceptions were magnified as Japan defeated long-standing empires in the East and challenged Western hegemony in the region. As Japan strengthened its world position, national characteristics such as colonialism, expansionism, occupation, and strength became cornerstones of the empire, and Japanese nationals worldwide were seen in a similar fashion that garnered both negative and positive reactions. This dichotomy placed the Japanese in an unusual space within Mexican society where, on the one hand, they were seen as important contributors to Mexico but, on the other hand, they were often despised based on their Asiatic origins imbued with the negative markers that Mexicans often attached to the Chinese diaspora.

By studying the Japanese, we observe the process of racialism that migrated from the Chinese experience to the Japanese and seamlessly crossed the national boundaries of the United States and Mexico, which in turn provides insight to the changing Mexican attitudes regarding immigration. Initially, Mexico encouraged immigrants in order to stimulate industrialization and modernization. However, Mexico was keen on importing European immigrants. When large numbers of European immigrants balked, Mexico shifted its recruitment efforts to what it considered second-tier immigrants: Japanese, Chinese, Koreans, and Lebanese. This modification resulted in Mexico altering its view on immigration from one strictly based on economic necessity to one based on culture, especially regarding what it meant to be Mexican. As Mexico altered its stance on immigrants, a debate emerged within Mexico on what it meant to be Mexican.

Finally, this study examines the changing attitudes related to broader relations between Mexico and the United States. Until recently, it was assumed that Mexico had very little agency in its relations with its northern neighbor. But in fact, Mexico used a diplomatic version of what James Scott termed "weapons of the weak" in order to challenge the hegemony of the United States.[16] In this manner, Mexico and the United States chose diametrically dissimilar positions regarding their treatment and attitude toward the Japanese. By comparing and contrasting these positions, it helps us understand the complex relations that developed that included conflicting immigration policy, a shared and chaotic border, anti-Asian sentiments, and significant Asian populations. The Japanese that resided in Mexico prior to World War II had an unusual experience because of their proximity to the United States, and the ambivalent relations between Japan, Mexico, and the United States made that experience increasingly formidable. And as Mexico experienced revolution and transformation in the early twentieth century, the Japanese became entangled with various political factions and administrations in Mexican history.

This study is based on a wide array of Mexican, Japanese, and US archival sources. Information for this study was gleaned from Mexican and US census records, Mexican and US periodicals, immigration reports from US and Mexican officials, and oral interviews conducted by government officials, journalists, and scholars. The holdings of the US National Archives and Records Administration (NARA) contain a large amount of information on the Japanese in Mexico, especially for the period prior to and during World War II. Additionally, Japanese language publications were used to provide some insight into the views from Japan regarding the movement of Japanese to Mexico.

The primary Mexican sources are the Archivo General de la Nación (AGN), which holds a vast amount of information on the Japanese experience in Mexico, and the Secretariat of Foreign Relations (secretaría de relaciones exteriores, SRE). The papers of Mexican presidents during the first half of the twentieth century contain detailed information on the Japanese experience. Important to any scholar on the Japanese experience are the papers and records of the Lázaro Cárdenas (1934–40) and Manuel Ávila Camacho (1940–46) presidential administrations. These two holdings contain important documents, images, and narratives on the Japanese during the 1930s and 1940s. The AGN also holds nearly 3,000 immigration case files on Japanese immigrants, each of which contains a wealth of information on marriage status, gender, religion, date of birth, place of birth, occupation, family, and destination within Mexico.

Of special note is the recently opened Dirección General de Investigaciones Políticas y Sociales; the secret intelligence files were made available in 1999. These files hold detailed information on the surveillance, detention, and arrest of Japanese Mexicans and nationals during the 1930s and 1940s. More important, these files provide some indication of the effort by the Mexican state to collaborate with the United States to counter Axis penetration in Mexico. Simultaneously, these archives provide insight into the treatment of individuals in the Japanese diaspora in Mexico during World War II. Lastly, gleaned from these files is the sense of agency and resistance the Japanese diaspora displayed under the difficult circumstances of World War II. The history of the Japanese in Mexico and Latin America was initiated by the need for modernization: Mexico wanted it and Japan needed to expand it. These national initiatives coalesced in the late nineteenth century and created the first and last government-sponsored immigration project in Mexico, but it started nearly fifty years of Japanese movement to Mexico.

The Book

The organization of my book is primarily chronological. I follow this approach in order to capture the unstable and erratic state of Mexican history and society during the first half of the twentieth century. At the same time, Mexican history is viewed through the lens of the Japanese experience during the nearly fifty years from their arrival to the end of World War II. After an opening chapter that provides the background and causes of the movement of Japanese to Mexico, the rest of the book explores the importance of Mexican history and how it shaped the Japanese experience in Mexico. Chapter 1 also provides the parameters for the triangular conflict that emerged between the United States, Mexico, and Japan in the early decades of the twentieth century.

Chapter 2 presents the reason for Japanese emigration in the early twentieth century and how it intersected with the Mexican Revolution. This chapter also discusses the impact of hemispheric Orientalism directed not only at the Chinese but also at the Japanese diaspora. This chapter studies the various roles of the Japanese population in Mexico that included settler, farmer, merchant, victim, and soldier. The involvement of the

Japanese as combatants in the Mexican Revolution is not well known, and an attempt is made to explain their participation.

Chapter 3 discusses the emerging formation of the Mexican state in the postrevolutionary period (1920–30), which created a system where the central government was not a leviathan forcing its will on the people. Rather, due to strong local and regional grassroots organizations and *caciques* (local or regional bosses), many regions throughout Mexico enjoyed substantial autonomy from a state-centered apparatus.[17] Thus, hegemony by the state was reached not by force but through negotiations with local and regional players that continually challenged the power of the central government. Chapter 3 argues that this "decentered" political apparatus created in Mexico after the 1920s contributed to a unique Japanese Mexican experience. Ultimately, for the Japanese in these regions this meant that state and federal government directives such as those that threatened the livelihood of the Chinese diaspora during the Mexican Revolution and the 1930s had little to no impact on the Japanese until World War II, and even then, many Japanese escaped the most repressive measures through negotiations with local and regional strong men who ultimately challenged and resisted national war measures directed at the Japanese.

Chapter 4 is concerned with the aftermath of Pearl Harbor in Mexico and the treatment of the Japanese Mexican population. Prior to the bombing of Pearl Harbor, the Japanese existed under a shield of invisibility, partly due to their smaller number, but primarily attributed to their assimilation and mixed marriages. However, as Mexico began to collaborate with the United States to extinguish any Axis threat, this imperceptibility quickly disintegrated, and their demonization intensified. This reconfiguration of the Japanese in Mexico is to a large measure due to the barrage of US and Mexican propaganda. As a result, US hegemony blanketed the hemisphere with a racial ideology that viewed Japanese not only as the enemy but also as inferior, which ultimately resulted in the hemispheric roundups of individuals of Japanese ancestry.

Chapter 5 demonstrates the unstable position of Japanese once the United States and Mexico declared war on the Axis powers. Although Mexicans of Japanese ancestry appear to have been treated better than their counterparts in the United States, specific case studies reveal that regardless of their location in the Americas, Japanese were vulnerable to overzealous officials who viewed all Japanese with suspicion. The chapter also explores how Japanese Mexicans and nationals were hunted, detained, interrogated, and sent to concentration camps in Mexico or to the United States.

Finally, chapter 6 presents the Japanese Mexican experience during World War II, specifically by examining the Comité Japonés Ayuda de Mutua (Japanese Mutual Aid Committee), a semiautonomous and quasi-Japanese association that provided assistance, among other things, to the Japanese population. This chapter is also an overall study of the Japanese reaction to their forced relocation and displacement. The discussion in the chapter attempts to assess the varied treatment of the Japanese Mexicans within Mexico by providing a comparison with their counterparts in other regions of the Americas. This chapter also explores how the Japanese exhibited forms of agency. Part of the Japanese community responded by organizing and, through self-isolation, "cocooning" themselves amid the adverse climate of World War II. Overall, and compared with other countries, Mexico displayed a level of empathy toward its Japanese population during World War II that was based on nearly fifty years of immigration, settlement, and integration. The Mexican state also recognized its leverage against its northern neighbor during World War II and used that capability to manipulate the United States with a level of skill and discretion that paid dividends for Mexico and its Japanese population.

CHAPTER ONE

Japanese Mexicans, Immigration, and the Public Imagination, 1897–1910

It is something I carry inside me. I am Mexican, but I am also Japanese, . . . Our grandfathers and fathers just wanted to work hard and adapt to their new country. Now, we have a greater awareness and we want to preserve the memory of their contributions to Mexico.

Carmen Mitsui, Sansei, Acacoyagua, Chiapas, 1997

The state of Chiapas invokes images of indigenous groups, the Zapatista uprising that began in January 1994, the ancient ruins of Palenque, or perhaps even the lush coffee plantations along the region of Soconusco, but one does not associate the state with the origins of the Japanese diaspora in Latin America that began in 1897. The epigraph above is from a Japanese Mexican and descendant of one of the original Japanese immigrants to Mexico celebrating the 100-year anniversary of the arrival of the first Japanese to Mexico. These Japanese pioneers landed off the coast of Chiapas and initiated a movement that spread to almost all regions of Latin America by the first half of the twentieth century. While the 1999 Mexican census indicated the total number of Mexican Japanese at approximately 15,000, by 2012 that estimate had increased to roughly 35,000.[1]

One of those individuals is José Martín Nomura Hernandez, thirty-one, the current municipal president of Acacoyagua, Chiapas, a small community of 7,000 people located along the southeastern coastal plain of the state and the community nearest the site of the nineteenth-century Enomoto Colony. José Martín is the great grandson of Francisco Nomura, who immigrated in the early twentieth century and eventually married a Mexican woman. According to José Martín, since the early twentieth century individuals of Japanese ancestry have dominated the municipal government of Acacoyagua. Another resident of Acacoyagua is Carmen

Mitsui, the granddaughter of Hisakiti Mitsui, who was part of the original thirty-four Japanese who arrived in Mexico in 1897. José Martín Nomura and Carmen Mitsui are representative of the Nikkei in Mexico.[2]

By the end of the twentieth century and as the 1997 centennial anniversary emerged, many of the Japanese Mexicans began to search for answers regarding their origins and the important contributions their ancestors made to Mexico. Carmen Mitsui stated, "It is something I carry inside me. I am Mexican, but I am also Japanese, . . . Our grandfathers and fathers just wanted to work hard and adapt to their new country. Now we have a greater awareness and we want to preserve the memory of their contributions to Mexico."[3] Similar to the sentiment expressed in the epigraph, Carmen's devotion to Mexico is attributed to the overall integration of the Japanese into Mexican society, which is partially explained by the absence of Japanese women during the early years of immigration. Because of this scarcity, many of the Japanese men married Mexican women and converted from Buddhism to Catholicism, as mothers became conduits for Mexican culture. Although some Japanese customs remained from the earlier period, overall Mexican culture and customs subsumed most traces of Japanese origin. The search for answers regarding their origins has led individuals such as José Martín and Carmen back to their Japanese roots—many are eager to learn and share the contributions their ancestors made to the development of Mexico. Indeed, the thirty-four Japanese that arrived in Mexico in 1897 were the impetus for the thousands, even millions, of Japanese who eventually spread throughout Mexico and the Americas in the twentieth century.

This chapter covers Mexico's decision to encourage immigration in an effort to push Mexico toward industrialization and modernization. This in turn created a national debate on immigration that resulted in Mexico decelerating its momentum as it vacillated between integrating its indigenous population into the national domain and using immigrants to accelerate the assimilation of the native population and usher in modernity. The chapter also explores the motives for the movement of Japanese to Mexico, which resulted in the arrival of the Enomoto Colony of 1897. The Enomoto Colony became the catalyst for twentieth-century Japanese immigration to Mexico. Also discussed, and germane to this study, are the complex foreign relations that engulfed Mexico in the first decade of the twentieth century and eventually developed into the triangular conflict with the United States and Japan that affected immigration. The early twentieth century also represents the continuation of "hemispheric Orientalism" in the Americas that developed with the arrival of Chinese immigrants, who were often disparaged regardless of location. With the arrival of a significant number of Japanese immigrants to the United States, Canada, and other regions of Latin America, such as Mexico, the general public in these various locations imposed a similar assessment of Japanese immigrants.[4]

Mexico and the Immigration Question: The Illusion of Whiteness

Generally, Mexico experienced one of the smallest movements of immigrants during a period of mass migration to the Americas (1880s–1920s). Historian Jose Moya placed this small movement into perspective when he wrote, "More Europeans arrived in the United States in a busy week than arrived in Mexico during the entire 35-year-long *Porfiriato*."[5] Beyond what has already been mentioned, a lack of European enthusiasm for Mexico can be attributed to limited agricultural land, countryside dominated by an indigenous population, a government that provided little in economic aid, and obstacles to industrial development that hampered Mexico well into the twentieth century.[6] Furthermore, Mexico's unstable political climate during the nineteenth century contributed to unfavorable conditions for immigrants that included a war for independence, foreign intervention, and civil strife in the 1850s, which was halted with the French invasion and occupation of Mexico from 1862–67.

Mexico's first concerted attempt to attract immigrants, especially white ones, occurred during the liberal Republic of the mid-nineteenth century (1855–76). The rationale was to attract immigrants from all ethnicities and religious denominations throughout Europe to create an agrarian-based population of small farmers.[7] In fact, the Liberal government held in reserve lands for the expected movement of immigrants from Europe that never arrived.[8] Mexico's premature attempt signaled a major dilemma that plagued the country for most of the nineteenth century: the nonexistence of an infrastructure for industrialization and economic growth. Although a full economic analysis is beyond the scope of this chapter, until the late nineteenth century Mexico lacked a foundation to push it toward modernization. According to Stephen Haber, Mexico's greatest economic deterrent during the nineteenth century was the lack of national markets due to high transportation costs, as well as an economic contraction caused by widespread banditry and internal tariffs that existed into the 1890s.[9] Although the tariffs acted as a buffer against outside competition, they also hampered commercial growth and development.[10] The intellectual elites of the country, seeing this stagnation and following the United States, began to advocate for a larger movement of immigrants to Mexico as part of a determined drive toward industrialization.

By the 1870s Mexican newspapers were writing editorials on the virtues of encouraging European immigration: "Mexico needs immigrants from the western races, people of the Christian countries that can introduce the customs and morals of Christian civilization and its capital."[11] These editorials and statements point to a resolute attempt on part of the Mexican state to recruit European immigrants imbued with discernible qualities that would help Mexico modernize and to maintain whiteness as the preferred racialized marker of superiority. In the Mexican case, the binary model of so-called race relations ran along the white-indigenous dichotomy and during the early twentieth century became a tripartite system of white-indigenous-mestizo categorization, with the state often promoting the ideas of whitening for the indigenous and mestizo populations.

Porfirio Díaz's pro-immigration policies emerged during the late nineteenth century and promoted Mexico as a place of immense opportunities for immigrants. Simultaneously, as US citizens began to purchase large tracts of land in Mexico, they also engaged in the recruitment of other immigrants, primarily Americans, in order to sell the land they had bought for premium profits.[12] In order to lure immigrants, land barons and speculators embellished those opportunities and painted an idyllic and romanticized landscape where arable land was abundant, as well as other natural resources, especially those associated with agriculture. For example, ads placed in US newspapers and magazines "exaggerated the quality of the soil, the nature of crops produced, and the climate."[13] And yet, in some limited locations, immigrants were able to eke out a living. In small numbers, immigrants from many regions were enticed to Mexico, and through private enterprise they established colonies seeking to replicate the success stories they had heard. Generally, American and European groups with religious affiliations such as the Mormons and Mennonites, Catholic associations, and the Chinese established colonies. By the late nineteenth century the region of Soconusco in Chiapas had fifteen colonies established by private companies, including the Japanese Enomoto Colony. Later in the early twentieth century, Japanese established colonies in the northern regions of Baja California, Chihuahua, and Sonora. The Chinese were also heavily concentrated in the north. With a small yet diverse immigrant population, Mexico continued to struggle with whether or not immigration and immigrants were in its national interest. The national discourse on immigrants and immigration followed a similar path in other countries in the Americas.

In parallel to other nations in the Americas during the early twentieth century, Mexico flirted and embarked on a desultory "whitening" policy that encouraged European and US immigration under a misconception that only such groups could propel the country into modernity. During the late nineteenth and early twentieth centuries, several studies emerged in Mexico that examined the need for immigrants. *Estudio sobre Inmigracíon y Colonizacíon* (*Study on Immigration and Colonization*) by Miguel Ramos Lanz, published in 1897, examined and compared European immigration to the United States, Brazil, Argentina, Uruguay, and Chile. Ramos argued that each of these countries had embarked on a path toward industrialization and that their European-based population was a significant factor. Ramos's study also points out that each of these countries developed policies and had particular laws that regulated and encouraged the movement of immigrants. More important, Ramos made the following claim that advocated a similar path for Mexico: "We should receive all Europeans with open arms and facilitate their permanent movement among us. The European pauper is superior in its production and consumption abilities to the Mexican Indian."[14] Mexican intellectuals were not alone in this assessment. Foreign governments, companies, and individuals blamed Mexico's lack of industrialization and consumption of foreign goods on the indigenous population. The Imperial German Office of the Interior released a report on economic conditions in Mexico and advised investors of potential problems in Mexico with a focus on the native population, labor troubles, and the use of Asian labor. This report, filled with negative commentary about the indigenous population and Mexican society in general, suggested the recruitment of white immigrants as a solution to Mexico's so-called backwardness.[15]

Another study from the first years of the twentieth century promoted European immigration to Mexico and encouraged the miscegenation of Europeans with the indigenous population with the objective of strengthening (whitening) the native population.[16] Juxtaposing the merits of Europeans and the flaws of the indigenous population remained constant in the early twentieth century. Furthermore, Mexico viewed non-European immigrants as a detriment to their modernization and immigration schemes. In fact, Asian immigrants, particularly Chinese, were seen as being beneath the indigenous population and a threat to Mexican identity. In spite of this, the petit bourgeois elements of the Chinese and Japanese diasporas were seen as a necessity for the expansion of Mexico's economy.

Contrary to this necessity, or perhaps a by-product of it, was the general negative perception of Chinese. These views reached tragic heights for the Chinese during the first three decades of the twentieth century. However, unlike the United States, Mexico did not view Asians as monolithic. The Japanese, as a nation and people, were viewed as a rising power, industrious, and a group that had reached, at least militarily, parity with the West. Japan's rapid modernization resonated with some elements of the Mexican population, which created different opinions and approaches to the movement of immigrants to Mexico.

As Mexico debated immigration and how to integrate its large Indian population into the national domain, Mexican elites advocated the removal of the indigenous population from lands that were considered vital to economic development. The Mexican elites of Porfirian Mexico were also obsessed with European culture and, in an attempt to refine their suspect *criollo* standing, created a simulacrum of European sophistication and posture that attempted to rival the opulence of the colonial era elite. In general, Mexico's Indian population was viewed not only as backward but also as an obstacle to Mexico's modernization plans. These views were not new to the *Porfiriato* but can be seen throughout Mexican history.[17] The irony, of course, as many have pointed out, is that Benito Juarez was a full-blooded Zapotec Indian, and Porfirio Díaz was a mestizo of Mixtec origin, some say almost "pure-blooded."[18] These were characteristics that both used early in their careers to attract alliances as each utilized the indigenous and mestizo populations to fight wars, but as each became national figures they gradually soft-pedaled away from those identities.

Elements of Mexico's nineteenth-century elites known as the *cientificos* made up of financiers, technocrats, and intellectuals promoted an additional component of whiteness based on the ideas of French philosopher and positivist Auguste Comte, who argued that being white was "a stage of civilization rather than a biological condition."[19] However, unlike Brazil's bifurcated population or Argentina, which primarily had a large European population for most of the nineteenth century, Mexico had not only a significant Indian population but also one that had been thoroughly mixed and stratified by the beginning of the nineteenth century to include Indians, mestizos, criollos, and a small black population. And by the beginning of the twentieth century it is well known that all groups in Mexico were equal before the law, at least in theory.

Mexican society remained resistant to Lamarckian schemes or any strategy that challenged over 400 years of mestizaje.[20] The mestizo and white population included many of Mexico's leading intellectual elites. This meant that a biological whitening process in the same vein as the United States or Brazil that viewed hybrid societies as inferior to so-called pure races would not fit the Mexican experience and would certainly be looked upon with suspicion by mestizos and criollos that made up part of the intellectual strata of Mexican society.[21] More important, as Alan Knight states, the idea of race was fluid in Mexican society, where an Indian could become a mestizo based on ethnic identification, assimilation, and education rather than racial ascriptions, and where collective transition was part of Mexico's overall development.[22] In other words, who exactly was an "Indian" was subjective. Manuel Gamio suggested these ideas even earlier when he stated, "Men such as [Benito] Juarez or [Ignacio Manuel] Altamirano could not be considered as natives, despite their genetic status, since they had become fully incorporated in modern culture."[23] Although not all *científicos* prescribed a racist ideology, for many the discourse often revolved around the backwardness of the Indians and the poor capabilities of the mestizo.[24]

From the early twentieth century Mexico remained dubious regarding a large influx of immigrants, and with the rise of *indigenismo*, Mexicans became even more concerned with the type of immigrant.[25] One author suggests that intellectuals of Mexico were adamant that immigrants not come in significant numbers so as not to change the basic character of the country, *la Mexicanidad* or its Mexicanness, specifically those who were not considered "white."[26] Indeed, as Mexico began to exalt the indigenous and mestizo populations, commonly described as backward and mongrels, to a "respectable" status in society, many of their so-called negative markers were shifted to non-European immigrant groups, Asians in particular. Much of the anti-Chinese sentiments in Mexico were organic in nature, but also clearly drawn from the US propaganda that circulated in Mexico during the early twentieth century, including one pamphlet that read, "The Chinese were those that added more misery, more criminals, and more beggars to the Mexican society. They were weak, ugly and addicted to opium."[27] Anti-Chinese sentiments appeared in Mexico very early in the twentieth century, with individual Mexican states enacting their own anti-immigrant legislation or spewing hatred about the Chinese.[28] For example, the Mexican newspaper *Excelsior* reported that the states of Sonora, Sinaloa, and Chiapas exhibited strong anti-Chinese sentiments. The same article reported that approximately sixty Chinese who resided in the city of Altar, Sonora, and operated laundries and bakeries were forced by a mob of Mexicans to flee the community and into the interior of Mexico.[29]

The Japanese were caught between two competing images. In many circles within Mexico the Japanese immigrant was viewed not unlike the

Chinese: nonwhite, degenerate, corrupt, unable to assimilate, disease-ridden, and a threat to the perceived purity of *la Mexicanidad*. Juxtaposed against this image were Japanese immigrants that belonged to a powerful country with economic and military strength and were often categorized as "white" by their government or the governments of Latin American nations.[30] These so-called markers of whiteness or Westernization ran parallel with the ascension of the Japanese empire in the late nineteenth and early twentieth century. Immigration and colonization became important platforms of the Japanese empire as it spread in many directions. Throughout the first half of the twentieth century, Japanese in Mexico struggled with these competing images and on occasion were homogenized with the Chinese by Mexican society.

Mexico viewed some immigrants as better than others and attempted to recruit particular Europeans in the early twentieth century. However, it became clear to top-tier immigrant groups, primarily Europeans, that opportunities in Mexico had been overstated and exaggerated, and the numbers of these groups never reached any significance. As this realization became apparent, Mexico increasingly began to accept secondary groups such as Chinese, Japanese, and an assortment of Lebanese immigrants.[31] As a consequence, Mexico's third largest immigrant diaspora was Chinese, not European, and the largest movement of Japanese occurred during the late *Porfiriato*.[32] Yet, by the end of the nineteenth century, Mexico's industrialization emerged from the infusion of foreign capital, rather than the arrival of large groups of immigrants. Nonetheless, beginning in the late nineteenth century, a small but steady stream of Japanese began a settlement process that left a lasting legacy in the Western hemisphere.

Japanese Emigration: A Brief Background

Formal and informal contact between Japan and Mexico can be traced back to the late sixteenth and seventeenth centuries. New Spain's contact with China and Japan developed via the colonization of the Philippines. Quasi relations that were established between Japan and New Spain (Mexico) fall into two significant periods: the colonial period, and the late nineteenth century when Mexico and Japan established firm ties.[33] It was in the latter period that Japanese immigration to Mexico received its impetus, a process that lasted well into the twentieth century. Like the Chinese, the Japanese diaspora went to various points throughout the world. However, unlike China in the late nineteenth and first half of the twentieth centuries, Japan embarked on two types of colonization: the first included military and civilian occupation such as those that occurred in Manchuria, Korea, and Taiwan; and the second involved movement of Japanese subjects to such places as the Americas where colonization was not occupation but a passive form of settlement focused on strengthening Japan through commerce and remittances.

Several factors in Japan and abroad inspired changes in the country's emigration policy in the 1880s. One was the country's imperialistic designs during the last quarter of the nineteenth century and into the twentieth.[34] Another factor was that a rise in the population and discontent in the Japanese urban and rural areas affected the economic welfare of the average farmer and worker. A third factor, the need for workers in the sugar cane fields, resulted in attempts by the government of the Kingdom of Hawaii to initiate a treaty that would allow Japanese immigrants to labor in the fields. Lastly, officials in Tokyo and Yokohama began to receive requests from other countries interested in importing workers.[35] The Meiji government's (1868–1912) emigration policy represented a step forward from the Tokugawa period (1603–1868), since it granted its subjects the freedom to sail the seas and settle in other countries. However, it should be understood that internal migration had been well established under the concept of *dekasegi*, the practice of leavings one's home place for temporary work long before the Meiji Restoration of 1868. Yet even by the early twentieth century, the Japanese populace did not look favorably upon the *imin* (immigrants).[36] In fact, many Japanese emigrants were viewed by their own country as uneducated or lacking a "national consciousness and were often criticized for abandoning the nation."[37]

Overall, the structural changes initiated by the Meiji Restoration of 1868 created a surplus in the workforce. The primary goals of the Meiji statesmen were to build industry and commerce and to use the military as a means of increasing its strength.[38] Japan also embarked on an aggressive colonization campaign throughout East Asia that included both military and civilian occupation. Domestically, as Japan's industrialization bore fruit, some regions experienced demonstrations and riots as many workers were displaced. Coupled with other economic and social factors already discussed, it was under these circumstances that the first Japanese immigrants left for Mexico.

Japan's national policy for emigration was directly linked to its continued need for modernization that began with the Meiji Restoration. However, by the 1890s Japan began to deploy external measures in search of additional methods and forms of modernity. This in turn facilitated Japan's determination that in order to maintain a state of equilibrium with

Western nations it needed to expand beyond its borders. Doing so, from the perspective of Japan, would bring it additional resources, wealth, territory, and knowledge.

Japan was not content with simply adopting Western technology and customs. Similar to its rapid industrialization, Japan was eager to learn about the West, especially the United States, to answer many of the enduring questions about its strengths and weaknesses. Thus emigration became one of the many mechanisms Japan used to study and adapt to its new role as an imperial power. By sending its subjects overseas to acquire additional knowledge that could be used for the empire, Japan hoped to acquire a competitive edge against Western nations that threatened its own hegemony in the East. And by studying the West and its nuances, Japan realized that modernity involved expansionism, occupation, and domination. In this manner, logic dictated that industrialization was only one variable toward the path of modernity. If Japan was to be seen as equal and modern among empires, the rational course of action was expansionism, colonialism, and emigration. From the Japanese perspective, "the terms 'expansion,' 'colonization,' and 'emigration' were used interchangeably, indicating that these were all aspects of Western power and influence in the world" that Japan needed to imitate.[39] However, unlike what developed in such places as Korea, Manchuria, or Taiwan, and in East Asia in general, where colonization was preceded by military invasion and occupation, Japan sent immigrants to the Americas as an informal enterprise of economic expansion by establishing agricultural colonies abroad, rather than through conquest. It is in this context that we see Japan's only quasi-government-sponsored attempt to settle Japanese emigrants in Mexico known as the Enomoto Colony.

Prior to the Enomoto Colony, Japan's emigration schemes were irregular attempts that ended with mixed results and the Japanese government pulling back the reins until a better system with locations beyond East Asia could be identified. Japan's ambition to send colonists to the Western hemisphere incubated until national circumstances and individuals coalesced to make such an attempt possible. These conditions emerged during the late 1890s when Japanese officials such as Enomoto Takeaki began to develop plans to send Japanese immigrants to the Americas. What became known as the Enomoto Colony in the southern state of Chiapas ultimately achieved one of the national goals: it became the first Japanese colony established in the Americas. Understanding the motives for the creation of the Enomoto Colony provides insight into Japan's national dilemma regarding modernization, expansion and immigration and its rise as an imperial power. Lastly, the Enomoto Colony became the catalyst for permanent Japanese communities throughout Mexico and Latin America.

The Pioneers: The Enomoto Colony

While Mexican intellectuals debated what type of immigrant best fit the national interest, the governments of Mexico and Japan reached two important agreements in the late nineteenth century. First, Mexico and Japan ratified the Treaty of Friendship and Commerce in 1888. This was the first treaty signed by Japan with a Western nation under the principle of equal and reciprocal terms. The treaty provided for reciprocal freedom of migration between the two countries. Second, on January 29, 1897, Manuel Fernández Leal, Mexico's secretary of development, and the Japanese consul general in Mexico, Murota Toshibumi, signed an agreement for the sale and colonization of land located in southern Chiapas. Four months later a group of thirty-four Japanese landed on the coast.[40] This was a remarkable event in Japanese emigration history and the history of Asians in the Americas for it marked the first official Japanese colony in the Western hemisphere. The impetus for this colonization began in the last decade of the nineteenth century and coincided with the ascension of the Japanese empire. A number of groups and individuals were involved in this initial venture, and Enomoto Takeaki, the former foreign minister and minister of the navy, heavily promoted the development of Japanese expansion overseas in the form of immigration.[41] Opportunity, enthusiasm, ambition, courage, and adventure easily describe all those involved in Japan's initial move toward Mexico. However, two critical characteristics eluded the original colonists: experience with farming and with a world beyond Japan.

Enomoto's vision of a highly profitable and expanding colony failed for a variety of reasons, some which are quite obvious. To begin, even before they landed in Mexico, the Enomoto Colony had already violated the agreement signed with Mexico by sending only single men. The agreement signed between Mexico and the Japanese Colonizing Society stipulated that families were to be sent in order to bring a sense of stability to the colony. Causes for its failure are numerous, but high on the list needs to be the haste of gathering emigrants who were too young and, most important, had no experience with farming and whose worldview consisted the island of Japan. None of the immigrants had any foreign experience, especially regarding the psychological strength needed to survive and adapt in a world thousands of miles away and in a tropical zone. In fact, from the various descriptions of the conditions encountered by the colonists, the majority quickly fell ill to a variety of maladies, including intestinal diseases from drinking unsanitary water, malaria from the infestation of mosquitoes, and sunstroke caused by overexertion in the tropical weather.

There is plenty of blame to be shared among the various players of the Enomoto Colony, but the ultimate demise of the colony must rest with its creator and namesake, Enomoto Takeaki. What remains puzzling is that after numerous explorations, surveys, and reports about the region of Soconusco, Chiapas, as the best location for the cultivation of coffee, the colony was unable to succeed in this area. Chiapas today, as in the past, is one the largest coffee-producing regions in Mexico. The identification of Chiapas as the most likely place to grow coffee was accurate on the part of the Japanese Colonizing Society, the entity that organized and funded the venture. There appears to be contradictory information from some of the colonists. As mentioned, the official reports conducted by the Japanese Colonizing Society indicated that the company had purchased land suitable for the cultivation of coffee. However, comments from some of the colonists state that the land was extremely rocky and the soil unsuitable for the cultivation of coffee. According to one of the colonists, Ricardo (Rokutaro) Arima, "Our original purpose was to produce coffee, but surprisingly all of the area was made up of rocky mountains. . . . Our plan for growing coffee was laughed at by the natives. Sometimes we planted crops at the wrong time."[42] Indeed, one report suggests that the Japanese surveyors were bribed by Mexican officials to write a positive report of the region and land under consideration for purchase.[43]

Japan also expected to reap economic remittances from colonists in Mexico to further finance its domestic industrialization, while simultaneously quelling domestic disruptions, which had erupted due to the displacement of many domestic workers, especially in the rural areas. A by-product of Japan's industrialization of the late nineteenth century was an increase in taxes, with the peasant class heavily burdened. For example, Japan's rapid modernization was carried out on the backs of the rural working class, which resulted in unrest, displacement, and poverty. It is also important to state that Japan's defeat of two important powers, China (1894–95) and Russia (1904–5), gave it a sense of invincibility and entitlement as the newest imperial power. Unlike its rapid and successful industrialization, Japan's immigration schemes did not immediately meet with success.

The Enomoto Colony's long-term goal of planting a permanent colony in Chiapas met with disastrous results; however, if the efforts of the colony are viewed within a larger context, the colony was a success. First, it established a small but permanent Japanese presence in Mexico that eventually expanded in the twentieth century. Second, and not initially apparent, the original Japanese colonists did find success either as individual farmers and entrepreneurs or as reorganized companies. Third, from the perspective of the Japanese empire, the colony created the momentum to carry additional Japanese emigrants to Mexico, and it reinforced the friendly relations that Japan and Mexico enjoyed until the outbreak of World War II. Lastly, because Chiapas was ground zero for the foundation of the Japanese community in Mexico and through successive generations, the state and national governments recognized the contributions the Japanese made to the development of the state. This is a contribution that would not be forgotten during World War II, when most of the Japanese in Chiapas remained undisturbed from the relocation efforts and displacement that affected other Japanese Mexicans. Yet, much of this success would not be recognized for decades, until it was realized that the attempt by the Enomoto colonists took a tremendous amount of courage and resilience, regardless of its outcome.

As Japanese immigrants began to emerge in such places as Mexico, the United States, Canada, Brazil, and Peru, they were met with suspicion and encountered anti-Asian sentiments throughout the hemisphere. The anti-Chinese movement that enveloped the Western hemisphere in the nineteenth and early twentieth century contaminated perception of the Japanese and conditioned the people of the Americas to homogenize all Asians. From the position of the hegemonic power in the region, the United States, the Japanese posed an additional threat beyond the standard race-based peril. Japan, as a rising imperial power became a potential danger to the supremacy of the United States both in the Western hemisphere and in East Asia. As a result, the United States launched a hemispheric wide policy of curtailing, controlling, and reconfiguring Japanese immigration to the Americas in what Erika Lee has termed Western hemispheric Orientalism. As Japanese immigration increased, a diplomatic dilemma developed between Mexico, the United States, and Japan.

Japanese Immigration: The Early Twentieth Century

In many ways, the US-Mexican conflict emerged much earlier than the twentieth century. Because of the US invasion and conquest of Mexico's northern territories in the nineteenth century, the overall relations between the two countries leading up to and through World War II had been marked with suspicion, mistrust, and mutual self-interest. Much of this suspicion was fueled by US intervention in Mexico and elsewhere in Latin America in the late nineteenth and early twentieth century. These relations demonstrate how the United States used its authority and position to dictate policy within and without its own borders, often becoming the arbiter on hemispheric ideology, including immigration. Japanese emigration to Mexico during this period of the early twentieth century is directly linked to Japanese emigration to the United States. As the United States increasingly viewed Japan as an imminent threat, it unleashed volleys of rhetoric and simultaneously exposed the underbelly of anti-Asian sentiment from the general public and government reports. For example, as early as 1907, US military reports indicated Japanese espionage taking place not only within the United States but also in Canada and Mexico with the intent on gathering information on the strengths and weaknesses of the United States. One report stated, "It must always be remembered, too, that every Japanese male or female, is a government spy, whether in their own country or in a foreign one."[44] This report also provided a general overview of the future conflict between Japan and the United States that included trade and control of important Asian markets.

As a result, Japan, under pressure from the United States, implemented a self-restrictive immigration policy generally known as the Japanese Gentlemen's Agreement (1907–8), which halted the official movement of Japanese laborers to the United States and ultimately diverted Japanese immigration to Mexico and other regions of Latin America. This in turn created a transborder predicament whereby many Japanese used Mexico to cross clandestinely into the United States which instigated the triangular clash between Mexico, United States, and Japan. This period in history also marks the hysteria and the development of the so-called Yellow Peril or a form of hemispheric Orientalism that did not abate until the end of World War II. Finally, Japan's ascension as an imperial power challenged Western dominance in the East, which increased tensions between the United States and Japan. This pushed Japan further away from the orbit of the United States and ostracized Japanese immigrants in the United States and elsewhere. Japan, therefore, cultivated its relationship with Mexico as a means to counter the United States in the Western hemisphere. The relations between Japan and Mexico became complex, friendly, and intertwined as Japanese immigration increased to Mexico.

The turn of the twentieth century witnessed an increasing number of Japanese entering Mexico. In 1900–8, the first phase of Japanese labor immigration, approximately 10,000 people from that country made their way to Mexico.[45] The Japanese made numerous efforts to develop colonies, but by and large, most failed. Not until 1905 did a considerable influx of Japanese take place. This surge in immigration to Mexico was not coincidental, but a reaction to the rising tide of anti-Japanese agitation and exclusion along the West Coast of the United States that eventually resulted in the restriction of Japanese immigration. As previously discussed, the movement of Japanese to the Americas was the result of multiple factors, but one that needs elaboration is the exclusion of Chinese immigration to the United States, which reverberated throughout North America, including Mexico.

The Chinese, the first Asian group to immigrate to the Americas in significant numbers, began their movement in the mid-nineteenth century, gained economic success in the United States, and challenged the hegemony of whiteness and the privileges associated with that status, including economic upward mobility. Immediately, Chinese were viewed as the "other" and described as "coolie" labor who failed to assimilate, were opium addicts, and corrupted white women. Erika Lee notes, "These images were almost identical in North and South America and were tied together by what I call 'hemispheric Orientalism,' a common racial ideology that traveled widely, defined Asian immigration as a threatening invasion, and was characterized by much borrowing and sharing of 'knowledge' about Asian immigrants across national borders."[46] As a result, multiple groups mobilized to bring an end to Chinese economic viability and solidarity, resulting in the passage of the US Chinese Exclusion Act of 1882.

The interconnectedness and linkages between the Chinese experience in the United States, Canada, and Mexico and the Japanese experience in the United States and Mexico are delineated by their treatment within the North American space controlled by the United States. As Lee and others have noted, by expanding the use of Western hemispheric Orientalism beyond the Chinese experience in the United States, a systemic methodology of racializing Asians becomes clear. Seen from this vantage point, the Japanese in the Americas became the next target of Orientalism as they increased in numbers first in the United States and then in other regions of the Americas and became victims of widespread racism, discrimination, and prejudice: "This racism was grounded in an American Orientalist ideology that homogenized Asia as one indistinguishable entity, positioned and defined the West and the East in diametrically opposite terms, and used those distinctions to claim American and Anglo American superiority."[47]

With this in mind, the United States made it difficult for Japanese immigrants to enter the region by employing various mechanisms such as limiting the number of Japanese brought over by vessels or imposing a head tax.[48] As these methods failed to stem the flow, West Coast communities switched from an economic rationale to a racial reasoning to restrict Japanese entry into the United States. In 1905 Japanese and Korean Exclusion Leagues were formed that thrust the dangers of the "Yellow Peril" to the forefront and were intent on stopping the invasion of the "Asiatic horde."[49] Finally, in 1906 San Francisco began placing Japanese children in "Oriental schools."[50] It became apparent that a pattern similar to that which excluded Chinese in the nineteenth and twentieth centuries was evolving for the Japanese diaspora with a restrictive immigration policy imminent. Coinciding with the rising tide of anti-Japanese sentiment in the United States was the increasing movement of Japanese to Mexico.

According to Mexican figures, the apex of Japanese immigration to Mexico occurred between 1890 and 1910. Mexican national census figures are more conservative in their estimates of Japanese immigrants living in Mexico at particular times. For example, the Mexican census indicates that twenty-two Japanese were living in Mexico in 1895 and forty-two in 1900, followed by 2,216 in 1910 and 1,728 in 1920.[51] However, emigration companies registered 8,789 Japanese bound for Mexico from 1900 to 1910. The Japanese emigration department registered 10,964 Japanese who traveled to Mexico between 1892 and 1910, but the Mexican census counted only 3,783 between 1900 and 1910.[52]

The discrepancies from the three different sources make it difficult to conclude an accurate number of Japanese immigrants to Mexico. One obvious problem is accounting for undocumented Japanese in Mexico, who followed the same modus operandi into the United States. It is evident that many Japanese used Mexico as a stepping-stone into its northern neighbor and entered Mexico from many areas of Latin America. Documentation confirms that many Japanese who traveled to the United States were at some point in Mexico before their arrival.[53] Remigration to Japan was not an option for the majority of poor Japanese laborers in Mexico, although a small number was recorded. Other discrepancies are due to some Japanese laborers dying in the fields and mines of Mexico and not counted. Also, some Japanese traveled from Mexico to other Latin American countries, and a large number were simply missed by Mexican census gatherers. table 1.1 illustrates the movement of Japanese into the United States through various countries and Hawaii. The movement also coincides with the development and implementation of the Japanese Gentlemen's Agreement. As noted in table 1.1, Hawaii by the early twentieth

Table 1.1. Japanese arrivals in the United States, 1907

	US Seaports		*Through Canada*		*Through Mainland Mexico*		*Hawaii*		*Total*	
Month	*Admitted*	*Rejected*	*Admitted*	*Rejected*	*Admitted*	*Rejected*	*Admitted*	*Rejected*	*Admitted*	*Rejected*
July	475	10	247	14	436	93	1,158	123	1,073	8
Aug	495	18	435	17	223	17	1,158	52	629	6
Sept	333	5	503	35	224	21	1,060	61	957	4
Oct	414	20	404	48	318	26	1,136	94	603	4
Nov	671	8	428	52	71	7	1,170	67	1,086	4
Dec	602	8	108	35	7	7	—	717	50	—

Source: Enclosure with letter of January 22, 1908, from US Secretary of Commerce and Labor.

century became an important conduit for the movement of Japanese to the United States, and also to Mexico.

Large numbers of Japanese contract workers arrived in Mexico between 1900 and 1908 to build various railroads and to work on sugar cane plantations and in the mines. Over 8,000 Japanese came to Mexico during this period.[54] Also, the Japanese tended to congregate in the northern zones of Mexico, particularly in the states of Baja California, Sonora, Coahuila, Chihuahua, and Sinaloa. Many Japanese were attracted to these areas because of the available employment in the mines and plantations, as well as the proximity to the United States. The southern regions of Veracruz, Yucatán, and Chiapas also recorded substantial numbers of Japanese contract workers.[55]

Some Japanese were also employed in nonagricultural occupations, which was a not characteristic of the immigrants arriving in Mexico during the first decade of the twentieth century. In northern Mexico some Japanese were self-employed or had skilled and semiskilled occupations.[56] However, during this period the majority of Japanese coming to Mexico worked as laborers. They often worked for foreign-owned companies that had been invited into Mexico to invest by the Díaz regime. The Mexican government tried to promote modernization of industries and agriculture in Mexico through capital investment and the adoption of modern technology from abroad. These foreign-owned enterprises seemed to prefer non-Mexican laborers rather than risk conflicts with hacienda owners who feared the flight of their work force for higher wages. By the turn of the century a considerable increase in Japanese immigration also took place in such places as the state of Coahuila, with the mining industry being the principal attraction.[57] As Japanese immigrants began to congregate along Mexico's northern border, several developments coalesced to raise tensions between Mexico, Japan, and the United States. In fact, this period represents the beginning of a nearly four-decade-long diplomatic entanglement between these countries regarding Japanese immigration and their presence in Mexico.

Pressured by the United States, Japan voluntarily restricted the movement of Japanese laborers to the United States in 1908, while Mexico did little to curb Japanese immigration or shut the back-door entry into the United States.[58] In general, the small number of immigrants to Mexico compared with other countries during this period is attributed to emigrants reluctant to settle in Mexico, rather than Mexican immigration laws. However, Mexico did create immigration laws similar to the United States but did not have the resources to enforce the prevention of individuals who were "paupers," or persons who might become "public charges."[59] Mexico also deemed the Japanese population in Mexico too small to create a quota. With pressure mounting and the United States concerned with the movement of Japanese to the United States through Mexico, Japan began strict enforcement over passports issued to immigrants bound for Mexico, and its efforts had a remarkable effect as illustrated by table 1.2. The surge between 1906 and 1907 was the result of the anticipated passage of the Japanese Gentlemen's Agreement, with over 9,000 passports issued

Table 1.2. Passports issued to Japanese nationals destined for Mexico by the Japanese foreign ministry, 1901–1918

Year	*Male*	*Female*	*Total*
1901	152	0	152
1902	187	0	187
1903	157	2	159
1904	201	0	201
1905	371	3	374
1906	5223	98	5321
1907	3897	48	3945
1908	16	2	18
1909	11	2	13
1910	33	3	36
1911	54	6	60
1912	58	16	74
1913	90	16	106
1914	93	9	102
1915	47	4	51
1916	66	6	72
1917	85	18	103
1918	184	31	215

Source: US National Archives, Records of the Department of State, Relating to the International Affairs of Mexico, 1910–29 (State Department Decimal File no. 812), 812.5595/4. As cited by Iyo Iimura Kunimoto, "Japan and Mexico, 1888–1917" (Ph.D. diss., University of Texas at Austin, 1975), 68.

to Japanese destined for Mexico. Nevertheless, even after 1908 Japan continued to issue passports for Mexico, contrary to the agreement signed with the United States, but it slowed to an insignificant number and probably were passports issued to nonlaborers such as students or tourists.

Mexican Response to US Imposition

To achieve a level of independence from stronger and domineering countries, Mexico launched a diplomatic version of "weapons of the weak," the foot-dragging and noncompliance often associated with groups facing a stronger foe.[60] The development of these tactics proved vital to Mexican foreign policy initiatives, and germane to this study is the Mexican diplomacy and subtlety which provided Japanese Mexicans important latitude not afforded to other Japanese in the Americas. In the end, I argue that lessons and experience learned in the political arena by Mexico in this early decade of the twentieth century kept Japanese Mexicans from internment in the United States and created alternatives for the Japanese in Mexico other than forced confinement in the manner of the United States when World War II emerged. More important, it allowed Mexico to negotiate from a position of strength with the United States on a wide range of issues. In the wake of the Japanese hysteria that developed in the United States, Mexico deployed an early version of what John Dwyer has termed "diplomatic weapons of the weak."[61] And it is in this sphere that Mexico challenged US hegemony and encroachment on Mexican sovereignty by embarking on strategic diplomatic obfuscation.

For example, in 1907, a Mexican debate emerged over restricting Japanese immigration to Mexico. However, unlike in the United States, Mexicans appeared to be more sympathetic to Japanese immigration, did not consider them a threat to their society, and to some degree did not fear their competition. It could be that this lack of fear stemmed from the fact that the Japanese, unlike the Chinese, had not penetrated Mexico numerically or economically to the extent of the Chinese. However, I submit that the views of the Japanese in Mexico went beyond economic and numerical rationalizations. Mexican intellectuals and writers alluded to this idea. An article articulated that "Mexico is very distinct from the United States" and also touched upon the issue of race and its use by the United States to exclude Asians from industry and agricultural labor. The following appeared in the Mexican newspaper, *El Imparcial*, and sheds partial light on the position of some Mexicans regarding the use of Asian and Japanese labor: "The Asian does not come because he wants to lower the economic conditions of the Mexican workers, we especially remind ourselves of the [Japanese] agriculturist and also the miners, there does not exist a reason that has determined the prohibition of their entrance into the Northern Republic."[62]

Bernardo Mallén, in his 1908 book altogether entitled *¿En donde está nuestra riqueza?* (*Where Are Our Riches?*), wrote of the prevalent attitude toward native workers and supported the notion of importing Japanese immigrants to supplant the national workforce. This perspective is well represented in the following passage:

> Japan could send all the necessary workers that we need to exploit the riches of our coasts, but only if we paid them a good wage and provided good food. Many nations were poor when its sons were indolent, rich when they were laborious. The best example is Japan, whose forty million inhabitants converted a poor island into a very rich and prosperous country, even more than China, which inhabits one-third of the world's population.[63]

During the *Porfiriato*, legislation did not exclude Asian immigration to Mexico, unlike in the United States. When anti-Asian sentiment emerged in Mexico after the start of the Mexican Revolution, most of it was directed against the Chinese and not the Japanese.

Although a public debate ensued in Mexico concerning Japanese immigration, very little documentation exists to reveal any Mexican designs to develop restrictive immigration legislation such as that created by Japan in the wake of the anti-Japanese hysteria in the United States. This is unusual considering that both Japan and the United States proposed restricting or stopping altogether Japanese immigration to North America without consulting Mexico. Mexico was certainly aware of the immigration conflict that emerged between the United States and Japan but chose a nonconfrontational and neutral approach to a delicate diplomatic predicament. One newspaper article reported that Mexico had entered into negotiations with the United States to prevent Japanese immigration, but there is little other evidence to support this view.[64] In this instance, Mexico was in a weak position, not wanting to offend its stronger northern neighbor but simultaneously wishing to maintain cordial relations with Japan that provided some leverage over the domineering United States. It is even possible that the only saber rattling Mexico could muster against the United States at this time were Japanese immigrants, which almost always put US officials into a frenzy. Perhaps this accounts for the hundreds of reports that suggested a massive Japanese influx into Mexico during the first decade of the Mexican Revolution.

By the early twentieth century US hegemony in Mexico and elsewhere in Latin America was prevalent. It is important to mention that the reach of US imperialism did not always necessitate military intervention. In fact, US-Mexican relations illustrate that the United States often deployed non-military dominance in the form of "diminutions of sovereignty through the exercise of power that included political, economic, and cultural forms."[65] It is fairly well known that US immigration policy spilled over its northern and southern borders that allowed the United States to become the de facto policing agent regarding immigration to North America. US immigration policy was only one agent of control regarding the Japanese diaspora in the Americas. In fact, one can say that US immigration policy regarding the Japanese emerged from the plebian citizenry of the United States that feared and felt threatened by the Japanese. Indeed, a variety of groups, organizations, and US government agencies played on these fears by launching a volley of propaganda that portrayed the Japanese empire as a menace, which in turn was superimposed on Japanese immigrants throughout the Americas. As a consequence, the Japanese, like their Asian cousins before them, the Chinese, were racialized, deemed undesirable and unassimilable, and reconfigured as a threat that had hemispheric ramifications.

As Mexico deflected US immigration policy and other impositions that challenged its sovereignty, another form of infiltration occurred. By the end of the first decade of the twentieth century, the anti-Asian sentiments in the United States gained momentum and reached a fever pitch. Much of this was the result of a heightened fear the US public sensed as the new century brought change that challenged the sense of entitlement that came with the privilege of whiteness. One of these challenges was the continued immigration of groups that countered the Northern and Western European immigration trajectory of the United States. These groups included not just Asians, but Mexicans, Middle Easterners, and Eastern and Southern Europeans. This fear in turn influenced and morphed into US restrictive immigration policy that targeted Japanese and eventually strained US-Mexican relations. The following section examines how the general public reacted to the arrival of Japanese immigrants, not just within national boundaries but also at the hemispheric level. I argue that the anti-Japanese movement reverberated beyond the confines of the United States and influenced the attitudes of Latin American countries and, in some cases, such as Brazil and Peru, led to anti-Asian legislation. Through the emergence of a culture of fear that labeled particular immigrant groups as undesirables, US immigration enforcement and policy extended beyond the US borderlands and into Mexico. The triangular conflict that developed between the United States, Mexico, and Japan had long-lasting implications and represents an important link in understanding the Japanese dilemma in the Western hemisphere. The following official and unofficial letters and correspondence illustrate an emerging fear of the Japanese and how such fears manifested as the racialism of an entire ethnic group.

Dispatches from the Surreal: Western Hemispheric Orientalism

By December 1906 dispatches from the US Embassy in Tokyo clearly showed the concern over developments along the US-Mexican border. American diplomats pressed Japanese government officials to enact legislation to restrict the flow of Japanese, not just to the United States but also to territory adjacent to the United States, principally Mexico. The following exchange between the US secretary of state and the ambassador to Japan illustrates the US position:

> If such Legislation as was indicated in my dispatch of the 26th could be inaugurated, I believe the [Japanese] Government could be induced to direct that the passport limitation be applied to not only Hawaii, but also to Mexico and other countries from which Japanese could pass into American territory.[66]

During this early part of the twentieth century the anti-Asian sentiments in the United States were the driving force behind the hysteria created regarding Japanese immigration to any place in the Americas, but especially the United States and its neighbors, Mexico and Canada. Although Mexico had individuals and groups from all strata of society that opposed Asian immigration, such as the Japanese, those views were countered by an overall tolerance or at the very least neutrality toward Japanese immigrants to Mexico. On the other hand, US society developed a pattern of opposing groups that challenged its racial equilibrium. The arrival of the first Asian group to the United States, the Chinese, during the mid-nineteenth century began a century long campaign of prejudice, discrimination, and exclusion against Asians that influenced and touched every corner of the Western hemisphere. As Japanese immigrants began to settle in such places as Mexico, US officials and the general public exhibited symptoms of paranoia as numerous reports alluded to phantom Japanese soldiers roaming the Mexican countryside or fifth columns established along the northern regions of Mexico. Regardless of their numbers in Mexico (the 1900 Mexican Census recorded forty Japanese in the country), and unlike China and the Chinese, Japan and the Japanese somehow posed a military threat, not from the perspective of Mexicans but from that of US officials and a suspicious American public.

As a consequence of the anti-Japanese movement in the United States and increased Japanese immigration to Mexico, the US-Mexican border came under intensified scrutiny and surveillance by the US government. US immigration policy in the late nineteenth and early twentieth centuries expanded the reach of US imperialism into countries bordering the United States by "extending American laws, ideologies, and systems of control to other countries."[67] Aggravating this situation were the sensationalized stories of a Japanese invasion of Mexico by hundreds of thousands of Japanese, Japanese sleeper cells disguised as immigrants, and the Japanese navy searching for a coaling station along Mexico's Pacific coast. For example, headlines such as "En Busca de Espias Japoneses" [In Search of Japanese Spies], "4,000 Operarios Japoneses Para Las Obras Ferrocarrileras" [4,000 Japanese Operators for Railroad Work], "1200 Japoneses Para Coahuila—Ninguno Llego Enfermo" [1200 Japanese for Coahuila—Not One Arrived Sick], "The Menace of the Japanese Conquest of Mexico," and "60,000 Japanese in Mexico" were common and fed the paranoia of Americans and the US government.[68] Most of these stories can be attributed to the anti-Japanese movement in the United States promoted by a variety of exclusion leagues, overzealous US citizens and military officers, newspapers, reporters, and a US propaganda machine used to pressure Mexico to limit Japanese immigration. The United States used the same mechanism to rebuke any Latin American nation that entertained the idea of allowing large-scale Japanese immigration or providing favorite nation status to Japan. It was Mexico, however, that received intense scrutiny because of its shared border with the United States.

The US government investigated almost every rumor regardless of how unlikely or bizarre the report. For example, in 1908 the United States conducted four investigations, perhaps more, based on letters it had received from the general populace. One letter from Edwin Cole to the secretary of war dated April 28, 1908, stated that three Japanese traveled from Jalisco to

San Blas, a port on the Pacific in the territory of Tepic, and were making careful notes of everything along the route, such as streams and ranches. Another letter to the US war department from a Mr. John A. Anderson dated May 6, 1908, included a translation from a Norwegian newspaper printed in Chicago on April 24, 1908, by someone named Olaf Olsen Berweit. In brief, the translated letter stated that a large number of Japanese reconnoitering parties had been engaged in mapping the northern border of Mexico. The author also spoke of the large number of Japanese traveling through the northern states of Mexico. This particular letter translated from Norwegian hits upon several sensitive issues that drove paranoia and fear on the US side of the border:

> More than 300 Japanese passed down from Juarez to Casa Grande, from whence they have tramped the whole distance through the Sierra Madre Mountains. "We intend" said some of those Japs "to go this way when we invade the United States." Some them [Japanese] also stated that they will return to Mexico the lost territories of California, Arizona, New Mexico, and Texas.[69]

The letters mentioned above were of the "run of the mill" character with literally hundreds of similar claims and observations found in newspapers across the United States and Mexico during the early decades of the twentieth century.

Conclusion

As the movement of Japanese, Chinese, Mexicans, and an assortment of Europeans and Middle Eastern groups increased in Mexico, the US-Mexican border became the staging ground for covert and overt entry into the United States and Mexico. As a consequence, the US open door policy shifted once again with a variety of groups targeted for exclusion, and by the second decade of the twentieth century the borderlands became a zone of intense immigration traffic. This atmosphere represented the start of the transformation of the US-Mexican border. This change can be attributed to the transpacific and transnational character of Japanese immigration to Mexico and the United States' exclusionary legislation, and to the militarization of the border, which gave rise to what Scott Michaelson has termed a "permanent state of racial emergency" for the borderlands.[70] As activity intensified along the border, so did the presence of the US military, Texas Rangers, and eventually the US Border Patrol. Those in any group associated with immigration became suspected criminals, but more important, the region became notorious for suspending due process of the law. It was into this atmosphere that the largest number of Japanese immigrated to Mexico. By the end of the first decade of the twentieth century, Japanese immigration to Mexico had peaked and was becoming an issue of concern primarily for the United States, but also for Japan and Mexico. Although compared with the Chinese the Japanese were generally treated well, some still became extremely concerned with their treatment in Mexico. The constant communiqués from the Japanese government sent to the Mexican government to protect Japanese subjects and their property indicated, at the very least, that the Japanese were swept up in the general anti-Asian movement.

Mexico, Japan, and the United States continued to be linked over concerns about immigration and the border. Public opinion in the United States was a stark reminder of the view and position of Asians. As one newspaper editorial wrote, "The frontier is like a sieve, and the Japanese are streaming in at every hole, now under one pretext, and now under another. They are coming secretly from Mexico and Canada, and openly with forged papers through Seattle and San Francisco."[71]

By the end of the first decade of the twentieth century tensions between the United States and Japan increased to the point that war between the two countries was openly discussed in newspapers and military reports. And, due to the cordial relations that Japan and Mexico enjoyed, the United States began to question the position of Mexico in the event that Japan and the United States went to war. For example, a US military report showing concern over Mexico's relationship with Japan and attempting to rationalize why Mexico might align itself with Japan provides additional insight into the complex web of diplomacy Mexico navigated in the early twentieth century. The report accurately describes the sentiments of some Mexicans and the general feeling toward the United States, which from the Mexican perspective translated into mistrust and suspicion regarding the motives of the United States. The report also brings to the surface the idea of race. Here, the Mexicans are described as vengeful, bloodthirsty, and inherently disloyal:

> It is universally understood that the Mexicans hate us cordially. For one thing they have never forgiven us for the War of '47, which sentiment,

together with their racial characteristics, would make them elated at an unexpected opportunity to seek revenge; and the only possible way to do this would be through some powerful ally.[72]

Overall, these initial efforts, which were difficult and had mixed results, encouraged many of the first Japanese immigrants (*Issei* or first generation) to settle permanently in Mexico's southeast.[73] The last elements of the Enomoto Colony had disintegrated by the first decade of the twentieth century, but this colony facilitated the greater movement of Japanese to Mexico in the first half of that century. Furthermore, the Enomoto Colony has the distinction of facilitating the movement of Japanese throughout other regions of Latin America. As Japanese immigration continued into the twentieth century, Mexico experienced powerful changes at the turn of the century, and immigration became a matter of national debate and concern that created internal dissension and a triangular diplomatic ballet among Mexico, Japan, and the United States that lasted until the outbreak of World War II.

The Japanese were dispersed throughout many areas of Mexico such as Chiapas, Oaxaca, Veracruz, and Guerrero, and by the early twentieth century some of the largest concentrations were in the northern states of Chihuahua, Coahuila, Sonora, and Sinaloa, with the principal enclaves in Baja California and Mexico City. Many Japanese were attracted to these areas because of the available employment in the mines and plantations and also the proximity to the United States. As with the Enomoto Colony, mass desertion characterized Japanese immigration to Mexico during the first decade of the twentieth century. These mass desertions, however, can be linked to a number of factors and not to a single cause. Those who remained in Mexico contributed to the development of Mexico, and many established roots in the country. Large numbers of Japanese contract workers arrived in Mexico to build various railroads and to work on sugar cane plantations and in the mines. The southern regions of Veracruz, Yucatán, and Chiapas also recorded substantial numbers of Japanese contract workers.[74] In the final analysis, the distribution of Japanese was widespread with enclaves in regions that provided economic opportunities and easy access to the fluid US-Mexican border.

The Japanese government, in accordance with the Gentlemen's Agreement, controlled the emigration of contract laborers to Mexico, which had risen noticeably from 1906 to 1908. In 1908, the US inspector of the Mexican district of the Immigration Service reported that there had been a gradual and marked decrease in Japanese arrivals, which clearly indicated that the regulations were effective and that there was an increase of Japanese departing for their home country.[75] It is interesting to note the attitude of the Japanese government toward immigration to the United States. The policy of self-imposed restrictions was adopted in order to avoid the enactment of a Japanese exclusion law similar to the Chinese. Maintenance of good relations with the United States and equal relations with the Western powers were the ultimate aims of this policy.[76]

For the next several decades, the United States and Mexico clashed over the movement of Japanese to the country and Mexican motives regarding its relationship with Japan. The United States remained wary of the Mexican-Japanese relationship, and until Pearl Harbor, Mexico maintained a friendly disposition with Japan and a level of tolerance with Japanese immigrants not seen in the United States. The cumulative effects of the Gentlemen's Agreement and the Mexican Revolution (1910) brought Japanese immigration to Mexico to a standstill. The Japanese that remained in Mexico witnessed and participated in the first revolution of the twentieth century. And although Japanese immigration to Mexico slowed dramatically, this did not stop rumors of impending schemes to colonize tens of thousands of Japanese in Mexico or that Japan was in negotiations with the Mexican government to establish naval bases in the region, which the general public and US government officials interpreted as a prelude to an invasion. The public imagination became increasingly phobic in the second decade of the twentieth century regarding the presence of Japanese in the Western hemisphere. As the first decade of the twentieth century closed, Mexico entered into the turbulent and violent period of the Mexican Revolution (1910–20). Like the rest of the population, the Japanese community was engulfed by the first revolution of the new century.

CHAPTER TWO

Japanese Orientalism and the Mexican Revolution, 1910–1920

No, Mexico is like a girl, who flirts with two boys, playing off one against the other in order to more easily land the one of her choice. Mexico really wishes to borrow money from the United States. In order to influence America to make her this loan, she circulates the story that Japan has offered to make it.

—American Consul Guaymas, Mexico, to Secretary of State, June 20, 1917

> We arrived [June 29] at Torreón de Cana about 5 PM. Owing to my acquaintance with Villistas during their stay at San Geronimo I had no difficulty recognizing some of them, which facilitated my being taken into the presence of Villa. . . . As I entered the room I saw Villa seated in a chair, looking quite different from the man I had known. His beard is long and jet black, and lacked attention. . . . He recognized me at once and asked me what I was doing so far away from San Geronimo. . . . [June 30-July 1] Both Sato and I have been provided with a rifle and pistol; Villa has asked me to ride in his carriage frequently. . . . General Villa now (July 5) plans the capture of Parral and begins to carry his scheme into effect this day. . . . Villa is in command of the main detachment. I am accepted as a member of his staff. . . . What ever happens to Villa's plan Dyo is determined to carry his plan into effect after Parral.[1]

Described above is the alleged infiltration of Pancho Villa's camp by three Japanese Mexicans hired by the US Military Intelligence Service to hunt down and assassinate the revolutionary leader. The three Japanese Mexicans are Tsutomu Dyo from Rancho San Geronimo, who entered Mexico in 1906; Juan A. Sato from Madera, who entered Mexico in 1906; and T. Fujita from Madera. The actual attempted poisoning of Villa is described in a report sent from the US attorney general, Thomas Watt

Gregory, to the US secretary of war, H. P. McCain. The attorney general began his letter with the following: "Herewith I enclose a copy of a very startling report made by one of our secret service men and sent from El Paso. The story seems too wild for anything, but as it mentions Captain Reed of the expeditionary force in Mexico, I thought you might care to run it down somewhat."[2] According to the report, Dyo and Fujita had been sent by Captain Reed of the American expedition in Mexico to General Villa's camp with a poison prescription, with instructions to administer it to General Villa and kill him. Dyo and Fujita state that the prescription was given to Captain Reed by an American Army surgeon with the Pershing expedition for this purpose.[3] Above and beyond the sheer audacity of the assassination attempt, the involvement of at least three Japanese Mexicans illustrates the complexity of the Japanese experience in Mexico. The turmoil of the Mexican Revolution forced thousands of Japanese in Mexico to choose alliances based on the necessity to survive, where by the end of the bloody phase of the revolution nearly 15 percent of Mexico's population either had been killed or became refugees in the United States.

This chapter studies the various roles of the Japanese population in Mexico that included settlers, farmers, merchants, victims, and soldiers. It also traces the small movement of Japanese to Mexico during the violent period of the Mexican Revolution (1910–20). During the Mexican Revolution, the movement of Japanese into Mexico slowed considerably due to civil strife, but the Mexican and US public continued to imagine hundreds of thousands of Japanese arriving on Mexico's shores. The alarm toward Japanese immigration had not abated but, in fact, increased as the Japanese empire continued its ascension, which the United States, fearful of its dominance, challenged at home and abroad. Furthermore, the involvement of the Japanese as combatants in the Mexican Revolution is not well known. The revelation that Japanese Mexicans were hired mercenaries indicates the Japanese experience in Mexico varied from the mundane to actively participating in some of the most controversial events of the era. The convolutedness of the Japanese experience in Mexico went beyond their involvement within the various ranks of the Mexican Revolutionary factions. Japanese Mexicans were also recruited for the US military's Punitive Expedition of 1916–17 in the hunt for Pancho Villa as scouts, at the very least, but also as alleged assassins.

My main focus with the Japanese during the Mexican Revolution is to describe the Japanese presence within various revolutionary factions; to illustrate the decreased, but continuous, movement of Japanese emigrants to Mexico; and to describe how the average Japanese resident in

Mexico experienced the Mexican Revolution. However, intertwined and obfuscating the Japanese experience not just in Mexico but also in the United States was the convergence of global, national, and regional developments during the second decade of the twentieth century. This tumultuous period began with the first revolution of the century and Japan's continued ascension as an imperial power. Complicating matters were the restrictions placed on Japanese entry into the United States that developed into a transborder dilemma where the United States attempted to use its hegemony of the region to expand its immigration policy beyond its own borders and dictate who could and could not enter the United States through Mexico. The position of the United States, for the first time, created a conundrum for Mexico, as it openly courted Japanese emigrants and maintained friendly relations with Japan. Simultaneously, the emerging schism between the United States and Japan revealed to Mexico that it needed to maintain a balance between exploiting this rift for its own designs, keeping the United States at bay, and remaining a US ally. However, the emergence of the Mexican Revolution in 1910 made it difficult for Mexico to preserve any sense of equilibrium.

World events created a long shadow over the presence of Japanese in the Western hemisphere. The eruption of World War I and Japan's continual rise as an imperial power served only to instill a sense of unease, fear, and agitation among Western hemispheric nations with the United States embracing a leadership role in these developments. As Mexico countered the hegemonic position of the United States for its own sense of sovereignty, I submit that it simultaneously and indirectly created a space for the Japanese by allowing their movement and settlement by going against prevailing US policy, a position not afforded to other Asian groups, such as the Chinese. Thus, in order to understand the Japanese experience in Mexico between 1910 and 1920, these national and global developments are explored in this chapter, but only in the larger context of those events, in order to remain focused on the Japanese situation in Mexico.

The Mexican Revolution: A Brief Background

During the era known as the *Porfiriato* (1876–1911) massive foreign investment not only spurred the development of capitalism in Mexico but also created stark class divisions and increased foreign control in general of Mexico's economy that included European capital.[4] As Díaz secured Mexico for foreign investment and development, the consequences of his stabilization programs became apparent as discontent from many areas of the Mexican population emerged by the first decade of the twentieth century. Thus, while many countries in the Americas were experiencing similar disruptions, Mexico became violently engulfed in a Revolution with the most brutal period from 1910 to 1920.[5] This began a tumultuous period for immigrants who had arrived and continued to migrate to Mexico. The Japanese who remained in Mexico faced additional challenges as it became evident that Mexico was headed toward upheaval and chaos. Another consequence of this violent era was the near standstill of immigration. Japanese continued to arrive in Mexico, but the numbers pale compared with the previous decade. Further, Japanese who arrived in Mexico in the years prior to the revolution found themselves participating in one of the most important periods in Mexican history.

A full analysis of why the Mexican Revolution emerged is beyond the scope of this chapter. However, it is important to place the revolution into a basic context to understand the situation that foreigners faced in Mexico, particularly those from East Asia such as the Chinese and Japanese. The initial interpretations of the Mexican Revolution during the early post-revolutionary period (1920–40) were grounded in populism, viewed as a spontaneous revolution and agrarian in nature.[6] By the end of the 1960s and in response to this simplistic account of the Mexican Revolution, scholars began to reevaluate this transformative period of Mexican society. Alan Knight claims that the Mexican Revolution was fought because of discontent in the peasant class; hence, the Mexican Revolution might be categorized as a peasant revolution, except that Knight is adamant in stating that the revolution was not a workers' revolution and had less to do with nationalism.[7] Others, such as John Mason Hart, present evidence that the Mexican Revolution was nationalistic in nature and that as foreign individuals and companies usurped Mexican land and displaced Mexicans, the country reacted and fought for national liberation.[8]

No doubt the Mexican Revolution defies easy explanation; clearly, a popular social movement coupled in some places with a sense of nationalism is evident. More important, the Chinese and Japanese felt the brutal force of both nationalistic passion and economic resentment. Furthermore, the Japanese in Mexico participated in the revolution on multiple levels that included fighting for various factions. There also appeared to be a fascination and perception, a myth, if you will, that any Japanese was a born military leader and needed to be placed into the ranks of the military or utilized in a manner to achieve military victory. Japanese farmers became scouts, spies, and alleged assassins. Japanese dentists and medical apprentices became field surgeons. This belief stemmed from the quick modernization of the Japanese military, their defeat of the Chinese and Russians in the late nineteenth and early twentieth centuries, and the growing strength of the Japanese empire. Also, some Japanese immigrants who arrived before and during the Mexican Revolution had seen military action in the Russo-Japanese War of 1904–5, and because of economic conditions in Japan, many sought opportunities abroad and found themselves in the midst of the first social revolution of the twentieth century.

Mexico and Japan: An Illusion of Conspiracy

While a few scholars mention the presence of the Japanese in Mexico during the chaotic period of the Mexican Revolution, some revealing images show Japanese immigrants, settlers, or sojourners with leading figures of the revolution and participating in many of its campaigns. Photographs taken shortly before and during the Mexican Revolution depict the Japanese as active participants. For example, a significant number of Japanese worked in the northern mines of Mexico such as Cananea in Sonora, El Boleo in Baja California, and Las Esperanzas in Coahuila and participated in the major strikes leading up to the revolution. Their involvement in the Mexican Revolution ranged from security detail with private armies, servants to a number of revolutionary leaders, rank-and-file soldiers, leadership positions, medical personnel, and hired mercenaries. Although no pattern is detected regarding which faction the Japanese were likely to join or if any of them adhered to a revolutionary ideology, a handful of Japanese worked for Francisco Madero, the *hacendado* of Coahuila and martyred president of Mexico. This may be attributed to Madero's friendship with various Japanese in Mexico.[9]

For most of the violent period of the Mexican Revolution, rumors circulated that thousands of Japanese were involved with the revolution. One source places the actual number of Japanese fighting during the violent phase of the Mexican Revolution (1910–20) at 800, although no evidence for that number is provided other than the sensationalistic media portrayals of Japanese soldiers in Mexico and overstated US Military Intelligence Reports.[10] This same source also states that the total number of Japanese deaths in the revolutionary armies was estimated to have totaled four to five hundred, which translates into a 50 to 60 percent death rate if 800 is taken as factual. It is well documented that Japan had sent observers, instructors, and technicians to Mexico, similar to other countries, but the Japanese received additional scrutiny based on false perceptions of thousands of Japanese in the Mexican Revolution, Japanese Imperial soldiers roaming the Mexican countryside, and an imagined military alliance between Japan and Mexico.

There is no doubt that Japanese-Mexican relations differed dramatically from those with the United States. Mexico and Japan each had grievances against the United States, which created, in some ways a natural friendship that predated the strained relations that erupted between Japan and the United States in the first decade of the twentieth century. However, on the one hand, such a friendship did not necessarily equate to an alliance that plotted against the United States. Portraying Mexico in this manner not only negates Mexico's ability to analyze the greater worldview, especially regarding its northern neighbor, but also undermines how Mexico deftly maneuvered through diplomatic minefields such as those that were present throughout the revolution and suspicions directed toward it from the United States. On the other hand, both Japan and Mexico used the tense situation before, during, and after the Mexican Revolution to keep the United States puzzled regarding the true nature of their affiliation.

Japan understood that Mexico and the United States had strained relations and attempted to exploit those conditions by probing carefully the limits of Mexico's friendship but also restraining itself from complete exposure to its involvement in Mexico. In this manner, Japan supplied weapons, munitions, military advisers, and technicians to leaders of the revolution, especially Venustiano Carranza, and reinforced its position with Mexico based on cordiality and caution. Japan also delicately explored Mexico's willingness to provide naval and coaling stations and although Mexico entertained such ideas behind closed doors, publicly it denied and refused any such overtures. By the early twentieth century, Mexican diplomacy with the United States remained unequal and strained, but Mexican relations with Japan were friendly, and the two countries increasingly viewed the United States with suspicion. In this manner, Mexico viewed Japan as a countervailing force against the aggression of the United States. However, it is also evident that Mexico understood that exploiting Japan-US tensions required a level of finesse to maintain equilibrium since it received arms and supplies from each country. More important, Mexico was aware that its relationship with Japan had its limitations and that its eventual position in the hemisphere relied on its relationship with the United States, and not Japan. Nevertheless, Mexico tested those limits up until the beginning of World War II. In many ways, as I argue later, these were the early signs of Mexico's "weapons of the weak" deployed diplomatically and successfully on many fronts during the first half of the twentieth century.

Japanese Penetration: Real and Imagined

Japanese immigration to Mexico during the second decade of the twentieth century began to show some patterns of settlement. By this period thousands of Japanese had moved into the northern sectors of Mexico drawn by the lure of work in the mines and its proximity to the United States. The experience of Taira Seishin fits this experience. Born in Ogimi, Okinawa, in 1886, Taira sought change, adventure, and opportunity in Mexico and left Japan in 1907. Taira's decision to go to Mexico instead of Brazil or Peru was based on Mexico's proximity to the United States. After arriving at the Mexican port of Salina Cruz, Taira made his way to the mining camp of Las Esperanzas in the state of Coahuila, where he worked only a few short months and moved farther south into Mexico. Although Taira initially desired to cross into the United States, he remained in Mexico for the remainder of his life, eventually settling in Mexico City.[11]

Another distinguishing marker for the Japanese in their formative years was their heavy presence in the agricultural sector and railroad industry. A significant number of Japanese also began to settle in the urban sectors such as Mexico City due to opportunities in nonagricultural professions. However, as the Mexican Revolution emerged and the violent phase developed, large numbers of Japanese gravitated toward Mexico's northwest states. This period also saw a shift from the Japanese day laborer to the small entrepreneur searching for a livelihood in such areas as farming or as small merchants along the border towns of northern Mexico, and the remnants of the Enomoto Colony founded a number of different operations in Chiapas.

As the Japanese in Mexico began to leave the agricultural sector, they first moved into industries that allowed them to utilize their experience such as those occupations related to agriculture: cereal buyers, rural real estate brokers, grocers, and owners of hardware stores, bars, and boarding houses in rural towns. In their next occupational phase the more successful Japanese began buying and operating machines for processing rice, corn, sugar cane, coffee, and other produce.[12] The Mexican Revolution, for the average Mexican, was chaotic and caused widespread displacement, with 500,000 Mexicans fleeing to the United States. Generally, no such quarter was given to Japanese due to the restriction placed on Japanese entering the United States, unless done so under covert means. As a result the Japanese in Mexico during the violent phase of the revolution survived by adapting to this new environment.

The Japanese population in Mexico remained relatively small and the number of Japanese who participated in the Mexican Revolution reflects that status. Nevertheless, there was a perception on the part of the Mexican and US press, the US public, and government officials that large numbers of Japanese were involved in the revolution, and of course this translated into a Japanese vanguard waiting in Mexico for the opportunity to invade the United States. The *New York Times* in 1914 reported that Japanese army officers were requesting permission from their government to enter the service of the Mexican Army. Simultaneously and similar to imaginary colonization schemes that involved the movement of tens of thousands of Japanese, the Mexican Revolution had a similar effect. Again, it is important to state that this paranoia or US neurosis was not limited to the public, but was also held by the US media and US government officials. More important, US intelligence officers created reports that portrayed Mexico swarming with Japanese colonists and soldiers and reports riddled and filled with hearsay, infected with the "Yellow Peril," but also by the more widespread phenomena known as Western hemispheric Orientalism. For example, the *New York Times* on January 29, 1914, reported 9,000 Japanese in Mexico, "most of whom are army veterans," the estimate rose to over 25,000 in 1916. On January 30, 1916, the *Boston Sunday Globe*[13] (1916) indicated that there were "90,000 Japanese in Hawaii and 30,000 in Mexico organized and ready to fight at a moment's notice." A July 1916 issue of *Forum* magazine reported that "the last estimate of our [US] military authorities shows one quarter of million Japs in Mexico." An officer on the staff of the War College in Washington estimated that there were 400,000 Japanese soldiers in Mexico.[14]

These sensational numbers are difficult to explain, especially since most of the numbers are not in line with reality. The most accurate numbers of Japanese in Mexico for the first two decades of the twentieth century are gleaned from a variety of sources, including data from US consular offices throughout Mexico, Mexican censuses, and the Japanese government. These sources, together with interviews of those who witnessed events, provide the best estimate of the Japanese population in Mexico during the revolution. For example, the majority of these sources indicate that the Japanese population in Mexico did not exceed 3,500 for the period 1910–20. The Mexican Census of 1910 indicates that the Japanese residents totaled 2,623 (2,456 males, 167 females). Passports issued by the foreign ministry of Japan, 1910–18, disclosed 964 nationals left Japan for Mexico. In the end the most likely scenario was probably very similar to the following report from a military engineer who served with Villa's forces: "I saw only four or five Japanese in the ranks of Villa's army. They were not handling machine guns, but with the exception of one, were connected with the infantry."[15] The numbers above reflected registered Japanese nationals and those that entered Mexico under Japanese passports. Not included are Mexicans of Japanese ancestry, which probably added several thousand more to the overall Japanese population in Mexico. Nevertheless, this does not come close to the sensational numbers mentioned by US newspapers.

The small Japanese population in Mexico between 1910 and 1920 can be attributed to several factors that included the surge of Japanese that entered the United States between 1907 and 1908, which depleted their ranks in Mexico, the chaotic period of the Mexican Revolution, and census enumerators simply undercounting the Japanese population. What then accounts for the dozens of US military reports and newspaper articles from Mexico and the United States that stated tens of thousands of Japanese resided in Mexico? Any attempt to answer this question requires an understanding of national and global events shaping not only Mexican-Japanese-US relations but also the mindset of the general public regarding shifting geopolitical dynamics that increased tensions between whites and Asians. More important, by the time the Mexican Revolution began, the Chinese and Japanese populations in the United States had become pariahs through racial exclusion. However, the restrictions and depictions of the Japanese as the *other* or unassimilable was only a means to an end. Japan and the Japanese represented a greater threat than the Chinese because of their quick modernization and ascension as an imperial power and so needed to be prevented from immigrating not just to North America but the entire Western hemisphere. Historian Erika Lee points to a pattern of unity between predominately white countries such as the United States and Canada that forged alliances to prevent the movement of Asians to North America. And with a series of race riots that erupted along the West Coast of the United States and Canada, in 1907 both countries began to view the "oriental problem" beyond national boundaries, thereby crystallizing "Western hemispheric Orientalism."[16]

Perhaps the knowledge of a small number of Japanese who immigrated to Mexico after their service in the Japanese-Russia War that culminated in 1905 with a Japanese victory, stirred anxiety and magically small numbers increased exponentially. From existing records a small number of Japanese who fought in Japan's early wars with China and Russia immigrated to Mexico. This was the experience of Atsuyoshi Schichiyo, who came to Mexico in 1910: "I took part in the Battle of Hoten, in Manchuria (February 10, 1906, the last major battle between Japanese and Russian forces). In the battle I commanded a grenade-throwing squad, and received from the Emperor a medal for bravery. After the war I decided to seek my fortune in Mexico. That was in 1910. The ship took us to Salina Cruz port, and I left immediately for Mexico City."[17] It is unknown how many Japanese such as Atsuyoshi participated in the Japanese military prior to arriving in Mexico, but based on the Japanese population in Mexico, the number must have been small. However, when stories such as Atsuyoshi's reached the US media, the number astonishingly grew, which in some small measure accounts for the large discrepancies between the true and imaginary numbers of Japanese in Mexico.

Clearly, the large discrepancy between the likely number of Japanese in Mexico during the Mexican Revolution (3,500–5,000) and the exaggerated reports from a variety of sources needs some explanation. There are probably several rationalizations for the degree of separation between perceptions of the Japanese in Mexico. First, the "Yellow Peril" created in the United States continued to swirl in the public domain, especially in newsprint that heightened the level of anxiety of the American public. When the anxiety is coupled with various strains of nativism, racism, and discrimination, the US public, including the media, began to take at face value any report, regardless how extreme, as the truth. In many ways, fear overcame rational thought but so did the increasing hatred toward the Japanese. This fear is responsible for not only the overstated numbers but also the process of dehumanizing the Japanese populations, which gained strength and ingrained itself throughout US society. These ideas and perceptions of the Japanese were also exported throughout the Americas. This in turn contaminated writers, the media, politicians, the military, and the general population regarding the Japanese throughout the Western hemisphere.

The Creation of a Hemispheric Menace

The Japanese presence in Mexico was not completely void of controversy during the Mexican Revolution. Throughout the revolution, Mexican and US newspapers and US government officials wrote sensational accounts of

Japanese infiltration into Mexico that went beyond immigration, such as the Mexican government abetting Japanese overtures, especially those of a military nature. And there was an endless stream of colonization schemes that portrayed hundreds of thousands of Japanese immigrating to Mexico. For example, in the northern state of Sonora, where a significant number of Japanese resided, the US state department reported on one of those schemes. Arturo del Toro, who had owned a hacienda in southern Mexico but was driven out by the Zapatistas, submitted one of these reports in 1919. According to Del Toro, in late 1918 on his way to the United States he encountered a group of Japanese including Japanese engineers who had traveled from Tokyo to examine land near Hermosillo, Sonora.[18] Del Toro also stated that he encountered another party of Japanese who posed as tourists. According to del Toro, one of the individuals was from Los Angeles, another from San Francisco, and the rest were from Japan. They took voluminous notes and photographs and showed a special interest in Guaymas along the coast.[19]

Although very little evidence surfaced concerning alleged Japanese schemes to purchase or lease land in Sonora, a simple rumor of such a possibility was enough to spur the US government to investigate the possibility. This is exactly what the American consul in Sonora suggested in his report to the state department. The report raises two concerns. First, Japanese could use the northern state of Sonora as a back door into the United States. This concern had been raised since the beginning of the twentieth century. Second, the American consul mentioned that the Japanese might acquire important economic advantages in various industries and become an economic threat. The notion of a "Japanese Menace" and a broader anti-Japanese sentiment continued to form the basis for the US policy to block Japanese entrance into the United States and to discourage a Japanese presence close to the American border. In his report to the state department, the American consul at Sonora stated the following:

> Should a large Japanese colony be established in the State of Sonora . . . they would be so situated as to command a back door entrance to the United States. They would acquire valuable pearl and other fisheries in the Gulf. They would secure very valuable lands capable of supporting hundreds of thousands of Japanese with their agricultural and perhaps mineral productions.[20]

Japanese colonization schemes were rumored to be in development on a yearly basis during the Mexican Revolution. As mentioned above, only several had any validity. Why was there so much hearsay into possible Japanese schemes? What was the genesis of the rumors? These are difficult questions to answer, but one conceivable explanation is that there was some element of truth to most of the unconfirmed reports regarding Japanese attempts to purchase or lease lands, as well as Mexican and American companies seeking out potential buyers. It is clear that Japanese capitalists had a desire for Mexican land and Mexicans and Americans were willing to sell theirs to the highest bidder. Another possibility involved German manipulation. According to Friedrich Katz, German aims in Mexico during the years 1911–13 were complex, but one of those aims was to provoke tensions, perhaps even war, between the United States and Japan, "that would neutralize two of its rivals was an old dream of German diplomacy."[21] To achieve its principal aim, in April 4, 1911, Germany circulated in the press that Mexico and Japan reached a secret alliance. It did not take long before the US press began to write sensational articles and the general US public went into hysterical mode. On April 9, 1911, an astonishing article appeared in *New York Evening Sun*, asserting the existence of such a treaty and even claiming that the US ambassador to Mexico, H. Lane Wilson, had seen it. The newspaper attributed the mobilization of American troops on the Mexican border to the treaty. The article and information had been planted in the paper by the German military attaché in the United States, Herwarth von Bittenfeld.[22]

Such a treaty, of course, between Mexico and Japan never existed, but the collateral damage was significant, especially from the perspective of public opinion and the increased agitation it caused regarding the presence of Japanese in Mexico and the United States. The treaty fabrication was followed by an anonymous article planted in the February issue of the *Atlantic Monthly* titled "A Letter to Uncle Sam," which warned of a "Yellow Peril" and suggested that "only an alliance of the white races" could put an end to the Japanese menace.[23] The planted stories, coupled with US paranoia of anything Japanese developed into a Mexican version of the "Yellow Peril" with a Japanese spy hiding under every rock or an invading horde landing every month. The US press drove much of this paranoia.

One of the most sensational stories emerged in 1913 in the *Cleveland Leader* written by Harry H. Dunn titled "60,000 Japanese in Mexico: Why Are They There and What Do They Do Besides Fish?" The article was accompanied by a handful of images that attempted to reinforce Dunn's assertions that the Japanese had designs other than fishing. For example, several of the images are of a military nature with one, according to Dunn, depicting the Japanese guards for Porfirio Díaz. A second picture allegedly depicting two Japanese officers in the Mexican Army, but actually appeared to be Japanese officers in the Japanese Imperial Army visiting Mexico. Another image shows several Japanese in traditional Japanese garb and is captioned "Japanese fisherman on Mexico's west coast and his plain and fancy wives." Besides insinuating Japanese had infiltrated Mexico, the images and story also attempt to view Japanese as morally corrupt and outside the boundaries and decorum of Western ethos. Generally, whether Buddhist or Christian, the majority of Japanese practiced monogamy, and not polygamy as suggested by Dunn's caption. However, the likelihood of the general reader of the *Cleveland Leader* making such distinctions were slim. It was this type of article that circulated through the first half of the twentieth century that contained, for the most part, unsubstantiated claims, but was digested by the public as the truth. For example, Dunn's article began, "Sixty thousand Japanese, all men and all former soldiers in the service of the Nipponese empire are in Mexico, a silent, patient, potential army four times as great as the entire federal military force of the Southern republic."[24] This quote would be repeated dozens of times in a variety of newspapers, popular magazines, and official government reports. It is difficult to define such hysteria, but a psychology of fear resonates throughout these reports regardless of its origins. The Mexican press and government officials differed little in their treatment of Asians in Mexico. However, as the following example will show, Mexico encountered the influence of the United States on many fronts.

Before the outbreak of the Mexican Revolution, Mexico developed a pattern of anti-Chinese sentiment that was organic, but also the result of anti-Asian attitudes that filtered in from the United States. As the anti-Asian sentiment enveloped the Japanese diaspora, the United States began concerted efforts to track and ascertain the motives of Japan and Japanese immigrants throughout the Western hemisphere. The surveillance of Japanese began in unlikely places such as Cuba, which had very few Japanese and those were often mistaken as Chinese. In 1910 a group of three Japanese located in Matanzas garnered the attention of Cuban and US officials because one of them was a veteran of the Russo-Japanese war and seemed "educated." Another report from the office of the military attaché in Guatemala indicated that a reconnaissance of "Central America" turned up no Japanese.[25] As a final example to illustrate the wide net the United States cast regarding its concern over Japanese immigration and activities in the Western hemisphere, a fifteen page report was submitted by the military attaché in Lima, Peru, which began with the following sentence: "For over three years the writer has constantly heard talk of the Yellow Peril in South America. This talk has generally centered about the west coast countries, particularly Peru, and especially with reference to the Japanese."[26] Overall, the report goes into great detail regarding the movement of Japanese officials and their Peruvian contacts. The report also furnished information on Peruvian-Japanese relations regarding Japanese colonies, military cooperation, and economic interests.

The infiltration and reconnoiter of Mexican ports by US agents coincided with the arrival of Japanese naval delegations at the Mexican ports of Manzanillo, Colima; Acapulco, Guerrero; and Salina Cruz, Oaxaca, which were also ports used by thousands of Japanese immigrants. The arrival of two Japanese training squadrons, aboard the S.S. *Asama* and S.S. *Kasagi*, occurred in January 1911 and was greeted by a delegation of enthusiastic Díaz officials and the Chancellor of the Japanese Legation in Mexico.[27] Eventually the Japanese delegation of nearly 200 naval personnel made their way to Mexico City. The arrival of the Japanese naval delegation garnered much attention from the Mexican, Japanese, and US press, as well as a flurry of US military reports. One US military report went into great detail about how Japanese Admiral Yashiro laid a porcelain wreath at the base of the monument at Chapultepec Castle in memory of the Mexican cadets who jumped to their deaths rather than be captured by US troops during the Mexican American War of 1846–48. The report indicated that Yashiro stated the following: "It is an honor and a duty to come and place this wreath of flowers at the base of the monument that is to recall for future generations the heroic deed of the young boys who knew how to die in defense of their country." The same report stated that the Chief of the Mexican secret police exclaimed, "Wait until Mexico and Japan get together; then with Japan to attend to the naval work while we attack by land, we'll make short work of the 'Gringos' or words to that effect."[28] Such reports and insinuations were common during the period of the late Porfiriato and the Mexican Revolution. The US military attaché received this last quote not from first-hand knowledge but from a secondary source, as was the case with many of the reports that circulated during this period regarding the movement or activities of the Japanese. Nonetheless, along with the sensational news reports and the general public outcry, such reports were part of the overall reconfiguration of the Japanese in the Western hemisphere. The involvement of a small number of Japanese Mexicans in the Mexican Revolution provided additional fuel for the hyperbolic and exaggerated claims of tens of thousands of Japanese in Mexico.

Japanese Combatants and the Mexican Revolution

The quick rise of the Japanese empire and its militarization caused concern for a number of US administrations and the US military. From the Japanese perspective, the presence and dominance of the United States and other Western nations in the East, in many ways, was responsible for Japanese militarization. And as I have mentioned earlier, Japan, throughout the late nineteenth and early twentieth centuries created a simulacrum of Western behavior in order to cope with Western aggression in the East, which it considered its sphere of influence. After several decades of adaptation, the Japanese went on the offensive and began to extend their military dominance in the region and by the end of the nineteenth century emerged as a dominant player in East Asia. The Japanese defeat of Russia in the early twentieth century signaled the rise of Japanese imperialism. This does not condone the Japanese occupation of various regions of Asia or the atrocities committed by the Japanese military up and through World War II. My point here is to shed some light on the Japanese position as it gained strength in the early twentieth century. Also, from a practical and prudent position, I agree that the United States needed to be concerned with the rise of Japanese imperialism. Yet, my argument is not necessarily with the military question, but rather, how interpretations and views of Japan and its military were superimposed upon all Japanese subjects without restraint. I submit that this imposition fed the various "Yellow Peril," war scares, anti-Japanese immigration legislation, and alien land and miscegenation laws in the United States, which in turn contaminated many regions of the Americas with negative images of all Japanese. In other words, US prejudices, policies, and legislation eventually influenced many regions of Latin America regarding the treatment of Japanese populations in the Western hemisphere. Japan's rise as a world military power also had other consequences such as producing combat veterans who immigrated to places like Mexico. Under extreme scrutiny in the Americas, a handful of Japanese veterans magically morphed into battalion strength fifth columns ready to invade the United States.

The Mexican Revolution also coincided with the emergence of other global conflicts, such as World War I, the US Punitive Expedition of 1916, and Mexican and Japanese overtures that were interpreted as the forging of a Japanese-Mexican alliance. These conflicts and episodes intensified the fears and anxieties of the US public. Yet, this process, as we have seen, began long before 1910. The fear of the Japanese presence in the

US and Mexico, as I have mentioned, was layered with racism and based on the belief that the Japanese were not only undesirable but also biologically unfit for citizenship, and in the process, their very presence diluted the purity of the white race. Mexicans had a very different approach to the Japanese, which I argue spared, with some exceptions of course, the Japanese from the nationalistic fervor that erupted with the Mexican Revolution. This was not the case for US citizens and Chinese residing in Mexico.

The Japanese experience during the revolution contained many variants, but also commonalities with the average Mexican. First, like so many Mexicans during this period, Japanese suffered high rates of unemployment due to being employed in occupations hardest hit by the revolution. As a consequence, many Japanese volunteered for military service with the various factions in order to simply survive. By and large, the Japanese in Mexico from 1910–20 survived not by fleeing but adapting to the violence and chaos of the revolution. In some cases their ethnicity created opportunities for survival. By this I mean that the Japanese were often released from captivity or their lives spared when captured by the various revolutionary factions because they were Japanese and quickly conscripted and commissioned as officers. Of course, this was based on the false assumption and stereotype that all Japanese males in Mexico were combat veterans or that the Japanese were inherently military leaders. The image of the militarized Japanese was so profound that Mexican military officials of all stripes were willing to accept groups of Japanese as conscripts with no questions asked. One source indicated that in March 1915 General Álvaro Obregón had written to First Chief Carranza stating that 800 Japanese soldiers had been offered to the Constitutionalists' Army by a Japanese.[29] However, most of these sources are linked to either US military reports or US consular dispatches, which tended to exaggerate such claims.

One of the most embellished US consular dispatches reported that 2,500 Japanese were being recruited from the United States to fight in the Mexican Revolution. Such a number would cause a logistical nightmare not only to recruit but also to maneuver across the US-Mexican border during a period of severe restriction of the movement of Japanese.[30] However, such exaggerations do not diminish the fact that some Japanese residing in Mexico were combatants and a handful had direct access to a number of revolutionary leaders. As I explain later, Japanese were allowed unfettered access to various revolutionary leaders such as Pancho Villa. And based on several accounts, two alleged Japanese assassins walked right into Villa's personal quarters for a face-to-face meeting without any precautionary measures taken to screen the Japanese. One simple explanation for this laissez-faire attitude is the previously mentioned stereotype. Mexicans believed that all Japanese were imbued with special military skills or knowledge that might contribute to their cause, and as a result, they were not only given a wide berth but also conscripted. This is exactly what happened to Nagantani Yasutaro:

> In Japan I was told that I would earn 20 yen a day in Mexico, and I was very eager to go there. I went to Mexico to work in the coalmines in Coahuila state. I was paid one yen 25 sen for work outside the mine. This was disappointing so I asked the Japanese supervisor about getting another job. He said that working underground paid more, but was dangerous. He suggested that I leave secretly during the night. . . . On the way to Tampico I was stopped by an attack of General Villa's forces. At that time a member of General González' staff, a Japanese named Fukota, asked me to join the army. I decided it was a wise thing to do, and became a surgeon's assistant.[31]

Kingo Nonaka's participation in the Mexican Revolution is quite interesting and illustrates the unconventional methods Japanese used to join the ranks of the revolutionary forces. Nonaka immigrated to the Oaxaqueña plantation near Veracruz in 1888, when he was fifteen years old. Nonaka indicated he could not endure the difficult working conditions of the plantation and fled to the city of Chihuahua. There he was rescued by a Mexican family, who had him baptized and treated him like their son.[32] Much later, Nonaka, who did not feel comfortable living idly on the hacienda of his benefactors, learned nursing in a nearby hospital and acquired a license to work in the infirmary. The careful assistance and cordial demeanor Nonaka gave to his patients became well known in Chihuahua, and his services were constantly requested.[33] Kingo Nonaka became one of the few Japanese officially recognized and awarded medals for his contribution to the Mexican Revolution. In November 1966, at the age of seventy-four, Nonaka received the Mexican Legion of Honor for his service, achievements, and participation in the Mexican Revolution. According to government records José Kingo Nonaka entered the revolution on April 15, 1910, and fought with the Constitutionalist Forces of the Division of the North under the command of General Francisco Villa and remained under this command until November 15, 1915. The citation indicates that Nonaka participated in military campaigns in Chihuahua,

Durango, Coahuila, and Zacatecas from 1913–14 as part of the medical corps.[34]

There are other well-documented cases, such as the career of Luis Bojorquez. Born in 1883 in Tokyo, he immigrated to Mexico in 1905, married a Mexican woman, and joined the revolution in 1913.[35] According to Bojorquez's military record, he joined the forces of Lieutenant Colonel Antunez of the Sonoran Battalion on February 13, 1913.[36] His combat record states that he fought in the campaigns of Santa Rosa, Santa María, and Empalme, where he was promoted to corporal in May 1913. He then fought at Culiacán with the 2nd Battalion of Sonora, where he was promoted to sergeant second class on October 20, 1913. He continued to fight battles from Sonora all the way down to Mexico City with the regiment known as Column Hill and was promoted to sergeant first class on June 10, 1914. The next campaign took him to Zacalelco and Puebla on January 5, 1915. On January 10, 1915, he was engaged in a shoot-out with Zapatistas. Bojorquez returned to the north and from April 6 to April 15 fought with Army of the Northeast at Celaya against the Villistas. On April 21, 1915, Bojorquez was promoted to the rank of lieutenant. After several other engagements in the north, by order of the secretary of war, he was promoted to the rank of captain second class on July 10, 1916. Luis Bojorquez remained in the military and later served with distinction in the cavalry.[37]

The story of Yamazaki Isokichi, who arrived from Kanagawa prefecture, in the early years of the twentieth century, provides insight into the many views of the Japanese in Mexico and the assumptions made about the Japanese. Furthermore, in this particular narrative Isokichi describes his encounter with a group of blacks in Mexico. It is unclear if the blacks were Mexican or from some other region, but the Japanese and blacks were each utilized for sport and amusement by their Mexican host:

> When I came to Mexico we had to walk from San Benito port to the inland towns. . . . It was in September 1915 during the rainy season. . . . We reached Cuitla (possibly Escuintla) and stopped at a house on the outskirts of town, gesturing for food. A young man appeared who spoke to us in English, which one of the group, Suzuki, understood. He asked us to come to his house, and gave us lunch. Afterwards he took us to the garden where there were several Negroes. He asked us to wrestle with the Negroes. . . . Suzuki adopted the Japanese wrestling stance and grappled with the Negro, and quickly defeated him. We wrestled seven other Negroes, defeating them also.[38]

The Japanese immigrants who came to Mexico at the beginning of the twentieth century never imagined fighting in a revolution, particularly one not in their native land. However, as the explosion of the revolution disrupted their lives and their attempts to flee into the United States were hindered by restrictive legislation and danger, many chose to fight. The case studies examined show that most of the Japanese fought for the revolutionary factions. Very few appear to have enlisted with Díaz or Huerta. It is not known whether this was due to most Japanese residing in the north or because some believed in the convictions of the various revolutionary leaders. However, what is certain is that some did not survive this period of violence, destruction, and disorder. José Kingo Nonaka and Luis Bojorquez serve to illustrate the level of integration and acceptance many Japanese in Mexico achieved, if not often recognized. The fact that some of the Japanese were placed in leadership positions and others were given battlefield commissions demonstrated the respect they garnered from the Mexican population. More important, the argument can be made that the Japanese in Mexico felt a sense of disenfranchisement and disillusionment from the *Porfirian* regime and took up arms against it, sometimes coerced into doing so, but others volunteered. From the various oral histories and interviews Japanese could be found in nearly every camp during the Mexican Revolution. However, the record of the Japanese experience in Mexico would not be complete if the focus was merely on the Japanese who actively participated as combatants.

Other Japanese remained somewhat removed from the daily tribulations of the violence and attempted to survive by continuing in their daily endeavors, occupations, or attempted to keep their businesses alive. This was the case with Iwase Mitsuo, who came to Mexico from Aichi Prefecture in Japan. His short but insightful words explore the contact between Japanese and the indigenous population in Mexico, but more important Mitsuo provides his thoughts regarding the Chinese and Zapotec Indians in Chiapas during the Mexican Revolution. Iwase and his Mexican wife owned a drug store in Arriaga, Chiapas:

> In this town 20 percent of the business is in the hands of the Chinese, and the Zapotec tribe runs 80 percent. Nevertheless, there are good opportunities here, even for an inexperienced person. The Mexicans, who regard them as an inferior race, despise the Zapotec tribe. But many of them, the males, went to school, leaving the females to run the business.[39]

The Japanese population in Mexico during the revolution suffered in a similar manner to the Mexican populace, but dissimilar compared with the Chinese population in Mexico. Unlike their Chinese counterparts, the Japanese were not singled out as foreign targets as nationalism swept the Mexican landscape. During the first few years of the revolution anti-Chinese hostility was rampant. The Chinese were frequently robbed and often killed as they transported merchandise on the open roads.[40] Revolutionary soldiers of every stripe seeking food and other necessities looted Chinese stores. Revolutionary leaders in need of cash and provisions extorted and imposed "forced loans" on Chinese merchants.[41]

The Japanese did not escape unscathed by the revolution. On numerous occasions Japanese in Mexico suffered assaults as a result of robbery or confiscation of merchandise, money, and sometimes land. A good example of this is Kajima Matsutaro who immigrated to Mexico from Hiroshima prefecture and describes his experience in vivid detail. Besides being captured by rebel forces, Matsutaro explains the horror of war and why some Japanese joined up with various factions, to prevent starvation:

> From 1913–1916 Mexico was in a civil war. In Mexico City we could hear gunfire day and night . . . we could not go outside because the gunfire was so near. When I opened the door, very carefully, I saw many dead and wounded people in the streets. It looked like hell. This was September 1914 . . . at that time there were about fifty Japanese in Mexico City, and most had left. They feared starvation and many Japanese men had joined the army to obtain food.[42]

Although a few incidents can be found in which Japanese were killed or property destroyed because of their ethnicity, there is no apparent concerted effort or pattern to target Japanese. Indeed, much of the evidence alludes to a belief that the Japanese were endowed with an innate ability to lead and fight, were militarily gifted, and were incapable of failure. These markers somehow made the Japanese different from their Asian cousins, the Chinese, and as a result the Japanese were more readily accepted because they served a utilitarian need for Mexico or at least that was the belief.

The lack of a discernible pattern of violence toward the Japanese may be attributed to a number of explanations. Robert Duncan has demonstrated that the region with the largest number of Japanese, Baja California, was peripheral to the revolution and did not experience the intense fighting and deaths of other regions. Furthermore, Governor Esteban Cantu (1914–20) exercised strong control over the area and a measure of independence that allowed him to prohibit the entry of Chinese and Japanese into northern Baja California. However, when protests occurred over the surprise arrival of some 1,500 Chinese laborers in September 1919, Cantu took harsh measures to stop the movement of Asians into the region.[43] Also, the Japanese population never reached numbers that would pose an economic threat to the general Mexican population. In 1910 there were approximately 13,000 Chinese in Mexico, compared with 2,200 Japanese.[44] During the decade of the revolution most of the Japanese who arrived came as fishermen, miners, or agricultural workers, and as they completed their work contracts transitioned into those respective occupations. However, the Chinese posed a greater threat because as they completed their contracts many did not take up laboring jobs but instead entered commerce as small independent entrepreneurs and occasionally in partnerships with American railroad and mine owners, thus becoming rivals of the lower strata of the Mexican working class.[45]

The Japanese in contrast did not experience this economic animosity at the level of the Chinese, again probably because the flow of Japanese immigration into Mexico was quantitatively negligible compared with that of the Chinese, the Japanese penetration into the Mexican economy remained small, and the Japanese had some official government supervision. Japanese in Mexico were always kept under the influence of their home country that controlled their subjects to avoid possible conflicts.[46] Furthermore, the Japanese government made concerted efforts through diplomatic channels, petitioning the Mexican government to protect their Japanese subjects. For example, on February 23, 1912, the Japanese Legation in Mexico petitioned the Mexican government to protect the interest, property, and lives of Japanese subjects:

> Throughout the state of Sinaloa the revolutionary bandits have begun to emerge. The character of their arrival is lawlessness. . . . They attack everyone without making any distinction between Mexican and foreigners. Life and property is in danger. One Japanese was attacked by the bandits, but luckily escaped. We request immediate protection.[47]

The situation for the Japanese remained similar the following year when an urgent dispatch reached the Japanese Legation stating the current environment required immediate intervention to protect the Japanese colony in Culiacán.[48] Although Mexican officials appeared attentive to the petitions by the Japanese government, the reality was that very little could be done in the chaotic climate of the revolution. This did not prevent the Japanese government from increasing pressure on the Mexican government to intervene by reminding the Mexicans of their treaty obligations:

> The Imperial Japanese Government have no doubt that the Japanese subjects shall enjoy, under your Government, the treatment of the most favoured nation, in all respects, especially regarding the protection of their persons, properties and interests as well as in the matter of satisfaction for their damages caused by the revolution.[49]

From the above description a significant number of Japanese fell victim to revolutionary factions seeking conscripts, bandits, and indiscriminate pillaging of property. However, to describe the Japanese simply as victims of the chaotic Mexican Revolution neglects those Japanese that played limited, but unusual roles during the period of the revolution. Evidence indicates that some Japanese readily signed up for military service for the adventure, while others actually fought and died seeking social change. Besides participating in the Mexican Revolution, Japanese also appear to have taken part in the US Punitive Expedition of 1916. The Japanese Mexicans who were "hired guns" defy the ordinary Japanese experience and provide additional understanding of the complex history of the Japanese in Mexico.

Japanese Mercenaries and the US Punitive Expedition

For Pancho Villa the year 1914 seemed to bring good fortune and his ambition of someday sitting permanently in the Mexican presidential chair appeared imminent. The United States had agreed to back him as the individual with the capabilities to unite Mexico under a new regime and bring order to the chaos. The United States did not see an enlightened leader in Villa or one possessed with democratic principles that could bring calm and hope to a nation. Rather, Villa personified the very qualities that the United States wanted and needed at this particular juncture, a tenacious and brutal leader who could suppress revolutionary factions, raids, bandits, and murder across the borderlands. Whether it was Pancho Villa,

Venustiano Carranza, or Alvaro Obregón, it did not matter, as long as the killing of Americans stopped and Mexican oil continued to flow. However, Carranza, the First Chief, refused to be outmaneuvered, and with one of the greatest war strategists of the revolution at his side, General Alvaro Obregón, Carranza planned a counteroffensive. By June 1915 Carranza and Obregón had handed Villa such serious defeats at Celaya, Léon, and Agua Prieta that Villa retreated to the mountains and lost the majority of his army. At this point the United States offered Carranza recognition if he could bring about stability and a government. After continued combat and defeat of Villa and Zapata forces and their retreat to their bases, the United States recognized the Carranza regime on October 19, 1915, as Mexico's new government.[50]

As Carranza went about attempting to reconstruct Mexico, Villa regrouped and maneuvered to sever the Carranza-US umbilical cord in order to force another regime change. On March 9, 1916, Villa with 500 of his men raided Columbus, New Mexico, killing seventeen US citizens. Six days later, March 15, 1916, the United States sent in a punitive expedition in search of Pancho Villa with the official objective of driving Villa and his men from the border region. Within two years Villa's dream to preside over Mexico came quickly crashing down.[51] By the end of the same year, not only had Pancho Villa been defeated, but a campaign to demonize him on both sides of the border began. Pancho Villa did not take his defeat and diminishing relevance easily. Simultaneously the United States stopped arms and ammunition shipments to Carranza. Carranza in turn demanded the withdrawal of US troops in April and in order to renew United States confidence and spur Pershing's retreat, authorized Texas rebels, aligned with the Plan of San Diego, to conduct raids into Texas from Mexico.[52]

The Plan of San Diego and the US Punitive Expedition were interlocked on multiple levels. First, the punitive expedition, although instigated by Villa's raid on Columbus, was a culmination of border clashes that erupted in 1915 where Americans were killed on both sides. Villa's raid was the tipping point from the US perspective. Rebels, whom eventually Carranza brought under his control, conducted many of the raids. Although it is possible that disgruntled Mexican and African Americans initially instigated the Plan of San Diego, in the end, much of the evidence points to Carranza's cooptation of the movement for his own political ends. Second, in order to bring the raids to an end, the United States agreed to recognize Carranza and his regime as the legitimate authority in

Mexico.[53] Finally, that recognition and Villa's response relegated him to persona non grata on both sides of the border. From Carranza's perspective Villa needed to be eliminated politically and if somehow Villa disappeared for good, well, that was all part of war.

It is in the midst of this military and political upheaval that we return to the Japanese experience. By this point the United States had become extremely nervous regarding the situation in Mexico with borderlands violence, the Plan of San Diego movement, and Mexico's oilfields, whose US and British control was in jeopardy. So concerned was the United States that a plan known as the Approved Mexican War Plan had been devised as a fail-safe option if and when it was determined that the United States needed to invade and occupy Mexico to protect its interests. The plan called for an invading force of 420,960 men and 500 guns (artillery).[54] Furthermore, it was well known that Carranza's regime had been receiving aid from Japan in the form of munitions and parts for manufacturing weapons in Mexico. These concerns coalesced as the punitive expedition entered Mexico. Within a short period Villa retreated into the mountains of Chihuahua where he enjoyed popular support. With Villa's whereabouts unknown, a variety of groups and individuals were used to locate Villa. The utilization of Japanese as scouts, spies, and alleged assassins became part of the hunt for Pancho Villa.

From the US military position, the use of Japanese appeared to be a good alternative to the use of Mexicans, who could not be trusted, and Americans, who lacked the experience for such missions. The initial reference to Japanese appears in a field report of Captain C. Williams, adjutant, for the period March 15 to June 2, 1916, which stated, "The San Geronimo Ranch [Mexico] is run by Japanese." This same report indicated that the punitive expedition made the area surrounding the San Geronimo ranch its temporary headquarters and it appeared that the Japanese at this ranch were recruited by the military.[55] The intelligence section of the punitive expedition and the predecessor to the Federal Bureau of Investigation (FBI) employed Japanese, while others were specifically assigned to various generals. For example, Nagamine Tonachi was assigned as an agent to General G.A. Dodd, 7th Cavalry Column, and Lucas Hayakawa was assigned as an agent to General George Bell, Commander El Paso District. Lucas Hayakawa and Gustavo Tatematsu were also employed by the FBI as secret agents code-named "Jah" and "Jat," respectively. The following is a list of Japanese individuals, some verified to be from Mexico, employed by various US entities (table 2.1).

Table 2.1. Japanese employed by the US Punitive Expedition, Intelligence Section, 1916[1]

Name	*Location*	*Entered Mexico*	*Service*	*Code Name*
Dyo, Tsutomu R.	San Geronimo	1906	Punitive Exp.	George
Sato A., Juan	Madera	1907	Punitive Exp.	Unknown
Suzuki T., Enrique	Pedernales	1908	Punitive Exp.	Unknown
Kawamur, R.	San Geronimo		Punitive Exp.	Unknown
Fujita, T.	Madera		Punitive Exp.	Unknown
Kato, A.	Punitive Exp.		Punitive Exp.	K
Tonachi, Nagamine			7th Cavalry	Unknown
Hayakawa, Lucas			FBI	Jah
Tatematsu Gemchi, Gustavo			FBI	Jat

Dyo, Sato, Suzuki, and Fujita were all assigned to the intelligence section of the punitive expedition and were under the charge of Lt. Nicholás W. Campanole. These four Japanese went on various secret missions, chiefly as scouts, to gather information, and to locate Pancho Villa. From April 1916 to March 1917, these individuals filed numerous reports from the field describing their observations, problems, and encounters. The reports were translated from both Japanese and Spanish. The Japanese scouts were paid five US dollars per day. By comparison, US civilian scouts, couriers, and agents were paid $100.00 per month.[56]

What followed is perhaps the most bizarre episode that involved the Japanese during the Mexican Revolution. In July 1916, Dyo, Sato, Fujita, and Suzuki continued with their mission of locating Villa for the American forces. However, according to some, two of the Japanese went beyond their reconnaissance mission and attempted to assassinate Villa with poison. US military authorities stated that if it did happen, the Japanese, on their own volition, went off mission and US military officers were not aware of such action. Nonetheless, a number of different sources and scholars have pointed to the strong possibility that the intelligence section of the punitive expedition authorized the mission to kill Villa. Because of the delicate nature and fear of possible repercussions, a systemic effort was made by the US military and civilian authorities to suppress the revelation of the assassination mission.

As important as the episode was, especially regarding the Japanese component, the period before and after 1916 continued to represent the complex triangular relationship that continuously flared and subsided during the first half of the twentieth century that engulfed Mexico, Japan, and the United States. As I have alluded to throughout this chapter, many of the revolutionary leaders, including Pancho Villa, had been on friendly terms with various Japanese residents, and several worked for Villa and his brother, Hipólito. The US Mexican Punitive Expedition was in reaction to Pancho Villa's raids into the United States along the US-Mexican border in and around the areas of New Mexico and Texas. According to Friedrich Katz, Charles Harris, and Louis Sadler, two Japanese initially approached First Chief Venustiano Carranza with an offer to poison Villa but were turned down by Carranza. Five months later, in August 1916, the same Japanese individuals approached US military intelligence officers of General John Pershing's Punitive Expedition into Mexico and offered their services to poison Villa. According to these sources, the Japanese were able to infiltrate Villa's camp and place poison in the coffee cup belonging to Villa. This episode was not made public during the period, so whether or not this would have affected other Japanese in the country remains unknown. Also, based on US military documents the Japanese in question were recruited by Pershing's punitive expedition.

Although the above mentioned books use archival material to support their assertions and there appeared to have been definite contact between Carranza and the Japanese and US military intelligence officers and the Japanese, what remains unclear are the motives for two Japanese subjects to carry out such a plot, especially since Japan had friendly relations with Mexico. The Japanese, overall, were well received, and Villa had an affinity for Japanese culture. From the evidence presented it remains unclear if an attempt was actually made or if the Japanese fabricated the attempt. Nevertheless, the fact that the Carranza camp and US military officers discussed such a plot in official reports makes it plausible. Also, according to Katz, a cover-up by the United States appeared to have occurred to prevent the story from becoming public.[57] Based on documentary evidence, an attempt by US authorities to conceal the alleged attempt, and an investigation into the plot to assassinate Villa, also makes it possible.

As mentioned at the beginning of this chapter, the actual attempted poisoning of Villa is described in a report sent from the US attorney general, Thomas Watt Gregory, to the US secretary of war, H. P. McCain. A special agent of the Department of Justice conducted an investigation with a reply received on October 4, 1916:

> Dyo, Fujita, Suzuki, and Sato et al. Alleged Villista Activities: Informant "Jah" advises that Japanese mentioned above have been employed as scouts from the General Pershing expedition in Mexico. . . . Informant "Jah" said that he desired to inform me of these countrymen of his who are working in Mexico. . . . Informant "Jah" reported to agent the fact that the two Japs, Dyo and Fujita, had been seen at Jimenez and Torreón with Villa and his forces, both holding the rank of colonel; therefore, informant "Jah" has become suspicious of their sincerity in their work with our government.[58]

The special agent above indicated their informant "Jah" (Lucas Hayakawa) is suspicious of Dyo and Fujita. However, if recalled, Dyo's report stated that in order to gain the confidence and maintain their cover, he and Fujita joined up with Villa's forces. And, if everything else is accurate, their cover allowed them to gain access to Villa and attempt the assassination. In the course of the investigation, additional individuals were interviewed, such as the Japanese interpreter, Tom Hillworth, of the immigration station in El Paso. Hillworth stated to the special agent that Dyo and Fujita informed him that they had been sent by Captain Reed of the American expedition to General Villa's camp with a poison prescription, with instructions to administer it to General Villa and kill him. Dyo and Fujita state that the prescription was given to Captain W. C. Reed by an American Army surgeon with the Pershing expedition for this purpose. Further, Dyo and Fujita state that in pursuance, with instructions from Captain Reed, they went into the camp of General Villa, taking with them the poison, and that Dyo did put a dose of poison in a cup of coffee set in front of General Villa, "[Villa] poured half his cup of coffee which contained the poison into another cup and handed it to a Mexican who sat on his right, and waited until the Mexican drank his portion of the coffee before he drank his own."[59] Based on the report, Dyo and Fujita quickly departed Villa's camp and returned to the American expedition without knowing the effects of the poison. Alarmingly, Suzuki was sent to the Villa camp to ascertain the outcome, which we know did not succeed. In the course of the investigation, General Pershing made a statement regarding the alleged assassination attempt:

> I have made a full investigation of this matter. All officers connected with secret service work of the Expedition in Mexico state that no officer had any knowledge or connection with any such plans as this Japanese report indicates. It is entirely possible that these Japanese had some such

> plan of their own, but I do not believe for one moment that any of our officers knew of it.[60]

Of course Pershing's comments can be interpreted as part of the cover-up to deny and maintain a distance between the Japanese attempted assassination and any US involvement. Indeed, Pershing states that if such an attempt was made, it was made without the knowledge or assistance of US military officers or handlers. The four Japanese, Sato, Fujita, Dyo, and Suzuki, continued conducting additional scouting missions in Mexico for the expedition until the withdrawal of Pershing's troops in February 1917.

The lingering question that remains is why four Japanese (three from Mexico) attempted to carry out such a dangerous mission. There are numerous responses and possibilities, but in the end this question remains elusive. Also, the possibility exists that the plot to kill Villa was a hoax created by the Japanese for unknown reasons. Direct evidence for the assassination attempt is missing. There is only circumstantial evidence from the informant "Jat" that such as attempt was made. Many theories abound regarding the motivation of the Japanese. One thing is certain and without question, US authorities employed a handful of Japanese Mexicans to help locate, not necessarily kill, Villa. Based on orders given to Pershing regarding the punitive expedition, the purpose was to scatter Villa's forces and relieve the border of the banditry and violence. Capturing Villa was also an option, but an order to kill or terminate with extreme prejudice is nowhere to be found in the official records. Yet, evidence indicates the US military and civilian authorities took measures to suppress dissemination of the affair and to absolve the officers and the command of complicity. At the very least the reports confirm the role of the Japanese Mexicans within the ranks of the US expedition, which also raises questions of its own.

What motivated this small number of Japanese Mexicans to join up with US forces? Was it the money, which paid five US dollars per day or the reward of $50,000 for Villa's arrest? Were these Japanese Mexicans, whose occupations ranged from miner to grocer, simply looking for adventure? Of the four Japanese sent on the scouting missions Dyo appears to have had a formal education well beyond the average Japanese immigrant of the early twentieth century. Most Japanese who entered Mexico when Dyo did in 1906 came with an agrarian background and an elementary school education. Dyo is also the individual who allegedly engineered the plot. His reports indicate that he was highly resourceful, daring but cautious, a keen observer, with a remarkable memory for detail, calm and affable. With this background, was Dyo more than a miner? Many of these questions will go unanswered. Nevertheless, the fact that Japanese Mexicans were employed by the punitive expedition provides further evidence of the complexity of the Japanese experience in Mexico.

Conclusion

Conditions in Mexico during the revolution were far from inviting. Nevertheless, the policy of Mexico seems not to have changed toward Japanese immigration. Unlike the United States, the Mexican government never restricted Japanese immigration and throughout the decade made efforts to recruit them. A Japanese newspaper stated, "The President of México pointed out to the vast stretch of country with sparse population capable of accommodating one hundred million immigrants, and added that the Japanese would be welcomed in Mexico for the development of her unbound resources."[61] As the violent period of the Mexican Revolution diminished, the Mexican government continued to view immigration as a viable option to bring some level of modernity and prosperity to the country. As Mexican society transitioned from violent upheaval to reconstruction, Japanese immigration also went through a change. When Mexico implemented its new constitution of 1917, it simultaneously entered into a new agreement with Japan for the recruitment of professional immigrants who would fill a void in Mexico. In April 1917, thirty Japanese immigrants with backgrounds in medicine, pharmaceuticals, and dentistry arrived in Mexico, which signaled a shift from farm laborers and mine workers to the recruitment of professionals that lasted until the beginning of World War II.[62]

In 1919 Mexico issued a statement that it welcomed immigrants. Official films depicting possible settlement areas were distributed on a large scale by the Mexican consulates. The invitation was extended particularly to Japanese and Germans. The Japanese were included among the 1,641 foreigners who were authorized to purchase landed property in accordance with Article 27 of the Mexican Constitution. And the federal government announced that free transportation would be provided all immigrants from the port of entry to colonization sites. In the summer of 1919 the Mexican government announced:

> All immigrants will have the same guarantees and facilities, irrespective of nationality, if they come to México with honorable intentions. The

> Secretary of the Interior has completed outlines of a law, which will provide a new system of colonization to help the activities of foreigners who come to México. A large immigration of Japanese is expected in the coming months.[63]

Although Mexico welcomed immigrants, officially Japan maintained a position of restrictive immigration to Mexico. However, the reality of the situation differed as seen in the following statements made in 1920. The Japanese foreign minister, Viscount Yasuya Uchida, declared that Japanese emigration to Mexico was controlled under an agreement between Japan and the United States, but officials of the Japanese Legation in Mexico, stated that Japanese immigration continued without any difficulty or obstacles.[64] Legation officials stated, "Immigration into México has always been very small and there is no prohibition against the emigration of Japanese to any country in which they wish to settle."[65] It is clear that legation officials differed with the foreign minister of Japan regarding emigration to México. Under the Gentlemen's Agreement of 1907 Japan agreed to limit the number of passports to Mexico in order to appease the US government. However, in practice Japanese continued to flow into Mexico at a smaller but steady rate. This, of course, was a great concern to the United States, which continued to push Japan to limit the number going into Mexico. And, regardless of the numerically small number of Japanese entering Mexico, this did not stop the countless reports that imagined tens of thousands of Japanese entering Mexico.

The friendly intercourse between Mexico and Japan intensified the diplomatic rift with the United States. A number of developments coalesced that heightened the anxiety on all sides. First, Japan's ascension as an imperial power challenged the hegemony of Western nations in the East. Second, Japan's growing presence in the West, in terms of not only its expanding military in the Pacific but also the expansion of the Japanese diaspora in the Western hemisphere signaled a demographic shift that tested US hegemony and fractured white supremacy in the region. Lastly, Mexico's open courtship of Japan and Japanese immigrants coupled with a public imagination developed into a nonexistent conspiratorial secret alliance between Mexico and Japan designed to thwart US influence in the Western hemisphere. The rift between the United States and Japan had grown significantly since the opening decade of the twentieth century and by 1920 a litany of anti-Japanese legislation had been created in the United States that infected the hemisphere and US relations with Mexico and Japan.

For every half-truth, dozens of false stories of Japanese penetration into Mexico developed, making it difficult for an accurate assessment of the Japanese and their role during this complex period. This atmosphere invited every diabolical possibility of Japanese motives for the Western hemisphere. The available evidence demonstrates that the Japanese had a variety of roles in the Mexican Revolution. As I have explained, the roles of the Japanese in the revolution were, in many ways, ordinary for the time and place. Like the typical Mexican, Japanese in Mexico fought, died, worked, migrated, attempted new business ventures, and simply found ways to survive under dire circumstances. Conditions such as those that existed during the revolution produced unusual situations for many people, but for the Japanese, whose population remained relatively small compared with other foreign groups, there were several captivating incidents and at least one alleged attempt to assassinate a revolutionary leader, Pancho Villa. These episodes occurred in the middle of the violent period of the revolution, are connected and intertwined, and while one can argue they are anomalies, the events illustrate the Japanese in Mexico were in some cases a cross between chimera and chameleons that, on the one hand, played unimaginable roles and morphed from mundane immigrant farmer, store merchant, to hired mercenary and assassin. On the other hand, Japanese Mexicans became combatants in the Mexican Revolution out of a need to survive, but also for the adventure. For many Japanese fighting for a revolutionary faction was the better alternative to desperately trying to survive during a chaotic period where employment was scarce. Mexicans viewed the Japanese as natural military leaders born out of the rapid rise of Japanese imperialism and Japan's defeat of Western nations, but also out of a stereotype pervading Mexican society that viewed all Japanese with an innate ability to fight. Although many of the Japanese in Mexico had received some military training while in Japan, it was not what you would expect for a battlefield commission, which was the experience for many Japanese who were given direct commissions as lieutenants. As a result Japanese Mexicans and nationals were conscripted into all revolutionary factions, given direct commissions, and placed into leadership roles, not on merit or heroics, but for simply being Japanese.

The Japanese who went to Mexico in the late nineteenth and early twentieth centuries came as farm laborers, merchants, miners, professionals, ex-Samurai, and both males and females immigrated to this region. The Japanese in Mexico were both urban and rural, Christian and Buddhist, and for the most part adapted to Mexican culture and customs. The

Americas became a region that held an unusual attraction for the Japanese as they emigrated to Brazil, Peru, Panama, Cuba, Mexico, Canada, and the United States. This movement remained so significant throughout the twentieth century that by the 1990s this affinity for the Americas resulted in over 90 percent of all Japanese living outside of Japan residing somewhere in Latin America.[66] Mexico became the unlikely place for Japanese immigration to begin in the Americas. Yet, because their origins remained tied to the Japanese empire, emigrants and long established Japanese Mexicans found it difficult to avoid having their motives regarded with suspicion. This burden increased in the 1920s and 1930s as Japan continued its occupation of the East and challenged the hegemony of the United States and other Western powers. Further, Japanese immigration to Mexico increased as Mexico entered the postrevolutionary period and internal developments created opportunities and obstacles for the Japanese diaspora.

CHAPTER THREE

The Japanese and Post-revolutionary Mexico, 1920s and 1930s

If the immigration of Orientals is not soon checked, it will drive Mexican labor completely out of the Mexican Pacific coastlands, said a member of the Mexican Congress.

—*Chicago Daily Tribune*, March 13, 1928

By the 1920s it had been over a decade since the Japanese government created a self-imposed restriction of labor to the United States, which in turn developed a diplomatic entanglement between Mexico, Japan, and the United States. Newspaper articles and the general sentiment continued to preach that the United States was better off without Japanese and the Japanese were best suited with a people more like them, such as Mexicans. One US paper stated, "We offend the Japanese, They Hurt Us . . . Mexicans and Japanese evidently do not conflict."[1] In the decade 1910–20 very little had changed with regard to the Japanese presence in North America. The economic viability of the Japanese in the United States remained challenged and the racialization of the Japanese at the hemispheric level persisted. As the violent period of the Mexican Revolution contracted, the Japanese community emerged psychologically traumatized but intact and stronger in some locations. During the post-revolutionary era there were numerous Japanese merchants who ran small businesses throughout Mexico that contributed to local, regional, and international markets. During the 1930s one particular Japanese Mexican rose to prominence within Japanese and Mexican business circles. Dr. Kiso Tsuru was considered the most important Japanese entrepreneur in Mexico in the decade leading up to the World War II.[2] A popular magazine of the early twentieth century concluded, "If one could credit any single person with attempting to advance Japanese trade in Mexico, it would be Dr. Tsuru."[3]

This chapter discusses the Japanese experience during the complex period known as post-revolutionary Mexico, roughly the two decades before

World War II. Mexico's attempt to rebuild was multifaceted and included reconfigured concepts of identity, nationhood, and debates on whether Mexico saw the need for immigrants during this period of reconstruction. Similar to other countries in the Americas, a discussion ensued regarding which type of immigrant best suited Mexico's needs and posed the least risk to its identity. Mexico, like other countries, was swept up by new scientific and pseudoscientific (scientific racism) ideas of the late nineteenth and early twentieth century. Ideas such as social Darwinism, positivism, and eugenics were discussed by many leading elites, some known as *científicos*, in the hope that Mexico could shed its so-called backwardness caused by its indigenous past and the hybridity or *mestizaje* that resulted from the mixing of Indians, Spaniards, blacks, mestizos, and mulattos.[4]

This chapter examines the challenges faced during the post-revolutionary era by the established Japanese population in Mexico. Although this period represented a time of change and upward mobility for the settled Japanese community, it was also a period of vulnerability as the economic crisis of the 1930s was coupled with an increase in nativism directed toward the Japanese. This chapter also covers the emerging formation of the Mexican state, which was not a hegemonic force, but rather, due to strong local and regional grassroots organizations, peasants, and *caciques* (chief or local leader), the government allowed substantial autonomy to many regions in Mexico.[5] As a result I argue that the "decentered" political apparatus created in Mexico after the 1920s contributed to a unique Mexican political apparatus, which directly affected the Japanese Mexican experience. The two decades leading up to World War II also epitomize the triangular relationship between Japan, Mexico, and the United States that continued on a collision course.

Post-revolutionary Mexico: Reconstruction, *Indigenismo*, and *Mexicanidad*

When the violent period of the Mexican Revolution (1910–20) came to an end, 1 million Mexicans were dead, millions had been displaced, hundreds of thousands sought refuge in the United States, and overall, Mexico's industrial complex was virtually destroyed. As the decade of the 1920s emerged, Mexico remained mired in revolutionary zeal, full-scale combat transitioned to localized upheavals, and the country began the arduous process of reconstruction. The new decade also tested Mexico on the diplomatic front as it engaged the United States on important issues that ranged from land and oil expropriation to its cordial and friendly relations with Japan. During this post-revolutionary era Mexico entered a reconstruction phase that prominently included an economic component as well as an ideological element with the state at the center of building a new nation and forging a new national identity. And although the process of nation building emerged in the 1920s, Mexican administrations continued to face recalcitrant caudillos, land reform issues, and a segment of the population that did not heel to religious reforms. The 1923 *Delahuerista* revolt, the *Cristero* Rebellion of 1926–29, and Saturnino Cedillo's rebellion in the late 1930s hampered Mexican progress, but did not halt the trajectory toward consolidation and modernization.

Key to implementing many of the revolutionary ideas was the reconstruction and modernization of Mexico. However, the process of modernization also came with a dark side that was initiated not by refractory caudillos, but rather, a new cadre of enthusiastic social scientists. These individuals, armed with scientific and pseudoscientific methods and myths went on the offensive and attempted to modernize Mexico from its basic infrastructure to its biological foundations. Thus, the threat to national unity remained internal and a debate raged whether the Mexican Indian was the savior of Mexico or the source of its eventual demise. Attached to these theories was a paradoxical debate on immigration where, on the one hand, immigrants were viewed as a necessary ingredient to propel Mexico into the modern age, but on the other hand, were regarded with apprehension because their presence might contaminate the very essence of the foundational cultural and biological origins that made Mexico unique. Whether imagined or not, this image of a unique Mexicanness hampered immigration to Mexico.

The genesis of *indigenismo*, the post-revolutionary version or an earlier one, was a construct from the non-Indian world and as Alan Knight has stated, "It involved the imposition of ideas, categories, and policies from outside. The Indian themselves were the objects, not the authors, of *indigenismo*."[6] The rise of *indigenismo* as articulated by such scholars as Manuel Gamio, Carlos Basauri, Luis Chávez Orozco, Justo Sierra, Moises Saenz, and others signaled the arrival of Darwinism, positivism, and eugenics to Mexico and their wide array of solutions to Mexico's internal problems.[7] However, as Alexander Dawson has articulated, *indigenismo* and the modernization of Mexico proved as allusive and illusory as the revolutionary state itself.[8]

These developments had consequences for Mexico's views on immigration. First, it limited enthusiasm for immigrants in general, but in particular non-European immigrants. Second, Mexico's immigration policy became linked with its rediscovered indigenous past that created a national debate on which course the country should take, that of the United States and Argentina with their emphasis on white Europeans or turning inward by highlighting the indigenous past and using this new identity to build a better and stronger Mexico based on revolutionary ideals. And, if the latter path was taken, what would become of Mexico's immigration schemes? Thus, the early phase of post-revolutionary Mexico coincided with two global phenomena that swept across the European and American landscapes; the first was social Darwinism in the late nineteenth century that morphed into the eugenics movement of the early twentieth century.[9]

What did all this mean? It meant that Mexico was determined to protect what it considered the bedrock of its national identity and one premised on over 400 years of *mestizaje*, primarily in the form of a Spanish and indigenous hybridity. This *mestizaje*, in all its forms, meant that Mexico had a uniqueness it could claim, highlight, and use to unify the nation. However, this exaltation of the indigenous past created a backlash against non-Indian and non-European immigrants when placed within the discourse of nationalism and Mexican identity. As *indigenismo* gathered strength and popularity in the 1920s, Mexicans were expected to value their "Indianness" and those who rejected it "were publicly chastised for their foreignness and lack of nationalist zeal."[10] These ideas of a unique *Mexicanidad*, coupled with the Mexican Revolution and nationalism, partially explain the small number of immigrants who came to Mexico in the early twentieth century. The rise in nationalism resulted in the development of anti-immigrant legislation and an increase in violence inflicted upon immigrants as they were caught up in the vortex of a Mexican identity crisis. While the United States, Brazil, Argentina, and even Peru accepted hundreds of thousands and even millions of immigrants, Mexico, by comparison, was hesitant at exposing itself to possible change to its basic character. In the end, Mexico tolerated small doses of immigration as long as no group gained a critical mass to challenge its identity. The relatively small Japanese community and movement to Mexico is representative of the overall position of Mexico and its desire to keep alive the illusion of *Mexicanidad*.

Japanese Immigration Resumes

By the time of his death in 1976, Dr. Masanosuke Ogita studied the history and language of the Chontales of the Oaxaca region of Mexico and was particularly interested in the lost poetry of this indigenous group. Over the span of several decades Dr. Ogita was able to record 200 ancient Chontal poems in their original language and much of his work was published under the title *Canción de Chontal* in the early 1980s. Dr. Masanosuke Ogita, who arrived in Mexico via Tehuantepec, Oaxaca in 1920, typified the changing characteristics of the Japanese immigrant coming to Mexico during the 1920s and 1930s; the newcomer was highly educated and with employable skills. Masanosuke Ogita also illustrated the affinity between Japanese, Mexicans, and in this particular case, the indigenous community. Indeed, Ogita took a keen interest in Mexican indigenous society and gained a strong friendship with the Chontales of the Oaxaca region. For over fifty years Masanosuke Ogita studied the Chontal and their way of life.[11] Dr. Ogita practiced odontology in Tehuantepec until his death. The two decades leading up to World War II delineated a stark contrast between the Japanese immigrants that arrived in Mexico before the 1920s and those that came during a time of extraordinary change in Mexico known as the post-revolutionary period.

Regardless of the national debates that raged during the 1920s and 1930s Japanese Mexicans continued their upward mobility as many shifted from the rural to urban sectors and from unskilled to skilled positions within the Mexican economy. This shift is partially attributed to the generational growth of the Japanese Mexican population that now included a Nisei and Sansei element. Also, Japanese immigrants that arrived during this era came with skills, advanced degrees, and capital, unlike their predecessors. Throughout the first two decades of the twentieth century, Japanese immigration to Mexico met stiff resistance from its northern neighbor, the United States, and less so from the Mexican government and its general population. Nevertheless, Mexico and Japan continued on a path of reciprocity regarding diplomacy and immigration. Furuya Shigetsuna, Japan's minister to Mexico, arriving at his post in November 1922, reflected on this interest in remarks. In his initial public statement he declared, "Mexico is a very wonderful country, endowed with the most abundant natural resources. Our political relations with Mexico are highly satisfactory, but it remains for us to develop our commercial and trade relations, and immigration, which will certainly bring benefits to both countries."[12] Japan had many incentives for sending its subjects overseas that included the adverse effects of natural disasters such as typhoons, large unemployment, a great earthquake of 1923, and an agricultural depression during the 1930s. Throughout the 1920s and 1930s immigration to Mexico became selective and restrictive based on internal developments and external conditions that squeezed the resources available to all groups. It was under these circumstances that Japanese immigration experienced a limited but steady movement to Mexico.

The 1930 Mexican census estimated the total number of Japanese residing in Mexico was 5,967.[13] In fact, from 1921 to 1936 the Japanese population in Mexico increased 300 percent.[14] An exact figure of Japanese in Mexico remained elusive and most estimates generally included only Japanese nationals and Japanese that had become naturalized citizens of Mexico. Often left off the census rolls were children and second-generation Mexicans of Japanese ancestry. For example, a pattern of guessing and undercounting the Japanese population was prevalent throughout the first half of the twentieth century in Mexico. In 1933 and based on Mexican official statistics, there were 4,583 Japanese in Mexico, but in 1934 the Mexican government revised that number to 8,609. In 1937 US officials estimated the number of Japanese in Mexico from 10,000 to 12,000 based on the movement of Japanese during the early part of the 1930s.[15] Regardless of source, the Japanese immigrant that arrived in Mexico during the post-revolutionary period was socially and economically different from the first generation that arrived in the country.

The Mexican government maintained a somewhat liberal policy that enabled the resumption of Japanese immigration, although it remained under pressure from the United States to limit or altogether prevent Japanese immigrants from entering Mexico. Furthermore, the original Japanese who remained and survived the Mexican civil war searched for a new beginning by the 1920s and showed signs of growth and change. As the violence subsided, the next phase of Japanese emigration and development emerged. The two decades that followed the Mexican Revolution signaled a new atmosphere for the Japanese, in which stability of the Japanese population would be accentuated by economic success and a general upward mobility in Mexican society. The next generation of Japanese, along with their relatives brought over during the 1920s and 1930s, established permanent communities throughout Mexico. Although faced with rising nationalism in the 1930s, Japanese emigration proceeded in a steady upward trajectory until the beginning of World War II. The Japanese that suffered, but survived the traumatic events of the Mexican Revolution, found a sense of place and empowerment in a country that became increasingly familiar to them.

Although Mexico continued to be pressured by the United States to deter Japanese immigration, Mexican officials were determined to find their own course and remain independent from US foreign policy. It is difficult to conclude whether the path chosen by Mexico regarding Japanese immigration was taken as a form of retaliation toward the United States or if the direction selected was a genuine effort at friendly diplomacy with Japan. Mexico and Japan had enjoyed cordial and equal relations since 1888. Nonetheless and regardless of external pressures, the early 1920s signaled a Mexican immigration policy that favored and encouraged Japanese immigration.

During the early 1920s, and on their own accord, Mexican officials in Japan began issuing visas to Japanese emigrants for destination to Central and South America, but a substantial number were permitted to land in Mexico because their passports carried the visa of Mexican authorities. This maneuver circumvented the agreement reached between Japan and the United States, in which Japan would limit the number of passports to Mexico. According to the American Ambassador in Tokyo, this matter caused considerable surprise to the Japanese government.[16] After American and Japanese officials investigated, new instructions were issued to Japanese local authorities in the ports from which vessels sailed. These new directives declared that Japanese bearing visas on their passports of authorities of countries other than the country for which the passport was issued would be held in violation of the regulations of Japan relating to passports and not be allowed to depart the country.[17] It was thought that in the future it would not be possible for Japanese to enter Mexico by making use of a subterfuge such as the one mentioned. Nevertheless, Japanese immigration resumed during post-revolutionary Mexico with the encouragement of the Mexican and Japanese governments.

The year 1924 marked important, if disturbing, developments for the Japanese in the Western hemisphere. First, for all their efforts to settle and blend into various countries and communities, the Japanese and other Asian groups were permanently barred from entering the United States with the passage of the Johnson-Reed Act (Immigration Act) of 1924, which undermined the agreements the Japanese had reached with the United States a decade earlier.[18] The Johnson-Reed Act became the prototype for like legislation in various countries such as Brazil, Peru, and Canada. The US 1924 Immigration Act effectively barred all Asians to the United States, which made Japanese immigration to Mexico an ideal alternative. Simultaneously, the US-Mexican border region remained contentious as a wide array of immigrants used Mexico as a "back door" into the United States.

Second, Mexico took an opposite approach by signing a new treaty with Japan that encouraged Japanese immigration. Japan and Mexico renewed their groundbreaking treaty of 1888 with the 1924 Treaty of Amity,

Commerce and Navigation, which superseded the original treaty signed by the two countries. The 1924 treaty allowed Japanese immigrants to bring their parents, children, and a wide spectrum of relatives. The terms included reciprocal freedom of immigration, and Japan removed all claims of damages caused to its subjects from 1910 to the date of the treaty.[19] Japanese immigration to Mexico took on a new dimension with the popularization of what the Japanese called the *yobiyose-imin* system established by the 1924 treaty, whereby to enter the country, immigrants required only an expressed invitation from someone already legally residing in Mexico and their sponsorship.[20] The only requirement was that they prove their family ties. With the new treaty and *yobiyose* system, the flow of immigrants increased, and they settled in many parts of the country and entered into diverse sectors of the economy. The *yobiyose* form of immigration lasted until 1932 when the Mexican government officially banned the immigration of foreign laborers except those with special skills, in partial reaction to the depression.[21] According to María Elena Ota Mishima, from 1925 to 1932, 2,183 Japanese immigrants arrived in Mexico as a result of the 1924 treaty between Mexico and Japan.[22]

Not all Mexicans were pleased with the continued friendly relations with Japan given that their northern neighbor had just barred all Japanese and considered them a threat to the hemisphere. Some Mexicans felt that the new treaty with Japan should be denounced as a "friendly" gesture toward the United States and many saw Japan as the aggressor regarding developments in the Far East. There were also indications that anti-Japanese feeling in Mexico at this time was more broadly based. This was reflected in popular opinion that the Japanese immigrants had not assimilated politically or culturally, and constituted "a nation within a nation. . . . Some Mexicans fear Japanese colonists as a menace to their sovereignty."[23]

Not only had some viewed Japan as a nation that had been friendly to Mexicans, but also Mexico became the first nation to sign a treaty with Japan based on equal treatment, not once, but twice, that cemented their cordial relations until the 1940s. A Mexican newspaper editorial wrote that Japan was "a country that has done us no harm, that has been our consistent friend, and that has shown us the utmost consideration in international relations."[24] However, as Japan invaded and conquered additional territory in such places as Manchuria and aggressively increased its military capabilities, it was difficult for Mexico to ignore such developments. Further, the more Japan agitated the US, tensions mounted between all three countries, with Mexico often on the defensive regarding its relationship with Japan and testing the boundaries of hemispheric solidarity and loyalty. Under these conditions and suspicions Japanese continued to immigrate to Mexico, but characteristically different from previous decades.

As discussed in the preceding chapters, earlier groups of Japanese immigrants to Mexico were primarily landless peasants and laborers. The majority of these early Japanese immigrants came from the overcrowded prefectures of Fukuoka, Hiroshima, Yamaguchi, and Kumamoto. They came as contract laborers and found employment on the plantations in the south of Mexico, in the mines and in railroad construction. Many died while some returned to Japan. There were few Japanese women in the early years of migration and the majority of men lived with native Mexican women. As a result, the offspring of these unions were largely absorbed as Mexicans.

Ota Mishima argues that during the first half of the twentieth century Japanese immigrants can be broadly classified into three occupational ranks and immigration status: (1) farm and railroad laborers who came to Mexico illegally or under a work contract, (2) fishermen who emerged in Mexico primarily after 1924 and immigrated under the *yobiyose* system, and (3) commercial and professional men and those who worked in other industries. These individuals came illegally, came under contract, or entered Mexico based on the 1924 treaty that allowed Japanese doctors, veterinarians, and dentists to immigrate to Mexico.[25]

Demographics, Occupational Patterns, and Shifts

The 1924 treaty propelled a new type of Japanese immigrant to Mexico that changed many of the characteristics from the previous generations. Japanese Mexicans also branched out into self-sufficient occupations.[26] According to Chizuko Watanabe,

> A steady transition from laborer to independent entrepreneur and professional occupations were observed from the end of the violent period of the Mexican Revolution to the beginning of World War II. Additionally, an investigation by the Japanese Legation in Mexico in 1913 showed that the number of Japanese owning businesses was still small and that most were engaged as laborers. From the total number of Japanese immigrants (2,737, including 165 females) only 223 owned independent businesses, mostly small grocery stores, bakeries, or pharmacies.[27]

By the beginning of the 1930s, Japanese in Mexico became business owners in increasing numbers and some of the immigrants were coming with considerable capital, resources or employable skills. The majority that entered under the *yobiyose* system in the 1930s were nonagricultural workers. To further illustrate this transition, it was reported in 1937 in the regions of Baja California, Sonora, Sinaloa, and Nayarit that Japanese residents were employed in diverse occupations that included engineers, farmers, ranchers, barbers, dentists, doctors, photographers, and entrepreneurs.[28] With the signing of the 1924 Treaty of Commerce and Navigation between Japan and Mexico, there was a marked increase in immigration and diversity of occupations.[29]

Table 3.1 indicates the change in occupations between 1925–1926 and 1926–1927. Farmers and farm laborers are still the largest group, but other laborers and servants are a small minority. The appearance of merchants and artisans, professional men, employers, capitalists and industrialists represented an improvement in education, in social position and in economic status, over the landless peasants who came in the previous decades. James L. Tigner makes a similar conclusion with Japanese

Table 3.1. Immigration of Japanese to Mexico, 1925–1927

Declared Occupations	*1925–1926*	*1926–1927*
Farmers and farm laborers	276	412
Merchants	146	153
Domestic servants	30	1
Unskilled laborers	21	36
Cabinetmakers	14	0
Electricians	6	0
Clerks	11	121
Mechanics	12	15
Professional men	36	42
Investors (capitalists)	2	60
Industrialists	3	2
Artists	7	13
Writers	2	9
Students	12	10
Various	22	49
No occupation	49	143
Total	649	1,066

residing in the Federal District in 1925: "Their population in the Federal District reflected the occupational diversity that would become a characteristic pattern: cafes, restaurants, bars, hotels, jewelry shops, barbers, auto mechanics, clothing shops, grocery stores, milk distributors, taxi drivers, candy stores and ice cream parlors."[30]

The end of the 1930s marked a predominance of commerce over many other occupations that increasingly became the norm. This can be attributed to a number of factors. First, immigration in the 1920s and 1930s included more merchants while people returning to Japan were largely of the agricultural and laboring classes. Second, the experience of Japanese agriculturalists in Mexico was not encouraging during the 1930s. Many lost their lands in the land reform programs of the government. Most were heavily taxed and exploited by corrupt politicians. Many felt insecure under the continual threat of anti-Japanese demonstrations. Third, the hunger for land and for an independent agricultural life, which was so much part of the tradition at home, gradually weakened in this new environment and a large number of Japanese sought the easier and more profitable life of the urban sectors. As a result, many Japanese drifted into small businesses, which proved more profitable and secure.

Some of the most prominent and successful Japanese Mexicans emerged during this period. Individuals such as Sanshiro Matsumoto, from Mexico City, whose father was a skilled gardener and grounds-keeper of the presidential residence, developed a large-scale nursery-florist business. At the outbreak of hostilities the family owned large nurseries in ten different locations around Mexico City, with nearly 200 Mexican employees. Kiso Tsuru, considered the most astute Japanese businessman in Mexico prior to 1941, was a self-educated pharmacist-doctor who went into the mining and oil industries exporting mercury, fluorite, and mica to Japan before the war. Both of these individuals played important roles before and during World War II and are discussed at length in later chapters.[31]

Marriage Patterns and Assimilation

Before World War II the assimilation of Japanese progressed further in Mexico than in most countries in the Western hemisphere. This can be attributed to the large proportion of mixed marriages. Early immigration was confined almost exclusively to young males. In Mexico the "picture-bride" system was not introduced until after the 1920s and then only in the agricultural colonies of Mexico's northwest. As a result, as indicated earlier, most Japanese men took native women, either as legal or common law wives. One source indicates that the ratio of Japanese men to Japanese women in Mexico was 5 to 1, making it one of the lowest ratios for any sizable group of Japanese in the Western hemisphere. Although legal marriage was not generally the practice between Japanese men and native Mexican women, 455 wives were registered in the Japanese Legation by the end of the 1930s.[32] It is generally accepted that the intermarriages between Japanese and non-Japanese was even higher. In the survey mentioned below nearly half of the Japanese men responded that they were single. The views from the surveyors indicate that the majority of those Japanese men who marked their status as single, were indeed married to Mexican women. These Japanese men were reluctant to state their true status based on the perception and "tendency among Japanese to look down on intermarriage, which saw endogamy as an ideal."[33] Most of the men living with native women became isolated from other Japanese, with their children identifying as Mexican. The only groups in Mexico maintaining a pattern of life that resembled a Japanese community in character were those in Baja California and Veracruz.

In a survey conducted in 1939 that included all the Mexican states with the exception of Baja California, a significant number of Japanese men were found to be married to Mexican women. The survey included 1,278 Japanese households. The households were overwhelmingly run by men, with 1,255 households headed by males and thirteen households headed by females. And similar to the 1935 survey, a majority of the Japanese married males had married Mexican women. The survey indicated that 424 Japanese males had married Mexican women and 291 Japanese men married Japanese females. This survey also provided the nationality and gender breakdown for the offspring born of these unions. The number of males born to Japanese mothers was 356 and females accounted for 737. The males born to Mexican mothers equaled 359 with 661 females. The number of Japanese men marrying Mexican women remained significant until the outbreak of World War II. To further illustrate this pattern, one source enumerated between 1930 and 1937 a total of 224 Japanese males had married Mexican women. During this same period, a total of four Japanese women married Mexican men.[34] Of course, the lopsided numbers can be explained by the strict cultural norms of the period that strictly prohibited Japanese women deviating from endogamy.

When the total number of children, 2,113, is added to the total number of adults 4,096, minus 424 Mexican women, the total number of Japanese and their offspring equals 5,785 individuals. When the Japanese population of Baja California is added to these numbers, estimated at 2,000 individuals in 1937, a total Japanese population in Mexico is approximately 7,785 by the end of the 1930s. This number falls within the middle range of the two extremes taken from a variety sources that place the Japanese population as low as 4,000 to as high as 12,000 before 1940.[35] It cannot be overemphasized that tracking the movement of Japanese into Mexico was often a guessing game since the Japanese entered under both legal and clandestine means. Adding to this dilemma was the inability of the Mexican government to track the children born of Japanese fathers and Mexican mothers. Furthermore, a significant number of Japanese in Mexico remained nonnaturalized. One source indicates that by 1930 the official figure for nonnaturalized Japanese in Mexico was 2,731 males and 1,580 females, or a total of 4,311. The number of Mexican-born children did augment the total considerably.[36]

The practice of endogamy was clearly evident before the 1920s, but Japanese males also engaged in exogamy since so many arrived without brides and married into the native population. One of the major results of exogamy was the influence of the Mexican culture channeled through the mother, which often obscured the Japanese origins. A good portion of the offspring of Japanese fathers and Mexican mothers were absorbed into Mexican society and had little to no further contact with the Japanese government officials. And, according to Chizuko Watanabe, "The offspring of mixed parentage tended to be Mexican culturally and were likely to marry Mexicans. When their Japanese progenitors died, they had little opportunity to maintain ties with the Japanese community."[37] Even those born of Japanese parents used Spanish as their first language, illustrating that assimilation among the Japanese in Mexico was an ongoing process. To this end, the children were mostly Mexicanized by the influence of their mothers who were Mexican.

A good example of this pattern is the experience of Yoshigei Nakatani. Yoshigei Nakatani arrived on the coast of Manzanillo, Colima, on November 26, 1932, aboard the *Gueiyamaru* with 100 other Japanese immigrants. Nakatani's decision to leave Japan is perhaps similar to other Japanese. Nakatani explained that his friend Kisimoto arrived at his home and said, "Look what it says here, a Japanese company in Mexico is searching for 13 clerks. When we arrived for the interview my friend Kisimoto was in a suit and I wore a kimono. . . . We met with H. Kato and he told us we were the first to apply and gave us the job."[38] However, when Nakatani and his friend arrived in Colima and began their journey inland, the poverty they witnessed caught them by surprise. In fact, Nakatani said, "We thought if this was Mexico, [it] could not be."[39] In order to adapt and survive, Yoshigei explained, in a country that was traditional, Catholic, somewhat discriminatory and hierarchical, a level of assimilation was required by necessity. Under these conditions Nakatani's choices were pragmatic. In fact, he made a conscious decision that it was necessary to start a family with a Mexican woman to root himself in his new country. A mere two years after his arrival in Mexico Yoshigei not only married a Mexican woman but also converted from Shintoism to Catholicism and gave his first son a Christian name, Carlos.[40] Yoshigei Nakatani's experience illustrates how Japanese viewed assimilation as a necessity to survive and prosper in Mexico and were willing to dispense with the Japanese culture to that end. Even with a global depression in place, Japanese such as Nakatani gambled on moving out of Japan in order to seek better opportunities. For some, Mexico offered perhaps an escape from the ordinary and a chance for adventure and economic prospects.

The end of the 1930s witnessed the dispersal of Japanese immigrants throughout Mexico with the largest concentration located along the northern regions, particularly Baja California.[41] The region became attractive after two Japanese colonies had been established at the beginning of the twentieth century in Mexicali and Ensenada. Baja, California, recorded 405 Japanese in the territory in 1921; 1,036 in 1925; 764 in 1930;[42] and an additional 165 from 1932–35.[43] An examination of immigration records for Japanese nationals in Mexico shows that approximately 400 individuals requested and eventually received citizenship through naturalization. Twenty Japanese residing in Baja California obtained naturalization from 1921 to 1932 and thirty-six individuals located in Sonora became naturalized citizens between 1920 and 1933. In the state of Coahuila, nineteen Japanese residents received citizenship from 1911 to 1934, while nine Japanese residing in Tamaulipas and Nuevo León requested and received naturalization from 1926 to 1932.[44]

Undoubtedly, there was a small but steady increase of the Japanese population during the 1930s who engaged in a variety of industries throughout Mexico, but the new immigrants tended to reside in Baja California and other northern regions of Mexico such as Sonora, Sinaloa, and Nayarit. In fact, Baja California became the largest and most insular Japanese community in Mexico. According to Daniel Masterson,

> Mexicali became virtually a Japanese enclave in Baja California Norte [table 3.2]. More than 300 Japanese families lived in the immediate vicinity of Mexicali, accounting for an estimated 80 percent of the

Table 3.2. Distribution of registered Japanese by state, 1939[1]

Baja California	1,389	Mexico City (DF)	829
Sonora	521	Coahuila	466
Chihuahua	423	Sinaloa	400
Veracruz	351	Chiapas	311
Tamaulipas	138	Jalisco	136
San Luis Potosí	109	All others	408

[1]"Japanese Population in Mexico (Lower California Is Not Included). Up to 1940," Field Notes on the Japanese in Latin America Mexico, NARA, Records of the War Department and Special Staffs, record group 165, box 978.

population of the area. As previously mentioned these Japanese in and around Mexicali worked in diverse occupations ranging from operating barbershops and restaurants to brothels.[45]

The 1920s and 1930s also represented a period when the Japanese community showed not only signs of assimilation but also elements of ethnic solidarity through the creation of institutions that were specifically designed to cater to the Japanese community. Also, since the 1920s the Japanese population had become more engaged at the political level and the Japanese government, in relation to the increase of the Japanese population in Mexico, raised the number of consulates in Mexico and its staff. Newspapermen and organizers became increasingly numerous and active and the dissemination of Japanese culture increased. The offices of large Japanese commercial houses and banks came to play a more important role in the life of the Japanese community. The Japanese government also began to lay the foundation for greater control of the Japanese population in Mexico, particularly through the creation of Japanese associations.

The Federation of Japanese Associations: Agents of Change, Agents of Control

Since the arrival of Japanese to in Mexico, the Japanese government generally showed a concern regarding the well-being of their subjects in Mexico. However, during the post-revolutionary period and due to the geopolitical dynamics that developed between Japan, United States, and

Mexico those concerns necessitated a different approach. In fact, what the Japanese government desired was greater control of the Japanese population in Mexico. To this end, by the 1920s the Japanese government began to utilize Japanese organizations within Mexico to exact a greater level of cooperation from the Japanese in Mexico. Also, as a more educated and sophisticated Japanese immigrated to Mexico, the Japanese government saw an opportunity to utilize such individuals for the benefit of the home country through the gathering of intelligence information on Mexico and the United States, and remittances for Japan. In this manner, Japan adopted a policy of careful state control over Japanese communities with substantial numbers. The methods employed by the Japanese government involved coercion, financial incentives, and instilling a sense of patriotic duty to garner the support of Japanese Mexicans and nationals. Even the manner in which the Japanese immigrants arrived in Mexico came with a level of governmental control.

All but a few of the later immigrants came under the auspices of quasi-governmental immigration companies. They arrived in debt to the company, and the company largely influenced their settlement and activities. The Japanese government gradually increased the pressure and many Japanese communities were brought under the authority and influence of the Japanese Legation in Mexico City or its consulates. Some settlers were tempted by offers of loans at low rates of interest. For example, during the *agrarista* campaign of the 1920s and 1930s, coupled with the onset of the Great Depression, a handful of Japanese lost their lands, causing great loss and financial hardship. Many of these individuals were rescued from financial ruin by the Japanese government, which provided long-term loans. The Japanese government offered other financial advantages, by generous aid in securing an education in Japan for their sons and by promising and giving protection against exploitation. Those who refused to cooperate were discriminated against in various ways, and were threatened with more serious reprisals. A highly organized and centrally directed Japanese community developed during the 1920s and 1930s. The experience of Japanese immigrants with corrupt Mexican officials and the observation of the exploitation of the Chinese, who had no governmental protection, led some Japanese, who might have otherwise protested, into enthusiastic support of Japanese governmental and quasi-governmental organizations who had control of the Japanese community.[46]

Regardless of their status in Mexico, the Japanese community, since the early twentieth century, had organized itself under various entities, but the most prominent were the Japanese association clubs that flourished throughout the country. These clubs functioned as intermediaries between the Japanese community and local governments, provided financial assistance, held civic events, and participated in local community events. These associations also functioned as a quasi-political entity for the Japanese communities and the heads of these associations were usually the most prominent and successful members of the community. The associations became very common throughout Mexico where a critical mass of Japanese resided. Because of the familiarity of the associations to the Japanese community, it comes as no surprise that Mexico banned such associations with its emergency measures during World War II and that the Japanese community fashioned its wartime organization after these associations. In this manner, the leadership of the Japanese community in Mexico made a conscious choice to centralize, for the duration of the war, its leadership and community.

Before the outbreak of World War II there were approximately sixty Japanese associations located throughout the country with the original in Mexico City, established in 1920.[47] The associations were loosely connected and although the Mexico City Japanese Association often served as a quasi-headquarters, overall the associations functioned in a decentralized manner, but under semi-control of the Japanese Legation. These associations were vital to Japanese immigrants arriving in Mexico and served principally as a form of protection. Similar to other immigrant groups, the Japanese associations that formed in the early twentieth century in Mexico were a lifeline for those arriving in the country with very little knowledge of their new home. Individual Japanese associations were established when a small critical mass was reached that warranted a sense of collectivism. Often, these new associations offered ethnic solidarity by maintaining many of the customs and language of Japan. Many of the associations were affiliated with either an ancestral village, a prefectural grouping, or were heterogeneous.[48] As these Japanese associations in Mexico matured they took on many functions that resembled mutual aid societies and came under stronger control of the Japanese government.

The local Japanese consul dominated branches of the association. Closely related to the associations were three Japanese schools in Mexico City, Navojoa (Sonora), and Mexicali. The associations in Mexico were also useful to the Japanese government. The local consular offices, with instructions from the Japanese minister in Mexico City, utilized the various associations for the dissemination of propaganda and in some cases used their Japanese nationals to gather information. The use of long-standing

Japanese nationals for the gathering of intelligence data on Mexico or the United States was not widespread, but intercepted Japanese diplomatic cables indicate the practice was in place prior to World War II. The cables also mentioned that the class of Japanese in Mexico, especially in and around the region of Baja California (farmers), were "simpletons" and not useful for intelligence gathering. In other words, Japanese farmers and laborers were viewed as uneducated and unable to gather information that might be pertinent for Japanese goals and designs. A better indicator of the unofficial link between the Japanese associations and the Japanese government are the relations between the last Japanese minister in Mexico, Yoshiaki Miura, and three prominent members of the Mexico City Japanese Association, Kiso Tsuru, Sanshiro Matsumoto, and Heiji Kato. This relationship is discussed in detail in chapters 5 and 6, but Yoshiaki Miura's contact with Tsuru and Kato went well beyond what is considered the average relationship between the Japanese government and members of the local Japanese association. This illustrates the level of control the Japanese government asserted on the Japanese population in Mexico.

Shinizo Yakichi, who is considered the founder and first president, with Sudo Masaho serving as vice president, established the original Japanese Association in Mexico in 1920. This first attempt was short lived, lasting only until 1923 due to disagreements over policies. The second attempt occurred in 1928 with its failure attributed to the same cause. However, in 1929 under the leadership of Jisuke Kato and Horiuchi Isaburo (Isaburo also played an important role in the Comité organized during World War II), the Japanese Association of Mexico City rose again with a membership of 162 individuals by 1942.[49]

Along with trade associations, the Japanese community in Mexico also established a variety of educational institutions. These schools were not unlike those created in other countries in Latin America with one of the goals being to maintain a sense of ethnic identity. In order to achieve such a goal a specific curriculum that focused on Japanese culture and identity was fashioned. However, such a curriculum was often interpreted as subversive, especially by US authorities that monitored the Japanese community. In 1929 one of the principal schools created by the Japanese was located in Mexico City and run by the Japanese Association. The facility included 7,000 square meters where fifty dayschool children and twenty boarding school children were given an elementary education. Other prominent schools were located in Navojoa City in the state of Sonora and in Mexicali City.[50] These schools adopted a program based on the

Japanese National School system that stressed Japanese rather than Mexican history and folklore and loyalty to Japan and pride in Japanese heritage, instead of duties as Mexican citizens, as one source put it.[51]

Japanese Mexicans and nationals also established a handful of other organizations and entities. For example, in 1934 the Japanese Trading Association was established, but dissolved and was replaced in 1940 by the Japanese Chamber of Commerce and Industry in Mexico. The principal undertakings of this organization included publication of a bulletin; a commercial exhibit on Japanese exports; a credit association; and consultations for new businesses. In addition to the associations there existed an organization called "Service Men's Association," which had a possible military connection. The Japanese Legation separately recorded the members, unlike the general record of Japanese in Mexico, kept this record secret. From a Mexican and US perspective, the highly centralized character of elements of the Japanese community posed a threat as a potentially dangerous instrument of official Japanese policy.[52] Nonetheless, these efforts at establishing commercial and educational institutions grounded the Japanese in their respective regions, while simultaneously creating a sense of ethnic solidarity.

While on many levels the Japanese community prospered, it did so because compared with the Chinese, the Japanese were able to avoid the intense nativism and overt racism that plagued the Chinese for a variety of reasons already discussed. Nevertheless, during the post-revolutionary period, Mexico, through a variety of immigration legislation, raised the bar for entry into Mexico. This was not extraordinary considering that as Mexico moved from the 1920s into the 1930s a global economic crisis became more evident. In line with other countries, Mexico barred the movement of general laborers considered competition for the majority of working class Mexicans. For example, the immigration policy of the government of President Lázaro Cárdenas was put forth in Section 14 of the Six Year Plan as follows: "In question of immigration of foreigners, the Government will consider the admission of three classes, namely those foreigners who will easily assimilate with Mexicans, with such preference to Latins; agriculturalists properly qualified as to aid in the development of the soil in Mexico; and technical experts."[53]

The impact on the Japanese was minimal since many of the Japanese that immigrated to Mexico during this period were from the professional class with the exception of cotton farmers of the northwest and, as already mentioned, the 1924 treaty between Mexico and Japan allowed for the movement of Japanese to Mexico. However, by the late 1930s a significant number of Japanese families in the northern regions of Mexico faced a different predicament that involved land reform and nationalism. In addition to these developments, the administration of Lázaro Cárdenas instituted a nationalization program that brought simmering tensions between the United States and Mexico to the surface, and by the late 1930s this situation was aggravated by events in Europe. Layered upon these internal and external conditions were attempts by Japanese Mexicans and the Japanese government at acquiring strategic war materials in anticipation of a global conflict.

The Mexicanization of Mexico: Land, Oil, and Sovereignty

As national and international forces coalesced during the 1930s, the Japanese in Mexico were not immune to these developments, which included continued land disputes, repatriation of thousands of Mexicans from the United States, the Great Depression, immigration, and the emerging world conflict. Indeed, the 1930s represented a period when the Japanese population in Mexico, outside of the World War II period, was at its most vulnerable. Throughout Latin America a general anti-Japanese sentiment continued to bubble to the surface and the negative reactions to the aggression of the Imperial Japanese government were often superimposed on the Japanese population throughout the Americas. And as Japan gained dominance in Asia in the 1930s, rumors circulated that Japanese immigrants were actually fifth columns planted for an eventual Japanese invasion of the Americas, especially Mexico due to its proximity to the US Anti-Japanese editorials began to emerge more frequently in Mexico's leading newspapers. In May 1933 an anti-Japanese article in *El Excelsior* appeared decrying a Japanese invasion, both demographically and militarily, within Mexico. Although the Japanese Legation countered the article, the anti-Japanese sentiments increased, especially in the northern regions of Sonora, Chihuahua, and Baja California, all with sizable enclaves of Japanese who owned land.[54] A central goal of the Mexican Revolution was land reform and Japanese in the northern districts controlled sizable arable territory.

Agrarian reform in Mexico had been ongoing for over two decades before Lázaro Cárdenas was elected president of Mexico in 1934. In its most ideal form the land reform instituted by the Cárdenas regime attempted to transform rural society and the nation. Some argue that Cárdenas used land reform as a political tool to quiet enemies and to gain support from the working class. For example, the confiscation of the secretary of agriculture General Saturnino Cedillo's land in 1936 was considered a political maneuver by Cárdenas to remove opposition to his campaign for land reform and other policies.[55] Certainly Cárdenas was not above such a ploy, but the results of his land reform were immense. And due to such an overarching reformation, landowners, regardless of nationality, felt the impact, as was the case with Cedillo. Colonies and individual foreign owners were targets of the agrarian movement. In March 1936, a band of fifty armed agrarians, headed by Raul Domínguez, chief of the Chihuahua Agrarian Commission, invaded a wealthy Mormon settlement in Juarez Valley, Chihuahua. Red-and-black flags bearing the words "down with the foreigners" were carried by the agrarians.[56] The Atencingo sugar plantation of William O. Jenkins, former American consular agent, on orders from the governor of Puebla, was confiscated and its 8,268 hectares of irrigated sugar cane land were given to 2,043 peasants, residing in forty villages at the rate of four hectares per family. This group was financed by the National Ejidal Credit Bank and was required to form a cooperative society supervised by the Regional Federation of Workers and Peasants, to which all the new *ejidatarios* belonged.[57]

It was under these circumstances that a significant number of Japanese in Mexico, experienced nativist and xenophobic attitudes from the Mexican population, in particular a group known as "*Agraristas*" (Agrarians), farmer-soldiers who seized property. On January 30, 1937, a large number of *Agraristas* in the Valley of Mexicali in the northern regions of Baja California invaded the private enterprises of Japanese companies and took possession of the houses, land, farming implements and livestock without governmental authorization or cause.[58] *Agraristas* took over the Maneadero property in 1938, "planted a red flag and proclaimed it a liberated area. Suzuki Tamanosuki was given a month to move, after which he developed a second Maneadero farm about fifty miles from the original and with financial support from the Mexican government."[59] However, these attitudes were uneven and primarily emerged from the northern Mexican states where the largest enclaves of Japanese were located and which was a region long known for its anti-Asian sentiments.

The 1930s brought additional challenges to the Japanese community that were directly and indirectly linked to national and international events. Even though global economies were gripped in a massive downturn, one area continued to provide not only profits but also strategic advantage and value, oil. Before 1938 the British Mexican Eagle Company owned or controlled 70 percent of Mexico's oil production. The British, United States, and Dutch oil interests extracted oil from the period of the Díaz regime through 1917 without paying any royalties or taxes to the Mexican government and after the adoption of the 1917 Constitution a royalty of 5 percent was paid.[60] Although the 1917 Constitution nationalized Mexico's land and subsoil and created conditions where foreign oil companies were required to relinquish the protection of their governments, a minority that controlled most of the oil refused those conditions.

In 1937 the Mexican government investigated the oil industry per labor legislation and determined that the oil companies were required to increase wages and social benefits by seven million dollars. When the oil companies refused to abide by all the conditions set forth and upheld by the Mexican Supreme Court, President Lázaro Cárdenas nationalized the oil industry on March 18, 1938. Initially the United States reacted negatively by refusing to buy Mexican silver and oil, while US and British oil companies demanded reparations. The United States also became concerned that Mexico might sell this important resource to countries such as Japan and found itself in a delicate position, as world events created factions and the Western hemisphere needed solidarity, not conflict. Mexico, on the other hand, through decades of internal and external problems, developed a unique set of diplomatic skills that allowed it to achieve a measure of success against its much stronger northern neighbor.

Weapons of the Weak

US citizens were heavily invested in land in Mexico and many suffered land loss during the revolutionary and post-revolutionary periods, which resulted in legal claims as well as heightened tensions between Mexico and the United States. Mexico's nationalization of land began a tumultuous period in US-Mexican relations. Intertwined with land reform was Mexico's determination to take control of its subsoil, especially the oil industry. When Mexico nationalized the oil industry in 1938, it crystallized tensions and mistrust that lingered from earlier land reforms. Thrown into this mixture was Japan's desire to acquire important strategic natural resources from Mexico, such as oil, which heightened the anxiety on all sides.

The list of acts of premeditated aggression against its southern neighbor is lengthy and it is sufficient to state that the US invasion and conquest of Mexico's northern territories left long-standing animosity and suspicions about US motives in Mexico and the Western hemisphere. The scholarship on these episodes is extensive and does not need repeating here.[61] However, I would like to quote Stuart Chase as a reminder of the enormity and gravity of US intervention in Mexico, who wrote in 1931,

> We have collected fabulous slices of Mexican territory. We took Texas in two gulps, the first, Sam Houston's "revolution" in 1836 and the second, the voluntary accession of the Republic of Texas in 1845. California and New Mexico we bought for $15,000,000. This sum would not buy one minor movie company in one suburb of one California city.[62]

Mexico became adept at understanding its opponents' negotiating weaknesses and playing off diplomatic rifts between nations, especially if it benefited the national interest. Mexico's ability and finesse were gleaned from decades of internal strife and its weak position in the region, where it faced a continuous onslaught from various US administrations. Under these conditions Mexico utilized a derivative of James C. Scott's theory known as "diplomatic weapons of the weak," as articulated by John J. Dwyer.[63] According to Dwyer, when Mexico was confronted by the United States on a wide range of issues such as the expropriation of American-owned rural land in Mexico during the 1920s and the nationalization of oil in the 1930s, Mexican diplomats skillfully challenged the United States and their European counterparts. These challenges came in the form of tactics that delayed any attempts at a quick and decisive settlement on the part of the United States or others making claims against Mexico "that are employed by weaker actors in a relationship marked by an unequal distribution of power."[64]

The deployment of these weapons is best illustrated with Mexico's confrontation with the United States over land seizures and the expropriation of Mexican oil. Mexico's strategies and tactics on how it was able to achieve diplomatic success against the United States at a time of economic uncertainty in conjunction with internal and external political strife indicates that the Mexican diplomatic corps was savvy, astute, and aware of US cultural nuances, that in many ways eluded their American counterparts. The ability of Mexico to keep the United States at bay during the 1920s and 1930s had a direct impact on the Japanese during the 1940s. The rift between Japan and the United States placed Mexico in an all too familiar position and the following quote, albeit in the parlance of the times, from a Japanese official demonstrates Mexico's early attempts at outmaneuvering the United States:[65]

> No. Mexico is like a girl, who flirts with two boys, playing one off against the other in order more easily to land the one of her choice. Mexico really wishes to borrow money from the United States. In order to influence America to make this loan, she circulates the story that Japan has offered to make it.[66]

As in previous decades the interplay between Mexico, Japan, and the United States is crucial in understanding the overall treatment of Japanese Mexicans and the motives behind the United States' hemispheric wide roundups of Japanese and Mexico's resistance against confining Japanese Mexicans during World War II. And, it was not a foregone conclusion that Mexico would fall neatly into the Allied camp during World War II. Mexico had friendly relations with Japan and traded extensively with Germany and Italy. When the markets for oil dwindled, Mexico began to engage Japan and Germany with barter exchanges for Mexican oil. When Mexico nationalized its oil industry, Japan assured Mexico that it was ready to buy all the oil produced in the country.[67] Between 1938 and 1940 Mexico exported over 510,000 tons of crude oil and oil products to Japan, over 11 million tons of to Germany, and over 6 million tons to Italy.[68] Seen in this context, the oil crisis presented concerns for the United States that went well beyond compensating US owners.

Notwithstanding the above, the United States changed course regarding its foreign policy with Mexico and Latin America during the 1930s that came to be known as the Good Neighbor Policy. Nonetheless, during the first half of the twentieth century the United States increasingly infiltrated Mexico economically in order to sustain leverage against the Mexican state without resorting to its usual military designs. The conflict over land, railroads, and oil illustrate the magnitude of this economic control. First, historian John Mason Hart indicates that by the time of the Mexican Revolution, foreigners held 35 percent of Mexican soil, with Americans controlling 27 percent or 130,000,000 acres.[69] This level of economic control of Mexico by the United States and other foreign entities is staggering.[70] Mexico's development and industrialization owes a great deal to American enterprise, but the consequences of that development created such disparities and inequalities that the social unrest that ensued manifested in the first revolution of the twentieth century that continued to be sorted out well into the 1930s. As the newly elected left-leaning president of Mexico, Lázaro Cárdenas maneuvered to consolidate power and reform, he simultaneously rattled the United States with his nationalization programs that affected land, railroads, and oil. And as previously mentioned, deteriorating relations between the United States and Mexico forced the Mexican government to rely more on European and Asian partners for the purchase of Mexican products.

Furthermore, Mexico's cordial exchanges with Japan and its often recalcitrant relations with the United States often found Mexico in an awkward position having to explain its position regarding Japan. When Cárdenas nationalized Mexico's oil industry in March 1938, relations between Mexico and the United States became strained, with some calling for intervention. During this same period relations between Mexico and Japan remained friendly, and economically, the two countries became further linked in the late 1930s as Mexico searched for markets to sell its oil. From the Japanese perspective, this was an opportune moment to garner a share of Mexico's natural resources, especially the type that were strategically important and needed to be stockpiled.

The issue of trade between Japan and Mexico became a topic of concern for the United States. Prior to 1941, Mexico exported a large array of products to Japan that included war materials such as oil, minerals, and mercury. In fact, in a newspaper article Japan's foreign minister in Mexico, Yoshiaki Miura, stated that if the United States continues to refuse petroleum sales to Japan, his country would have to purchase oil from those nations that would like to profit from their resources. Minister Miura then outlined the trade between Mexico and Japan: Mexican exports to Japan 1939 in pesos, 9,394,000; 1940, 24,043,000; 1941 (January through March) 7,626,000. Mexican imports from Japan: 1939 in pesos, 7,268,000; 1940, 17,512,000, and 1941, 4,806,000.[71] However, as hemispheric solidarity came to fruition, Mexico signed various defense pacts with the United States, one that included the sale of all surplus commodities to the United States in order to keep them from any Axis nations. Mexico's "friendly" relations with Japan remained relatively unscathed until the Japanese attack on Peal Harbor, and even then, Mexico did not declare war but broke diplomatic relations. At the national level a handful of Japanese Mexicans became successful entrepreneurs during the post-revolutionary period, that directly aided the Japanese efforts to gain natural resources for their strategic military value.

Kiso Tsuru: The Enigmatic Japanese Mexican

Japanese business enterprises gained traction in Mexico during the 1930s with substantial holdings in the mining and oil industries. Japanese

Mexicans also became important players in a number of industries within Mexico, especially those that had potential benefit during times of war. As a precautionary measure Japan and Japanese sought to protect their established commercial interests by transferring them to Mexican wives and children born in Mexico.[72] During the 1930s one particular Japanese Mexican rose to prominence within Japanese and Mexican business circles. Dr. Kiso Tsuru was considered the most important Japanese entrepreneur in Mexico in the decade leading up to the war.[73] Indeed, the United States identified Tsuru as more than just an economic dynamo. From military intelligence reports, Tsuru has been branded as the head of the Japanese intelligence network in Mexico. Because of Tsuru's organizational abilities he was certainly capable of simultaneously running over half a dozen companies and Japan's intelligence infrastructure in Mexico. However, much of the evidence demonstrates Tsuru was a brilliant entrepreneur and trusted confidant of Japanese Ambassador Yoshiaki Miura but not the head of Japan's intelligence network. From the US and Mexican perspective, it is understandable how such a supposition was made. Tsuru's name surfaced in many classified documents associated with Japan's efforts to acquire war materials, which gave the appearance that Tsuru was not simply a businessman.

Tsuru directly or indirectly organized all the important Japanese commercial enterprises in Mexico for the fifteen years leading up to World War II. Tsuru's exceptional ability to maneuver between Mexican and Japanese business and political circles made him a paradox regarding what is considered the general Japanese Mexican experience in Mexico prior to and during the war. Yet, Tsuru's experience provides great insight into the complexity of the Japanese situation in Mexico, while simultaneously helping us understand the intricate nature of that existence. The handful of Japanese enterprises that attracted the most attention from Mexican authorities were primarily organized and managed by Tsuru. All of these companies were engaged in the development of strategic war materials that were shipped to Japan to aid in their war efforts prior to 1941. Tsuru's companies were involved in petroleum exploration, drilling, pharmaceuticals, extraction of resources, and the mining of minerals.

Tsuru owned, controlled, or was a key stakeholder in three major companies that had substantial holdings in Mexico. La Compañía Mexicana de Petróleos, "La Laguna" S.A., was formed in 1934 in Jalapa, Veracruz, to exploit the oil fields in the region. The Japanese, through Tsuru, leased 250,000 acres of oil land in the state of Veracruz. Although La Laguna was a Mexican entity, it was indirectly and highly financed by the Japanese government through another company known as Taiheyo Sakiyu Kaisha (Pacific Petroleum Company) out of Kobe, Japan. The Japanese government and Japanese individuals owned 80 percent of the stock and was represented by Tsuru in Mexico, but the Japanese government provided the company with working capital. In July 1941 that working capital amounted to $350,000 US dollars.[74] Tsuru was also president of Compañía Internacional de Drogas S.A.[75] Compañía Petrólera Veracruzana, created in 1935 was financed in a similar fashion, by the Japanese government, for the oil fields in and around the region of northern Veracruz and Tamaulipas. This company was also associated with Tsuru. He combined Veracruzana and La Laguna, with the latter as the holding company and Tsuru as its financial director.[76] Tsuru also directed the Turo Mining Company, Nippon Suisan Kaisha, and it was also reported that Tsuru was to have handled all of the financial aspects for the Isthmus (Tehuantepec) Pipe Line, which was to have been built by the Japanese.[77] The rationalization for the pipeline was purely economic. Japan hoped to cut down on mileage and cost by circumventing the Panama Canal by shipping Mexican oil across the isthmus to Salina Cruz and then to Japan.

Numerous intercepted Japanese cables, through a United States cryptoanalysis project known as Magic, mention Tsuru working diligently to secure war materials for Japan. The following is an example of an intercepted message between Japanese officials in Tokyo and the Japanese minister in Mexico, Yoshiaki Miura.[78] In this message is a discussion of how Tsuru attempted to convince the Mexican government to barter Japanese rayon, a semisynthetic fiber used in the manufacturing of clothing, for Mexican fluorspar or fluorite, a mineral used in metallurgy that allows the melting of steel at lower temperatures. However, Tsuru ran into many obstacles in this endeavor:

> Although Tsuru appears to have been making arrangements for barter of artificial silk [rayon] for fluorspar through influential circles after the Presidential Order, he asked me concerning a plan and he agreed with my explanation of the foregoing. Tsuru is finding out exactly the position of the President and the Economic Minister through a person close to the President, General Banierosu [Kana spelling], received the reply that any movement whatsoever at this time would be futile and that one should wait for an opportune moment.[79]

Furthermore, Tsuru is mentioned in a variety of sources that included the Servicio de Migración Registro Nacional de Extranjeros, Mexico's secret police investigative unit known as Investigaciones Políticas y Sociales, US military intelligence division reports, intercepted Japanese diplomatic messages, and personal diaries of Japanese Mexicans living in Mexico during this era. The fact that Tsuru's life and activities were extensively chronicled indicates Tsuru was a prominent resident of Mexico before and during the war. The experience of Tsuru provides insight into the various roles Japanese Mexicans and nationals played in Mexico prior to and during World War II, where on the one hand, long established Japanese felt a sense of loyalty to Mexico, yet on the other, many remained connected to Japan, especially culturally. A Japanese Mexican recalled when war broke out between Japan and the United States, "there was an increasing tendency among the Japanese in Mexico to blindly support Japan's military expansion to the Asian continent after 1931. Furthermore, some Japanese who had lived in Mexico for decades, considered Mexico their second country, changed their nationalities and even Hispanicized their names, remained willing to follow the direction of Japan." [80]

Dr. Kiso Tsuru is an excellent example of this conflict. Tsuru, who came to Mexico in 1918 through Salina Cruz, Oaxaca, and was nationalized in 1935, built a strong reputation as an astute businessman establishing La Compañía Internacional de Drogas, S.A. in the 1930s and eventually settling in Isabel la Catolica no. 85 in Mexico City.[81] Serious Japanese interest and investment in Mexico began around 1934 when Tsuru and an associate, Yukio Nagamatsu, began an oil drilling operation. After several setbacks, Tsuru's company eventually received the backing of the Japanese government due to their desire for Mexican oil. By 1941 Tsuru was considered the best-connected businessman of Japanese ancestry in Mexico and as a result the Japanese government sought his skills, advice, and expertise, especially regarding war materials. Further, Tsuru worked closely with Carlos Almazan, an engineer and close confidant of Luis Cabrera, an attorney and strong critic of the United States, who became the head of the Junta de Administración y Vigilencia de la Propiedad Extranjera. Tsuru, because of his ambition, drive, and willingness to deal with the Japanese government, in some ways resembled your typical "war profiteer." However, I argue that Tsuru's role in Mexico navigates the complex nature of the Japanese experience in Mexico.

By the late 1930s Japan had become so desperate to gain resources such as mercury and oil that Japanese officials in Mexico City openly approached the Mexican President and his minister of economics in an effort to gain concessions, only to be rebuked. Shortly thereafter, Japan embarked on a plan to gain war materials in secret through the back door and hoped to barter rayon for mercury with Tsuru as the middleman.[82] However, because of Tsuru's contacts in Mexico and business dealings with Japan he became a security concern to the United States and Mexico. Unfortunately for Tsuru, corroborating evidence was found when the Japanese diplomatic corps in Mexico was repatriated to Japan in 1942. During a search of former Japanese diplomatic personnel, documents were found in the house formerly occupied by the Japanese naval attaché, Captain Kyoho Hamanaka, which revealed Tsuru's importance, especially his dealings with Mexican officials. Another document stamped "extremely confidential" that was addressed to Katauo Abe, commanding officer of the Naval Affairs Bureau, as well as to Konomu Onjaku, commanding officer of the Munitions Bureau, and Takazuni Oka, commanding officer of Division 3, Navy General Staff, also implicated Tsuru. The report reviewed in detail the efforts of the Pacific Petroleum Company and the Laguna Corporation (headed by Tsuru) to secure oil in Mexico together with the failure of all drillings to produce as expected. The report was dated August 29, 1940, and was prepared by Captain Katsuya Sato, who was the Japanese Naval Attaché in Mexico at that time.[83] A US intelligence report even had Tsuru connected to the caudillo of San Luis Potosí, General Saturnino Cedillo, which stated, "[Tsuru] at one time connected with General Cedillo in a revolutionary attempt." These were unsubstantiated claims, but nevertheless indicated a close scrutiny of Tsuru, especially by US officials.[84] Tsuru also appeared to have been implicated along with Carlos Almazan and Carlos del Rio in an attempt to smuggle mercury from Manzanillo, Mexico aboard the Japanese SS *Asuma Maru*. Tsuru's mining company in Oaxaca extracted large quantities of mica, mercury, lead, and zinc in Guerrero and fluorite in Taxco.[85] A note left by Japanese naval attaché Captain Katsuya Sato provided an indication of Tsuru's motives. Sato was concerned that Tsuru's enterprise, the Laguna Company, was not performing and suggested to the Japanese government that all operations of the Laguna Corporation be taken over by the Japanese government and the Pacific Petroleum Company, adding, "From the time of establishment Tsuru has been a problem and attempting to gain too much personal profit."[86] Sato's general sentiments were that Tsuru was overly concerned with profits and less with the motives and aims of the Japanese empire.

Others had a different impression of Tsuru with some Japanese adamant that Tsuru was a loyal Mexican, but the fact remained that he entangled himself with the Japanese government in their covert attempts to import war materials from Mexico. Eventually Tsuru and his enterprises became part of the blacklist created by the Allies within Mexico and he was shut down. Did Tsuru deliberately attempt to help the Japanese war effort? Was he simply a profiteer? Or was Tsuru, as one article put it, "protector in chief of the Japanese in Mexico?" The US FBI had numerous files, which tended to indicate that the Japanese government had used Tsuru and his commercial enterprises as fronts to gather information and obtain war materials, although no positive evidence ever substantiated that Tsuru was an intelligence asset or actually engaged in espionage.

At the outbreak of the war all of Tsuru's entities were quickly confiscated, shut down, and Tsuru was arrested. Unlike some of his counterparts Tsuru was not sent to the United States for internment, but remained in Mexico City as part of the relocation efforts by the Mexican government. Shortly thereafter, Tsuru used his talents during the war to protect Japanese in Mexico. When Mexico ordered the relocation of Japanese Mexicans, Tsuru along with Heiji Kato and Sanshiro Matsumoto were hand picked by Yoshiaki Miura, minister to Mexico, to organize and look after the interests of all Japanese in the country. This apparent close contact with the highest representative of the Japanese government in Mexico appeared to further implicate Tsuru as a possible agent of the Emperor. However, it is more likely that Yoshiaki Miura simply recognized the organizational talents of Tsuru, Kato, and Matsumoto, who and with their extensive contacts seemed the logical choice to help organize the Japanese population in Mexico during a period of uncertainty. These three individuals also became the charter members of the Comité Japonés de Ayuda Mutua during World War II.

Conclusion

Mexico's discourse on race and racialization swung from Darwinism, positivism, eugenics, *indigenismo* to "*mestizophilia*." Charting this discussion on race partially explains the different treatment of the Japanese and Chinese in Mexico and reveals a racial ideology that viewed Japanese closer to whiteness and the Chinese as a threat to Mexican ethnicity and identity. The imperceptibility of the Japanese in Mexico resulted in an inconsistent policy regarding their position and treatment. In the end, Mexico developed two distinct trajectories for the Chinese and Japanese. The Chinese felt the full brutality of racism and the anti-Chinese movement, while the Japanese encountered a Mexican society more willing to include them based on preconceived notions of whiteness.

Nevertheless, the Japanese presence in Mexico created many challenges as the multilateral relations between Mexico, Japan, and the United States became strained over the course of the 1930s. The Japanese experience in Mexico remained tenuous and even though the overall population remained relatively small they continued to be seen as a threat, not just to Mexico, but also to the United States, and eventually to the hemisphere. Although the economic and social character of the Japanese immigrant to Mexico began to change in the 1920s and 1930s they increasingly became targets of nativism, nationalism, and anti-immigrant legislation. The invisible armor that once cloaked and protected the Japanese in Mexico gave way to an ever-transparent design to sabotage their efforts and livelihoods in a nation that largely showed little concern over their presence. The Japanese continued their movement to a country that in large measure accepted them, even as national debates on immigrants, immigration, and nationalism engulfed Mexico.

Through the early decades of the twentieth century Japan and Mexico maintained friendly relations and the oil sales to Japan during the 1930s are indicative of those interactions. Simultaneously, Mexico was very much aware that the United States, not Japan, remained its most important ally, but that it needed to exert a level pressure to gain concessions from the United States. In this manner, Mexico's sales of oil to Axis nations such as Japan, Italy, and Germany during the 1930s were an additional gambit. Considering the weaker position Mexico maintained compared with the United States, it is not surprising that Mexico chose this position in order to indicate to the United States that Mexico had other markets to which to sell. As the United States inched closer to war in 1941, it mounted a policy of accommodation with Mexico rather than conflict in order to achieve a level of hemispheric solidarity to guard against Axis penetration in the region. Mexico also understood that with the possibility of global war it held a significant amount of clout in the hemisphere, especially regarding its natural resources and it used its position to achieve specific concessions from the United States and keep it at bay. In some ways the United States maneuvered Mexico into making decisions that favored the United States and that had international implications in the late 1930s revolving around land, oil, and foreign ownership in Mexico.

The expropriation of oil and its conclusion allowed Mexico to implement basic tenets of the Mexican Revolution and exert its sovereignty to the dismay of various foreign entities, enabled the United States to close decades old land claims and compensation for the oil companies, and made it possible for both countries to set aside differences to implement defense pacts to strengthen bilateral relations. That Mexico and the United States reached this level of cooperation is surprising considering the tumultuous relations they shared after the start of the Mexican Revolution.

Unfortunately, the aims of the Imperial Japanese government often enveloped Japanese Mexicans as it attempted to gain a strategic advantage for natural resources such as oil, mercury, or other minerals. And as had been the pattern, anything Japanese was viewed with suspicion with the United States wary of Japanese activities in Mexico, regardless of whether the persons involved were Mexican citizens such as Dr. Kiso Tsuru. The next chapter examines the propaganda blitz that occurred after the bombing of Pearl Harbor. Suspicion directed at Japanese Mexicans and nationals became more pronounced after December 7, 1941 and from the US perspective Japanese fifth columns were indeed operating in Mexico. These fears created an uncertain future for Japanese Mexicans and for the Japanese diaspora in the Western hemisphere.

CHAPTER FOUR

The Long Reach of the American Empire

Japanese Mexicans, US Hegemony, and Mexican Propaganda, 1941–1945

The Axis powers have set up in Mexico a subversive organization so formidable in its ramifications and so efficient in its operations that the stability of the Mexican Government is at stake.

—"Secret Memorandum for the Chief, Latin American Section," June 2, 1941

In October 1942 a poster could be seen throughout Mexico depicting three individuals hanged by the neck, and with the following text, "*Así es el nuevo orden nazi*" [This is the New Nazi Order]. The poster, titled "Nazi New Order," by Taller de Gráfica Popular (Popular Graphic Art Workshop, or People's Graphic Workshop, TGP) artist Robert Mallary, was one of the first lithographs created by TGP that promoted the propaganda campaign of the Mexican government for the war effort (figure 4.1). The use of artists and their ability to reach and speak to the masses was part of an overall propaganda blitz that Mexico deployed in the early 1940s to rally the country for war and to silence US concerns of Mexican apathy toward the war effort. Even when Mexico declared war in May 1942, the United States remained unconvinced that the Mexican public supported such declarations. After Mexico announced its proclamation of war, a US-based writer assessed the situation and wrote the following:

> Does this decision mean that the generality of Mexicans are persuaded, that they now trust the United States, that they unitedly believe that Mexico's interest is served by joint action with the United States in ending the threat of the Axis, in working out a free brotherhood of democracies in the western world?[1]

Figure 4.1. "Así es el nuevo orden nazi" [This is the Nazi Order]. The poster, titled "Nazi New Order," is by Taller de Gráfica Popular artist Robert Mallary. Taller de Grafica Popular created many images to promote the war effort and reach the masses in Mexico. Source: Verna Carleton Millan, "Propaganda War in Mexico," *Inter-American Monthly*, September 1943, 16–19.

Suspicion and concern from the Mexican public remained high in the early years of the 1940s, so much so that the country showed little enthusiasm to get involved with European or US affairs. Unlike the previous decade when Lázaro Cárdenas astutely rallied an eager nation against US aggression and imperialism as he nationalized American-owned land and the oil industry, Manuel Ávila Camacho faced a country reluctant to get involved in a war whose aims remained unclear to most Mexicans. As Camacho took office in 1940 he faced a public with varied views on the war in Europe where, on the one hand, many felt a sense of indifference toward Europe and its ongoing conflict. On the other hand, a significant portion of the Mexican public understood the dangers of the European conflict and the need for Mexico to make a strong stance against not only the aggression of fascism but also the tyranny of Nazism spreading across Europe.

This chapter examines the propaganda blitz that was launched by the United States and Mexico after each had entered into World War II. Prior to the bombing of Pearl Harbor the Japanese in Mexico existed under a shield of invisibility partly due to their smaller numbers compared with other Asian groups, but primarily attributed to their assimilation and mixed marriages. However, this invisibility quickly disintegrated and their demonization commenced. This reconfiguration of the Japanese in Mexico is due in large measure to a barrage of propaganda and attributed to individual journalists and government agencies, who, for propaganda purposes, racialized the Mexican Indian and the Japanese so that any Indian might be a subversive Japanese and any Japanese could pass as Indian to hide among Mexico's populace. Individuals from the other Axis nations, such as Germans and Italians, did not encounter the level of hatred or racialization experienced by the Japanese in the Western hemisphere. The racial discourse of World War II had a distinct *otherness* attached to it that existed long before the outbreak of the war. The treatment of the Japanese at the hemispheric level is connected specifically to the racialization of the Japanese in the United States. As a result, US hegemony blanketed the hemisphere with a racial ideology that viewed Japanese not only as the enemy but also as inferior. When the United States entered World War II it unleashed a massive propaganda machine to sway public opinion and to deal with intractable Latin American countries to procure the allegiance of every country in the hemisphere.

Part of this campaign required that the hemisphere remain in a constant state of fear of Axis infiltration. This was partially achieved by journalists such as Betty Kirk (discussed later), and the United States–supported *Inter-American Monthly* and *En Guardia* popular magazines, which initiated a hail of negative articles and images of suspected Japanese "fifth columns" and Japanese saboteurs disguised as Mexican Indians, merchants, or barbers. These magazines saturated the US and Latin American newsstands. In this manner and at a hemispheric level, every Japanese was racially profiled as a potential threat to national security. Although Mexico became a strong ally of the United States and the war effort, it often found itself at odds with the United States over its Japanese population. The Mexican population simply did not view the Japanese in the same light that the Americans did. The Mexican population did not display the same nationalistic fervor as the Americans after Pearl Harbor and for good reason: Pearl Harbor was not Mexican territory. As President Manuel Ávila Camacho and his secretaría de gobernación (secretary of the interior), Miguel Alemán, acquiesced to US demands to hunt down any Axis infiltrators and limited civil liberties during the war, they simultaneously balanced such efforts by accommodating Japanese Mexicans whenever possible.

The Long Reach of the American Empire

By the beginning of the 1940s Mexico had a population of Issei, Nisei, Sansei, and a smaller group of Japanese nationals with diplomatic cover.[2] A definitive number of Japanese in Mexico is difficult to gauge, especially for the 1940s. Several different rationalizations attempt to account for the flaws of the 1940 Mexican Census and its inability to provide reliable data on foreigners in Mexico. According to sources, the 1940 Census was never fully released by the Mexican government, primarily due to a lack of funds to publish the materials.[3] Delia Salazar Anaya, a Mexican demographer, indicates the same census failed to accurately enumerate the foreign-born population because many refused to identify their legal nationality due to the ensuing global conflict.[4] More significant was confusion over how Mexico defined nationality.

When war erupted in Europe with Germany's invasion of Poland in 1939, trade with Latin America became disrupted and "fifth column" fears were heightened throughout the region. From the US perspective, such an economic disturbance might bring political destabilization and push Mexico and other South American countries toward the Axis powers.[5] Overall, nearly 6,000 Japanese nationals and 13,000 Mexicans of Japanese ancestry resided in Mexico on the eve of Pearl Harbor.[6] The small number of sources on Japanese in Mexico neglect to enumerate the Japanese who became naturalized citizens and their offspring. When these numbers are taken into account the combined Japanese population in Mexico is over 19,000, a significant revision from sources that only tallied Japanese nationals or naturalized citizens. On the whole, the Japanese population posed no numerical threat and certainly was not large enough to shift demographics or change *la Mexicanidad*.

The epigraph at the beginning of this chapter appeared in a secret memorandum in early summer 1941 from the US war department's Latin American section. The four-page memorandum outlined the general Axis threat in Latin America, which in turn, from the perspective of US officials, posed a danger to the United States. According to this report, "The extent and effectiveness of the Axis forces may be estimated from the following brief summary of their organization and activities. Statements concerning a few of those activities are not based on documentary proof at present available to this office, but are the result of analysis of trends and opinions of observers on the ground."[7] Overall, the report lays out various groups and organizations whose potential for subversive activities raised a security risk if not 'checked.' The obvious groups mentioned in the report included German immigrants and naturalized German Mexicans, Italians, and Japanese. The report also mentions threats from fascists groups such as the Spanish Falange and individuals attached to or who supported the Nazis party and any affiliation with the Gestapo. However, thrown into this mix were Mexican labor groups such as the Confederación Trabajadores Mexicanos, the Mexican Communist Party (Partida Comunista Mexicanos, PCM), and so-called patriotic groups. Indeed, the report stated, "It is the Mexican who is in the best position to do serious harm to the United States and the cause of democracy."[8] This concern regarding Mexico reverberated throughout the World War II period and attempts to rectify the perception that Mexico was inundated with subversives and provocateurs manifested on multiple levels. One of those manifestations was a coordinated propaganda campaign unlike anything ever seen before that placed Mexico at the forefront of both the Allied and Axis nations as they jockeyed for influence with Mexico.

For the forty years leading up to World War II, the Japanese were depicted, almost universally, as enemies to the state and the Western hemisphere. This image was carefully crafted in the United States and disseminated throughout the region. During the late nineteenth and early twentieth century, US influence in the Americas was nearly absolute through its military, economic, and political authority. Indeed, one scholar indicates that the United States "sent warships into Latin American ports a staggering 5,980 times between 1869–1897 to protect

American commercial interests."[9] Just as staggering was the economic control of US corporations over the natural resources of Latin America, in particular Mexico, where by the outbreak of the Mexican Revolution, US companies controlled nearly all the mining and oil industry. As a result, many Latin American countries were influenced by the onslaught of US propaganda and took punitive measures against their Japanese populations. However, some countries like Peru needed very little nudging and deployed anti-Japanese legislation in their country long before World War II. As Daniel M. Masterson points out, Peru, like the United States and Canada, began to develop anti-Asian legislation in the early twentieth century directed primarily at Chinese and Japanese in the country. Peru's anti-Asian efforts culminated with the passage of its 1936 Immigration Act that prohibited the immigration by "racial groups" and other restrictions simply meant to discourage the movement of Japanese to Peru.[10] Based on anti-Japanese sentiments throughout the Americas, an overarching pattern of racialization of the Japanese at the hemispheric level emerged before the 1940s, which fueled the Japanese hysteria during World War II.

When the United States and Mexico entered World War II in 1941 and 1942, respectively, the US government employed few people with a solid understanding of Mexico beyond what was read through popular magazines or newspapers. As a result, US military intelligence relied heavily on individuals whose "knowledge" was gleaned from having lived for extended periods of time in Mexico, whether or not these individuals truly had an understanding of all the nuances of Mexican society. In many ways journalist Betty Kirk (discussed later) falls into this category. Furthermore, Kirk and others were an extension of a well-designed official US propaganda machine seeping through the writings of US and foreign journalists based in the United States, Mexico, or Latin America. This cadre of individuals who wrote scathing articles on the presence and dangers of Japanese living in the Americas pushed an anti-Japanese agenda through the use of reportorial journalism.

After the bombing of Pearl Harbor, reports of a Japanese invasion of the Americas substantially increased in newspapers and US government reports, as did the hysteria. An examination of many of these reports indicates that most were the result of overzealous and uninformed US military officers, biased journalists, unsubstantiated reports of Japanese sleeper cells, and the panic caused by anything that resembled a Japanese saboteur, including the morphing of the Chamula and Otomi Indians into Japanese waiting to undermine US and Mexican national security. In fact, American fears of a Japanese force infiltrating into Mexico are discernable as early as the first decade of the twentieth century with dozens of articles suggesting Japan's intent to invade.[11] Regardless of any solid evidence, the first two decades of the twentieth century witnessed a flood of information, mostly based on rumor that alluded to an imminent attack by the Japanese and their desire to establish a military base somewhere along the Pacific Coast. On this last point, the Japanese were certainly desirous to establish a military presence in the Western hemisphere to counter the US military presence in East Asia. As mentioned earlier, Mexico used this to gain concessions from the United States without fully committing itself to any such Japanese designs. Overall, the hysteria and frenzy over motives of the Japanese in the Americas prior to the 1940s laid the basis for their treatment during World War II.

The FBI created a detailed report titled "Plan of Japanese Invasion through the Republic of Mexico." The invasion report was part of the 468-page analysis on Mexico developed in 1942, with sections devoted to each Axis nation and the threat it posed to the United States if and when it decided to use Mexico as a conduit for an invasion of the United States. Similar to my earlier comments, these invasion plans were not the result of Mexico or the United States intercepting military plans for an invasion, but rather was based on data gathered through hearsay and newspaper articles circulating rumors of invasions that the FBI included in its report as conclusive evidence. For example, while en route for internment in the United States in February 1942, Captain Kyoho Hamanaka, the Japanese naval attaché in Mexico, "voiced his implicit belief in Japanese victory and the extension of Japanese influence in Latin America."[12] Hamanaka further explained what his government could do to Mexico and other Latin American countries in its desire to extend control and boastfully iterated that Japan could send one battleship, two heavy and two light cruisers, ten destroyers, and one airplane carrier to the port of Acapulco, Mexico, and land and maintain a force of 10,000 soldiers. Hamanaka's very words were incorporated into the FBI report with a detailed map that illustrated Hamanaka's verbal invasion plan.

The FBI also used a February 2, 1942, newspaper article from *La Opinion*, a Mexican language newspaper published in Los Angeles, California, articulating another Japanese invasion plan. According to the writer of the article, Waverly Root, the Japanese would cut communications and advance northward along the Mexican coast and with a fleet of small fishing boats formerly operating in Mexican waters, in conjunction with Japanese naval units, seize the Gulf of California and the Peninsula of Lower California. At Navojoa, Sonora, the Japanese force could establish an air base and with the Japanese fifth column together with Nazis in the area, aid in the military operations. The Japanese would then disembark troops at Tortuga Bay and aim to capture Ensenada, Baja California, from which point they would attack San Diego, California. The source used for this newspaper article was the Syndicate of Railroad Workers in Western Mexico, who relayed their information to President Manuel Ávila Camacho.[13] The FBI report also contains information that resembles material from Betty Kirk's *Covering the Mexican Front*:

> Japan's military mission is to open a gateway through the states of Sonora and Sinaloa for an attack upon the southern border of the United States. These states sparsely populated and undefended, were honeycombed with Japanese "farmers" and "fishermen," and the Japanese fishing fleet, operating in Magdalena Bay, knew every inlet and cove.[14]

Both of the scenarios just mentioned were plausible, but unlikely. Japan was not interested in invading the Americas. Japan was interested in keeping Mexico neutral and out of the camp of the United States. Such invasions as those discussed by Kyoho Hamanaka and *La Opinion* countered such objectives. If Hamanaka had actually uttered the plans above, it can be characterized as a captured sailor boasting and venting to his captors. As a trained naval officer and attaché, chances are slim that Hamanaka would have divulged plans for invasion of the United States. In addition, the article in *La Opinion* plays upon the fears of the Mexican and American public by resurrecting rumors that had been circulating for decades about imaginary Japanese designs for the region. For example, for decades leading up to World War II, the US media, government officials, and military intelligence often wrote that Japanese fishing boats in Mexico were actually Japanese naval spy ships in disguise. According to these reports the Japanese boats, rather than fishing, conducted reconnoiter operations and were mapping the coastlines for an invasion. And in Navojoa, Sonora, rumors circulated that it was a bastion for Japanese soldiers and fifth column elements. The importance of such reports lies not in their veracity, but in how such reports and newspaper articles were a catalyst and source for a massive report by the FBI on Mexico with detailed invasion plans based primarily on rumor and allusion. Additionally, such reports coupled with a nervous public fueled the hysteria of Japanese fifth columns and an imminent invasion, which in turn configured all Japanese into saboteurs, imperial soldiers, subversives, and terrorists well depicted in the propaganda literature disseminated by the Office of Inter-American Affairs (OIAA),

Figure 4.2. The title of the article where this picture appeared was "Jap Threat to Latin America." The actual caption read "Japanese children in class of secret school. Children are often taken to school after midnight to absorb Japanese ideology from saboteurs rattling books. Schools are thorn in the flesh of multiracial Brazil, whose government tries hard to unify her forty-million children." *Inter-American Monthly*, June 1942.

reports by the FBI, or unreliable intelligence gathering. And as figure 4.2 illustrates, even school children were depicted as possible threats to the Americas.

A Prelude to War

During the 1930s and early 1940s, hemisphere-wide initiatives were introduced to relieve tensions created by US foreign policy decisions that had rattled numerous Latin American nations during the first half of the twentieth century. First, Franklin D. Roosevelt announced the Good Neighbor Policy in his inaugural address on March 3, 1933, which was reinforced by his secretary of state, Cordell Hull, at the Seventh Inter-American Conference held in Montevideo in December 1933 outlining a new US strategy of nonintervention.[15] As US foreign policy shifted away from direct intervention and the global status quo began to unravel, the United States found it prudent to extinguish any lingering animosity to lay the foundation for a Western hemispheric front against Nazism and fascism. As early as 1936 the United States put in motion its hemispheric plan for solidarity by sponsoring the Inter-American Conference for the Maintenance of Peace held in Buenos Aires. The result of this conference was the "principle of consultation," which ultimately meant that an aggression against one American nation would be considered an aggression against all.[16] Put another way, collective security of the hemisphere was emerging due to the threat from abroad. An early effort at this approach came in September 1939 with the Panama Conference where a US resolution was submitted and approved that became known as the General Declaration of Neutrality. This declaration of neutrality was coupled with the Declaration of Panama, another US initiative that created a security zone for the Western hemisphere.[17]

Developments in Europe brought major changes to the Western hemisphere. In late 1939 the United States and Latin American countries were more concerned with keeping the war away from the region than with its defense. Thus, as Europe plunged into war Western European nations such as Great Britain and France immediately recognized the importance of the Western hemisphere and the potential for Axis penetration. As a result, in 1939 the British and French created the Inter-Allied Propaganda Committee to counter German propaganda in Mexico and sway Mexican opinion toward the Allies.[18] The fall of France to Hitler in May 1940 increased the possibility of Axis penetration in the Western hemisphere. To counter this possibility the 1940 Act of Havana declared and rejected the transfer of possessions between European powers and the taking of European territories in the Caribbean if necessary to protect the hemisphere from German encroachment.

Mexico also viewed the changing global atmosphere as a means to seek economic concessions in order to relieve the pressure from the United States that stemmed from continuing claims against it, but Mexico also saw this as an opportunity to commit to the fight against tyranny. By the end of the Cárdenas administration many within and without Mexico felt Cárdenas' social programs had leaned too far to the left. In fact, nearly half of the state governors in Mexico were in opposition to President Cárdenas and his social initiatives. The 1940 election of Manuel Ávila Camacho ushered in a center right president for Mexico to the pleasure of the United States and business community.

In December 1940, shortly after the election of Camacho, negotiations between the United States and Mexico began for a defense agreement and the construction of naval bases in Mexico. On December 26, 1940, the Mexican government gave permission to the United States Army to use Mexican airfields en route to the Panama Canal. On March 7, 1941, the Foreign minister of Mexico, Ezequiel Padilla, announced that Mexico would aid in the defense of the Western hemisphere should any nation in the Americas be attacked by a foreign power. In June 1941 Mexico solidified its position with the Allies and announced the Douglas-Weichers Agreement, which stipulated that Mexico would sell all strategic minerals to the United States. On July 10, 1941, Mexico prohibited the exportation of "basic and strategic materials" to all non-American countries as well as to any country that had not established similar export restrictions.[19] As the United States strengthened ties with Mexico it began a mobilization effort that included the direct penetration into the political, cultural and economic spheres of Mexico. It also meant that American aid and assistance was turned off and on at will depending on the level of cooperation and alignment of Latin American countries with US policies.

Propaganda Leviathans

During the late 1930s and early 1940s the United States mobilized to counter Japanese penetration into Mexico. As a pretext the United States pushed hemispheric cooperation, development, and modernization. What erupted was a massive propaganda war with US penetration into Mexico and the rest of Latin America to saturate the region with US goals and views on the war. However, this campaign of words and views was much more than simply convincing Mexico and the rest of Latin America that the Allied fight was the right fight. The United States embarked on a mission to penetrate and change Mexican culture to make Mexico more conducive to economic infiltration and social conditioning by American corporations and US government agencies. Numerous US government agencies infiltrated Mexico during World War II, but the Office of Inter-American Affairs stands out due to its sheer size and efforts in Mexico and other regions of Latin America. It should also be recalled that the OIAA had a predecessor and relied on this historical past to create the largest propaganda machine during World War II.

In many ways, the establishment of the OIAA in 1941 was fashioned after, or at the very least, resembled two entities. The first was the Committee on Public Information (CPI), a US propaganda office that emerged as the result of US entry into World War I in April 1918. At the time CPI was the largest propaganda unit in existence and became the prototype for the development of propaganda for the sole purpose of swaying public opinion toward war. One of the major achievements of CPI was its deep incursion into US newspapers and its sweeping campaign to gain the confidence of the American public for the war aims of the United States. Further, CPI published the *Official Bulletin*, a state-supported newspaper in the United States that reached a circulation of 118,000 at its height.[20] Similar to the journalists used during World War II by the OIAA, CPI had a cadre of journalists willing to not only write for the US government but also slant their stories toward the aims of US policy, collude with the government to censor information, and lie to the American public.[21] From the position of CPI its effectiveness at utilizing the US press was an extraordinary success, but after the war writers and journalists hit back recognizing that their credibility as trustworthy reporters of the truth hung in the balance. The backlash against the saturation of propaganda from World War I resulted in journalists and newspaper owners taking back control of their news reporting.[22] As successful as CPI was in winning the minds of the US public, it did little in swaying public opinion or enlisting the help of the other republics in the Americas. The short duration of US involvement in World War I may have contributed to its limited aims regarding the reach of its propaganda message. However, before the outbreak of World War I another organization emerged that in conjunction with the development of CPI, provided US strategists of World War II with another model to shape their propaganda machine.

The second entity, the Pan American Union (PAU), was created initially under the name "International Union of American Republics," in 1890 at the First International American Conference in Washington, DC, and at the behest of the United States.[23] The PAU was under the control of the United States, specifically the secretary of state, with an executive committee made up of the US secretary of state and four members taken in rotation from the Latin American countries. As stated in its 1923–27 report, the PAU's mission was to work cooperatively for the "broader economic, financial, and cultural interests of all the Republics of this continent and prompt collection and distribution of commercial data and information."[24] Thus, under the auspices of the US government the PAU reached into all sectors of commercial and cultural interests in Latin America. I submit that the OIAA was simply a wartime version of the PAU and adopted many of its objectives and ideas:

> The Pan American Union is in constant touch with educational and scientific institutions, philanthropic associations, and commercial organizations, placing at their disposal all the facilities of the Pan American Union in the solution of the problems which they are called upon to solve, and at the same time endeavoring to bring them into close touch with one another in order that they may be mutually and increasingly helpful. The contacts thus formed afford effective means of bringing about better understanding and closer relations between the nations and peoples of the Western hemisphere.[25]

Other points in common between the OIAA and PAU include the OIAA's affiliation with the US Department of State and that the PAU issued a monthly publication titled the *Bulletin* in English, Spanish, and Portuguese. In fact, many of the goals of the *Bulletin* appear to have been adopted by the OIAA sponsored *Inter-American Monthly*, which "continues to be the official record of actual conditions and trends, both material and cultural, in each of the countries members of the PAU, particularly with respect to commerce, legislation, education, public health, labor, social services, industry, and international communications by land, sea, and air."[26] Furthermore, the PAU and OIAA considered their publications as authoritative and keenly insightful to the Latin American way of life as stated first by the general director of the PAU:

> That it is [Bulletin] widely regarded as the authoritative interpreter of the Latin American Republics is shown by an increased use of its material in the government departments of the American Republics; in the extensive reprints constantly appearing in the Latin American and United States Press; in the growing desire for its cooperation in movements related to *inter-American affairs*, public and private; and in the increased recognition accorded it by economic, industrial, and social organizations throughout the American Continent.[27]

As articulated by the PAU, much of the labor of the organization was devoted to acquainting the people of the various American Republics with each other's history, economic and social development, their particular contributions in the fields of art, music, literature, and drama, and of encouraging movements that have for their purpose the fostering of common cultural interests. Lastly, the PAU created an effective mechanism for the distribution and dissemination of information, that if used for the purpose of propaganda could achieve its desired effect. In addition to its *Bulletin*, the PAU maintained a public relations department to supply the press of the United States and Latin America with news items and photographs. The PAU also utilized the radio to initially broadcast Latin American music, but eventually and more important, to disseminate speeches on Pan American themes. To this end, the PAU became an important conduit for the commercial and cultural exchange of ideas between the American Republics. It also appears the PAU may have influenced the development, implementation, and designs of the OIAA to strengthen the US position in the Americas.[28] Not mentioned in the PAU report is any attempt at Western hemispheric defense initiatives, but this is to be expected as the PAU saw itself primarily as a commercial and cultural entity. The importance of Western hemispheric mutual defense emerged in the late 1920s and early 1930s as it became clear that US policy of unilateralism and intervention in Latin America was counterproductive to regional commercial cooperation and defense, and as the European and Asian conflicts unraveled the political status quo of their regions, it was only a matter of time before the Western hemisphere was drawn into the confrontation. This last point made it imperative for the United States to shore up anti-American sentiments in Latin America brought about largely by its long history of intervention.

The Impact of the Office of Inter-American Affairs

To infiltrate the minds of the Latin American republics, operations were conducted by an array of US agencies, but the OIAA, initially created under the name "Office for Coordination of Commercial and Cultural Relations between the American Republics" in 1940 to "respond to perceptions of a massive threat to the security of the United States," merits some attention.[29] The OIAA became the largest propaganda machine during World War II, dwarfing any like agency from the Allied or Axis power countries. In its infancy the OIAA received a paltry $75,000 annual budget, but as it gained in importance and influence, its budget increased to $3.5 million and swelled to $60 million by 1943.[30] The Communications and Cultural Relations Divisions of the OIAA became the main arm of US wartime propaganda in Latin America.[31] The OIAA, because of concerns over Mexico's and in general Latin America's perceived lack of enthusiasm toward the war effort, put in motion a plan to create a state of fear in the Americas concerning enemy infiltration into the region with the hope of mobilizing Mexico's civilian population. In some regards Mexican apathy toward the war was accurate, and a number of Latin American countries leaned closely to pro-Nazis and fascist ideology. Furthermore, over 100 newspapers and magazines circulated throughout Latin America that were either sympathetic to the Axis nations or received financial assistance from them.[32] In fact, according to Monica Rankin, "the OIAA could also pressure periodicals to shift allegiances by threatening to cut off their supply of news print."[33] The OIAA went beyond this by developing its own publications, using an array of journalists, writers, and pseudospecialists on Mexico and Latin America to push the US and Allied agenda to counter any apathy in the hemisphere.

This propaganda apparatus, created and unleashed with the design of swaying and changing public opinion on the war, was especially worrisome to the Japanese in the Americas because, first, individuals of Japanese ancestry in the Americas were the largest of the Axis nations, and second, their configuration as undesirables began long before the outbreak of World War II, with anti-Japanese sentiments just below the surface in most Western hemispheric nations. The demonization and level of distrust of the Japanese in the Americas began to reach new heights with the outbreak of World War II as popular articles reached the general audience and increased suspicions. These popular articles increasingly suggested any indigenous person could be Japanese in disguise or that all Japanese were a threat. Additionally, beyond the negative discourse constructed by the court of public opinion, various US agencies adopted similar views as they developed fact sheets, reports, and studies aiding and abetting the racialization and fear of the Japanese population in the Americas. The monolithic image of all Japanese as the enemy created an atmosphere where a constant state of surveillance, harassment, relocation, and confinement were seen as the only possible solution to the Japanese population in Mexico and elsewhere in the Americas.

The Terror of the Machine: The Racialization of the Japanese

Any discussion on the Japanese experience in Mexico during this period must be filtered to distinguish the real, the imagined, and sometimes a combination of the two. The OIAA used many methods to keep the propaganda machine churning. For example, the OIAA had two major monthly publications to propagandize and disseminate information to the English and Spanish-speaking worlds: *En Guardia: Para Defensa de las Américas*[34] (*On Guard: For the Defense of the Americas*), a Spanish language magazine filled with images depicting the war effort, and the *Inter-American Monthly*, an English language publication used to promote the US and Allied positions on the war (see figure 4.3). Because of the popular nature of the glossy magazines, they were attractive to average people in their respective regions, and each had a substantial readership.

These monthly magazines were part of the overall design to promote inter-American cooperation through commercial and cultural interests during the 1940s. In the 1942 inaugural issue of the *Inter-American Monthly*, Nelson A. Rockefeller, the coordinator of OIAA, wrote an article, "New Economic Frontier," where he expounded on the need for economic solidarity in order to "secure the hemisphere against the enemies of freedom."[35] The *Inter-American Monthly* was designed for popular readership in order to reach a wide audience and in this manner mold and slant general sentiments about the war effort in a pro-US fashion. Central

Figure 4.3. Propaganda free-for-all. *Inter-American Monthly*, September 1944.

to the objectives of the United States was the need to make it appear that the United States supported an equal partnership with its Latin American neighbors while surreptitiously maintaining its hegemony through defense pacts and economic inducements. Throughout the war period these monthly periodicals used articles and images to convey the sweeping solidarity of the Americas, which the Axis powers had no chance of breaching, even when that solidarity was vulnerable.

The *Inter-American Monthly* attempted to achieve these objectives by disseminating positive propaganda about the cooperation between the United States and Latin America in a series of articles that ranged from regional military cooperation to economic relationships, popular culture, and US aid to various countries south of the Rio Grande. Furthermore, each issue carefully and deliberately discussed the dangers of Axis "fifth columns" in Latin America and that through hemispheric cooperation these countries could eradicate such perils. It is important to understand that most of these articles were based on flimsy evidence and used sources that had ulterior motives regarding the Japanese presence in their communities, such as competing merchants with cause to fabricate evidence about their Japanese neighbors. Based on this propaganda every Japanese Mexican became a suspected saboteur and Japanese merchants were reconfigured as hidden Imperial soldiers. The *Inter-American Monthly* not only racialized Japanese and Indigenous groups in Mexico but also created and sustained a constant state of suspicious alertness against everything Japanese. For example, a 1943 *Inter-American Monthly* issue featured an article by Betty Kirk, "Mexico's War on Hidden Japanese," accompanied by a map of Northwest Mexico and the Baja peninsula (see figure 4.4) which identified thirteen locations of Japanese activity and had the following caption, "West Coast Centers of Jap activities before Mexican Government cracked down on them."[36] Kirk's article failed to mention that these locations were the major ports of entry and settlement for Japanese immigrants. By the beginning of World War II Baja California had the largest concentration of Japanese in Mexico. The activities the Japanese were engaged in were primarily fishing and cotton farming in and around the Baja California region, which required boats and trawlers that were often suspected of engaging in espionage.

The same issue contained two photographs: one of Hoshiko Brothers mercantile store in Mexicali and another of two men inside a barbershop (see figure 4.5). The sensational caption read, "Japanese agents often operated as small merchants, such as the Hoshiko Brothers in Mexicali, and as barbers, like [the] one shown above in Ensenada."[37]

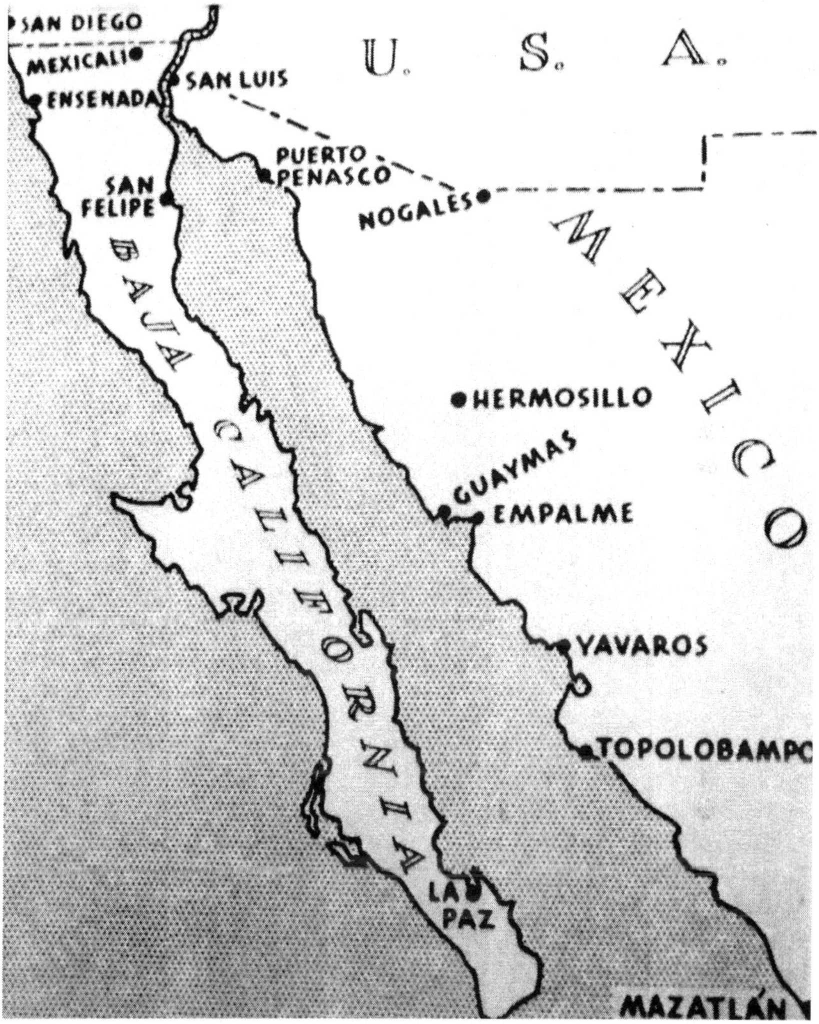

Figure 4.4. "West Coast centers of Jap Activities before Mexican Government Cracked Down on Them." *Inter-American Monthly*, January 1943

The article provides no evidence of the Hoshiko brothers' involvement in espionage as alluded to and the image taken of the barber with a client not only appeared to have been two Mexicans but also could have been taken almost anywhere in Mexico or perhaps even in the Southwest United States. As mentioned earlier, Japanese Mexicans used the barber

Figure 4.5. Japanese fifth column fears. *Inter-American Monthly,* January 1943.

trade as an accessible means to earn a living and a significant number were employed in this manner. Nonetheless, the images were powerful in their insinuation that all Japanese were suspect and were used as part of the public's indoctrination into the Axis threat in the Americas. The OIAA also encouraged mainstream forms of popular culture, such as the *Saturday Evening Post,* to create exposés on the Japanese population throughout Latin America using identical techniques to the *Inter-American Monthly* that reinforced to the public the wary and suspicious nature of the Japanese population. These images also highlight OIAA's prevalent use of popular culture, reportorial journalism, and propaganda.

This next example illustrates how the United States took a broad approach in reaching its audience and conveyed multiple messages with the use of popular culture through the OIAA sponsored *Inter-American Monthly*. A February 1944 issue featured a "Yaqui" Indian in full baseball catcher's gear (see figure 4.6) with the article discussing how the American pastime had become equally popular in Latin America. If we are to believe that the individual underneath the catcher's mask is actually a "Yaqui" Indian, then we can also assume that that author is making several underlying assumptions about Mexico's indigenous population. First, that modernity is defined and linked to the United States and can only be transmitted through US culture and customs. Second, fundamental to the article is a discussion on how Latin Americans have discarded the antiquated sport of bullfighting for the progressive and modern sport of American baseball. Bullfighting is associated with the colonial empire of Spain and depicted as leftover cultural baggage from a conservative and nonprogressive era of colonization. And since baseball is a "team" sport and requires "unity," Latin Americans learned valuable lessons required during times of war.[38]

Figure 4.6. "A 'Yaqui' Baseball Player—Promoting Modernity and Solidarity." *Inter-American Monthly*, February 1944.

US and Mexican officials used various forms of popular culture to connect with the masses that reached beyond race and baseball in order to convince the Americas the Axis threat to Latin America was real and not imagined. One of the most incendiary images supplemented Betty Kirk's article mentioned earlier, that attempted to convince the general public

Figure 4.7. "Looking like the Enemy," Betty Kirk's tableau on racial profiling. *Inter-American Monthly*, January 1943.

of Japanese infiltrating into Mexico by disguising as various indigenous groups.

The images in figure 4.7, aligned side by side, were viewed with the following caption: "Which is the Japanese? The old Chamula Indian from the state of Chiapas, left, and the young Otomi from Hidalgo, right, bear a striking racial resemblance to the Japanese, center, now held prisoner in Mexico's penal colony in the Island of Tres Marías"[39] The photographs appeared in a 1943 edition of the *Inter-American Monthly* in an article titled "Mexico's War on Hidden Japanese." The *Inter-American Monthly* is a sample of the propaganda machine created by the United States to engineer a state of hemispheric peril. More specifically, Kirk's article, photos, and maps illustrate the wide net of suspicion thrown at the Japanese diaspora throughout Latin America in order to manufacture a hemisphere-wide defense against Axis penetration into the region.

The images also provide important insight on the process of racialization and the use of racial profiling of the Japanese and indigenous populations in Mexico. In this case, Betty Kirk deployed the optical illusion or sleight of hand in order to confuse the reader and cement the propaganda of fear that all Japanese in Mexico are a threat. More important, Kirk's article provided the basis for the justification of the racialization of Mexico's Japanese population by stating, "The Jap bears a racial resemblance to the Mexican Indian. When mingled with the pure Indian type found in the undeveloped regions, a Japanese can pass without notice, if he is garbed as the Indians are and speaks their colloquial language. Such disguises are part of the armor with which the Japanese Fifth Column is girded to carry on its subversive work."[40] Such statements, positions, and attitudes were commonplace during this period. In fact, a similar juxtaposition was entertained decades earlier in a US popular magazine known as *The Outlook* in an article titled "The Hyphen in Mexico." The author proclaimed, "One thing that may lead the observers to form an exaggerated opinion of the number of Japanese in the country south of the Rio Grande is the fact that those Mexican Indians of an Oriental cast of the countenance already mentioned look even more like Japanese than like Chinese."[41]

As the Americas became entangled with World War II, the Allied and Axis nations struggled for the hearts and minds of the region, and Mexico became an important staging ground for such efforts. Indeed, mobilization for the war effort went well beyond the recruitment of troops. For the United States and Mexico it became vital that public opinion and support for the war remain unfettered to deter Axis penetration into Mexico and other areas of Latin America. In order to gain public support for the war a massive propaganda campaign was unleashed in Mexico. Betty Kirk's article is but one example of that battle.

Betty Kirk's diatribes against the Japanese in Mexico and Latin America were not limited to the single article mentioned. Kirk's articles and book chapters were heavily quoted by other authors, which entrenched the negative image of an already suspect Japanese population in the Americas.[42] The average reader made no distinction between Japanese officials in Mexico, such as military attachés, who by design carry out suspicious activities for their home country and Japanese Mexicans. Kirk's recipe for racializing groups, such as the Japanese and Indians of Mexico, morphed into an amalgamation of race, ethnicity, and nationality where the Mexican Indian, Japanese national, and Japanese Mexican became fused and undistinguishable from each other. Authors like Kirk, through their writings, provided the popular discourse justifying the round up and detention of the Japanese population.

According to Josephus Daniels, who was the US ambassador for Mexico from 1933 to 1941, and who wrote the introduction to Betty Kirk's book, *Covering the Mexican Front: The Battle of Europe versus America*. Kirk became a foreign correspondent in Mexico a year after Lázaro Cárdenas was elected president of Mexico (1934). Kirk began covering Mexico for a number of US and British newspapers and magazines; her only credential was having lived in Mexico for an extended period of time, which somehow qualified her as an expert on Mexican affairs.[43] Nevertheless, Kirk's various publications resonated with the public and within the confines of US government agencies that developed case studies on the Japanese diaspora in Latin America and assessed Mexico's ability to counter any fifth column activities. One author, Stephen Naft, lifted, verbatim, Kirk's article "Mexico's War on Hidden Japanese," published in January 1943, as part of a study he prepared for the OIAA titled *Japan's Menace to the Americas*, internally released to the US government in 1943 as well.[44] And, as mentioned earlier, Kirk's article was written for the *Inter-American Monthly*, an OIAA-supported publication. Thus, Kirk and Naft were each commissioned by the OIAA to propagandize for the agency, with Naft relying entirely on Kirk's position on the Japanese in Mexico. Finally, Naft used a subsection of Kirk's book, titled "Japan's Skeleton Army," to drive home Japanese fifth column fears. These articles, filled with half-truths, hearsay, and propaganda and lacking sources, coupled with a long-standing mistrust of the Japanese in the Americas, created a hemispheric wide frenzy toward the Japanese diaspora, but more important, these positions made their way into US government reports to develop policy regarding the Japanese in the Americas.

These types of articles and fears were not limited to just the United States or Mexico. In June 1942 the *Saturday Evening Post* ran a five-page exposé on the Japanese in Brazil titled "The Japanese Pincers in Brazil." With the exception of the title and author, this article is identical to Kirk's "Mexico's War on Hidden Japanese," with the obligatory images of Japanese men, women, and children all somehow undermining the Allied war effort for Japanese emperor Hirohito. This particular article contains depictions of Japanese-Brazilians and their daily lives, but the images are transformed into fifth column fears by the captions attached by the author. When such images are repeated and reinforced by the Inter-American Monthly, the image of the Japanese menace becomes all to real (see figure 4.8). The images and captions below are of Japanese Brazilians and typical of articles on Japanese in Latin America during this period.[45]

Although Brazil played an active role in the Allied effort during World War II, its contributions are often forgotten or diminished. Brazil allowed the United States to build airfields and to have control over its navy and air forces during the war. Brazil, with the largest Japanese population in the hemisphere (nearly 200,000), did not round up and intern any of its Japanese. In some cases and similar to Mexico, Brazil required some Japanese to relocate away from "strategic" locations. However, a large number of Japanese had settled in frontier regions of Brazil in and around São

Figure 4.8. Throughout the Americas, propaganda portrayed ordinary Japanese children, schools, and merchants as a subversive threat. By reconfiguring ordinary Japanese of the Americas, they became, in the eyes of the public, the "Jap Threat to Latin America," as pictured in this image. *Inter-American Monthly.* Courtesy of US Library of Congress.

Paulo and Paraná in areas considered so remote as not to pose any security risks. The logistics of rounding up 200,000 Japanese made it unrealistic, and Brazilian authorities also understood that Japanese farmers were vital to their agricultural industry.[46] Nonetheless, Brazil, under the dictatorship of Getúlio Vargas, implemented nationalistic policies that closed down

Japanese language schools and restricted their movement, which applied to all foreigners in Brazil. And, according to Fidelis Reis, a federal deputy from Minas Gerais, "Asians were almost a great menace because their alleged failure to assimilate would guarantee the presence of 'yellow cysts in the national organism,' which would be as great a danger to Brazil as the concentration of Asians in California was to the United States."[47]

Although the process of racializing the Japanese predates World War II, entities such as the OIAA, and the US government in general, escalated fears and tensions within Japanese communities throughout the Americas through a 1940s version of racial profiling. I argue that the United States influenced the views of the Japanese in Mexico and Latin America. In fact, legislation limiting the movement of Japanese to Brazil and Peru was fashioned after the US 1921 and 1924 immigration acts, which established a quota system for the movement of immigrants to the United States. However, after the bombing of Pearl Harbor, the Japanese in Mexico and elsewhere were reconfigured from undesirables unsuitable for American societies to spies, saboteurs, and threats to democracies. As this image gained a foothold in the imagination of the public, the demonization of the Japanese escalated to dehumanization as depicted in popular culture and the mainstream media. This image primarily constructed by the United States and exported, intensified efforts to hunt down any so-called fifth columns in Mexico. And, as discussed later, US propaganda, influence, and pressure were directly responsible for the roundups, arrests, and deportations of thousands of Japanese in the Western hemisphere. The OIAA spent a considerable amount of time, energy, and money convincing the United States and Latin American public that Japanese individuals were threats to their way of life. Using a variety of approaches, the OIAA organized a propaganda campaign to bring countries like Mexico in line with US positions on a level never seen before or since.

Although a full-scale examination of OIAA's methodology of delivering propaganda is beyond the scope of this study, it can be said that it used almost every conceivable means to achieve its objectives. By this I mean the OIAA, in general, used economic incentives and threats, and culturally saturated every Latin American country with music, theatre, cinema, radio, and the use of graphic novels by enlisting prominent artists, musicians, directors, and actors. The OIAA used US and Latin American journalists to dispense US policy and positions on the war effort. The OIAA also created newsletters, funded newspapers, and created glossy magazines in its endeavors to drive home its message of hemispheric solidarity. To effectively propagandize and reach the masses throughout Latin America, it was vital that the appropriate method of delivery be used, and this varied from country to country. Propaganda also had to be tailored to specific audiences within the country as determined by geographic, demographic, social, and economic considerations. For example, because each Latin American country had groups with varying degrees of literacy, multiple delivery systems were deployed. There were deliberate attempts to convey messages to Latin America's middle and upper classes by using the most widely used form of communication for those classes during this era, print media and radio.

Overall, the popular periodicals, the *Inter-American Monthly*, *En Guardia*, and the *Saturday Evening Post* were just one weapon in an arsenal created to combat any pro-Nazi or pro-fascist sentiment in Latin America. The evidence of this period indicates strong leanings toward Germany and Italy by some Latin American countries, including Mexico. One of Nelson Rockefeller's primary missions as Coordinator of the OIAA was to fill Latin American newspapers and airwaves with US official policy in order to discourage opposing views and increase hemispheric solidarity. Brazil, with the largest Japanese population in South America, initially resisted US efforts and segments of Argentina's and Chile's populations were openly supportive of fascism and Nazism.[48] In Mexico, US officials painted La Unión Nacional Sinarquista (National Synachist Union of Mexico), in operation during the late 1930s and 1940s, as a pro-fascist and pro-Nazis organization. American intelligence reports indicated that the Sinarquistas might have been collaborating with the Japanese in Baja California.[49] According to a Mexican government report La Unión Nacional Sinarquista was formed in 1937 in Leon, Guanajuato by a group of "fanatics" who numbered approximately 400 young middle-class professionals with the following goals: "To plant in Mexico a new Christian social order through a patriotic militia and unite all Mexicans for a better country. Our motto will be Fatherland, Justice and Liberty."[50] The scholarship on the Sinarquistas indicates they were generally considered to be a pro-Catholic organization primarily made up of farmers at the base and middle class professionals at the leadership level.[51] Although the Sinarquista literature points to a strong anti-totalitarian position within their ranks, from the Mexican and US perspective this organization still posed a risk to Mexico and the region.

Although President Manuel Ávila Camacho was aware of German and Japanese attempts at espionage within the country, the United States remained concerned that many in the Mexican government leaned too far toward the Axis powers. In fact, María Emilia Paz, writes that American officials concluded that the "only sectors of Mexican society that could genuinely be regarded as anti-Axis and prodemocratic were the organized labor movement and the Mexican Communist Party."[52] Based on this perceived lack of enthusiasm for the war, the Mexican government amplified its propaganda machine to ignite Mexican zeal for the war effort. Like their American counterparts, the Mexican government used many forms to disseminate their propaganda. The use of art became a prevalent medium to illustrate the Allied fight against the Axis nations, while concurrently advancing the US policy on the war. Along these same lines, leftist artists and the Mexican government used an array of visual imagery to convey their concerns about fascism and Nazism, how ordinary Mexicans contributed to the war effort and the general social conditions in Mexico from the 1930s through World War II.

Mexican Perception of US Propaganda

A portion of the Mexican public had little interest in a war fought thousands of miles away and for many the memory of the Mexican Revolution remained vivid. Prior to 1941 Mexican support against the Axis nations vacillated and much of this ebb and flow is attributed to the historical treatment of Mexico by US imperialism, which left long lasting animosity and suspicion. Furthermore, many Mexicans remained suspicious of US and British financial interests and aims and felt that perhaps this war was not about defeating tyranny but further exploitation of the working class in Mexico. From the Mexican perspective there was also the observation that US and British visitors to Mexico came merely to sojourn, whereas the Germans and Japanese sought to make Mexico their permanent home, became citizens, intermarried with Mexicans and treated the Mexican people more as their equals socially and commercially.

In addition, prior to Mexico joining the war in 1942, Axis sympathizers in Mexico used a large of array of propaganda techniques to sway public opinion. A large number of newspapers and periodicals were pro-fascist and pro-Nazi. Papers such as *El Hombre Libre*, a Catholic paper, and the *Omega* carried such headlines as "Virile Attitude of Argentina and Chile before the Violence of Mr. Wells" and "Jews over America," respectively. Other groups in Mexico sympathetic to the Axis nations included the National Sinarquista Movement founded in 1937, and Acción Nacional founded in 1938 and loosely connected to the Spanish Falange. Axis propaganda had penetrated deep into Mexico in its attempt at keeping

Mexico neutral during the war. The Japanese bombing of Pearl Harbor in 1941 and Mexico's declaration of war in May 1942 created a shift toward the Allied effort. Another important factor in changing public opinion was the Good Neighbor Policy and the perceived need for hemispheric solidarity. With this momentum Mexico enlisted all sectors of society to neutralize and counter Axis propaganda throughout the country.

Emulating the OIAA and with its assistance, but on a smaller scale, the Mexican government and other political entities produced their own forms of propaganda aimed at different segments of its population. In this section my discussion focuses primarily on the use of art as a medium for propaganda purposes. In many ways the role of Mexican artists as disseminators of propaganda for the government or as agents of change for their communities can be traced to the nineteenth century with their most influential period emerging with the outbreak of the Mexican Revolution, especially the period after 1920 and the advent of cultural institutions supported by various Mexican administrations.[53]

With the emergence and rise of fascism and Nazism battles were fought along multiple fronts including the ideological that used art as a weapon of choice for propaganda purposes. All sectors and sides of World War II deployed this intellectual combat by the foot soldiers of the artist communities. Mexican artists began to illustrate the dangers of fascists and the goal of world domination by Hitler and the Nazis. Further, in their attempts to keep the Mexican population neutral during the war the Axis powers went on a propaganda free-for-all utilizing all means at their disposal such as groups within Mexico considered pro-fascist or pro-Nazis or at the very least sympathetic to the Axis war effort. To counter these efforts Mexico went on the offensive and unleashed a barrage of propaganda that illustrated Mexican solidarity with the Allied war effort. In these important endeavors, artists from Mexico united with the Mexican government to create images of a Mexico in harmony with the Allies and ready to combat the aggression of Germany, Italy, and Japan. With its rich history of graphic and satirical art and many celebrated artists of the early twentieth century, Mexico was well prepared to use this medium for propaganda purposes.

Mexican Art and Propaganda: Beyond Aestheticism

As briefly articulated, long before the outbreak of World War II, Mexico had a tradition of producing graphic art in newsprint, engravings, wood cuts, and broadsides. José Guadalupe Posada's years of greatest influence popularized many of the techniques just mentioned by incorporating them into the daily lives of the Mexican people, producing art relevant to the masses, and making art accessible. The onset of the Great Depression in Mexico only deepened the conviction of many artists that capitalism and the exploitation of labor were important subjects to address within their art. With nearly 500,000 Mexicans repatriated from the United States, the economic global collapse, the rise of fascism and Nazism in Europe gave a sense of urgency to the art produced during this period. Diego Rivera's mural *Detroit Industry* (1932–33) remains one of the great artistic masterpieces of the twentieth century while simultaneously providing an important social commentary on society.[54]

Furthermore, the Spanish Civil War of 1935–39 provided material for Mexican artists to comment on the fear and rise of fascism and the threat it posed to the left. Indeed, emerging leftist artists of Mexico gained invaluable experience speaking out against Spanish Falangists or fascists during this period. In fact, a small group of young and veteran Mexican artists such as Leopoldo Méndez, David Siqueiros, and Pablo O'Higgins started a collective known as the Liga de Escritores y Artistas Revolucionarios (League of Revolutionary Writers and Artists, LEAR) in 1933 as a popular front against the rise of fascism. These were many of the same individuals that started Lucha Intelectual Proletaria (Intellectual Proletarian Struggle) in 1931, LEAR's predecessor. This collective lasted from 1933–38 and became the catalyst for TGP, an important artist collective from Mexico City that continued the tradition of Mexican graphic art that was utilized to combat fascism, Nazism, and promote the war effort for Mexico.[55] LEAR was a highly politicized collective that grounded many of the artists to the PCM, although membership was required. Nonetheless, this group was influenced by the international communist struggle and introduced into their organization basic precepts such as class struggle and created in 1934 *Frente a Frente*, a newsletter used to promote the communist struggle, which was also a space for art that followed a similar ideology.[56]

Pablo O'Higgins, Leopoldo Méndez, and Luis Arenal founded TGP in 1937.[57] TGP became one of the most important collectives in Latin America and widely respected elsewhere. The Mexican government enlisted the help of the artist collective TGP during World War II to create poster art, broadsheets, and printmaking for the promotion of Mexico's war efforts and to rally its citizens. During World War II the primary artists for TGP were Alberto Beltrán, Angel Bracho, Fernando Castro Pacheco, Leopoldo Méndez, Ignacio Aguirre, and Raúl Anguiano. In many ways,

TGP reflected the Posada tradition of using a Mexican visual style to connect to its mass audience in the form of lithographs, prints, woodcuts, and linocuts. As a collective, TGP supported the efforts of the Lázaro Cardenas administration and its expropriation of the oil industry by creating art for the campaign. During the 1940s TGP supported Manuel Ávila Camacho's drive to unite the country during World War II. The founders were also connected to the communist party and the antifascist movement.[58]

Ideologically, many Mexican political groups contributed to this propaganda campaign, with the PCM providing an excellent example. In 1945 PCM published *Un Programa para Unir Más a la Nación* (*A Program to Further Unite the Nation*), a forty-page exposé on uniting the Mexican people, preparing the communist party for the next presidential election, industrializing the country, and an attack on the Axis powers. As fascism ascended in Europe during the 1930s and 1940s PCM became one the strongest supporters of the Allied effort due to the threat fascism posed to the left, especially to the Soviet Union. As a result the PCM launched a strong propaganda campaign of its own to garner Mexican support for the Allies, but also to promote the PCM agenda regarding the direction of the country. *Un Programa para Unir Más a la Nación* is an example of PCM propaganda that served multiple roles. Within the text the authors provided the nation with twelve major points to further the development of Mexico.[59] For example, the exposé opened with its first stated goal as "Conquista de la Victoria Completa y Organización de la Seguridad y la Paz" (Achievement of Complete Victory and Organization of Security and Peace), which promoted the destruction of fascism and supported the various declarations espoused by the Allied nations.[60] The PCM also issued a call for national unity that could only be achieved through a fair and equitable distribution of wealth and placing national interests above the interests of individuals or groups. The PCM also viewed such ideologies and groups as Nazis, the Spanish Flange, the Sinarquista Movement, and the National Action Party as detriments not only to the PCM but also to achieving national unity within Mexico.[61] *Un Programa para Unir Más a la Nación* was filled with images such as the two below that depicted the Allies defeat of the Axis powers, but also addressed internal concerns such as national unity, equality for the indigenous population, and the allocation of resources to the workers in Mexico (see figure 4.9). The cartoon caricature of Hitler, Hirohito, Franco, and Mussolini and their defeat by the Allies is not unusual, but it is important to point out this was not Mexican or US government propaganda; rather these images were developed and disseminated by the PCM who considered fascism and Nazism

Figure 4.9. Mexican Communist Party propaganda. From *Un Programa para Unir Más a la Nación*, Archivo General de la Nación, March 1945.

a threat to the Soviet Union and the communist movement, in general. Images like the ones above reveal the importance of art and its use as a propaganda tool. Whether Mexican, United States, Japanese, or German, the state liberally utilized various forms of art as a medium to reach the masses with their message. Nation states understood the power of art and used all means at their disposal to create images that sold their message.[62]

Conclusion

Decades before the bombing of Pearl Harbor the United States laid the groundwork to consolidate a hemispheric defense against the Axis powers. This was achieved first with the rise of US imperialism in the late nineteenth and early twentieth centuries. Second, military coercion was supplemented with economic dominance of Latin America. Third, US culture had pervaded so deeply throughout Mexico that a Phelps-Dodge engineer stated, "It takes just four years to complete the Americanization of the Mexican."[63] The reach of the American empire reigned so absolute throughout Latin America that even its domestic policies reached beyond its national boundaries. More important, the United States' development of misinformation agencies during World War I and the creation of the international Pan American Union allowed it to hone its skills at churning out propaganda that infiltrated the Western hemisphere economically, politically, and culturally.

The creation of the OIAA was a natural progression and necessity from the US perspective. The propaganda campaign unleashed by the United States after Japan bombed Pearl Harbor on December 7, 1941, and eventually by Mexico, achieved many of its objectives. First and foremost, the United States and its legions of agencies that spread throughout Latin America brought all of the Western hemisphere under the banner of the United States and Allied Powers. Through the use of propaganda, especially the print media, the United States was able to convince much of the hemisphere that behind every door and under every rock was a Japanese waiting to wreak havoc. By creating this sense of fear, the United States and Mexico justified the necessity to hunt, interrogate, detain, and if necessary, intern individuals of Japanese ancestry. This, of course, came at the expense of ordinary Japanese Mexicans and nationals in Mexico who were further racialized during the war. The use of journalists from the United States and throughout Latin America reshaped the war effort and views toward the allied perspective and was paramount in reconfiguring the Japanese as "public enemy" number one. The racialization of the Japanese diaspora dehumanized and demonized an entire ethnic group and resulted in a near universal Western hemispheric internment program.

The United States, already the hegemonic force in the hemisphere, also used financial incentives rather than military force or occupation to persuade countries like Mexico that it was in their best interest to join the allied effort. The OIAA played an important role in these developments. Although this chapter spoke mostly of its propaganda efforts, the OIAA had many subagencies that included economic development, media, and public health that utilized their respective areas to provide incentives to Mexico and other Latin American nations. As the United States spread its propaganda throughout the hemisphere, it simultaneously prodded reluctant Latin American republics to join the campaign. In the initial war years Mexico was seen as less than enthusiastic toward the war effort.

To counter this perception Mexico unleashed its own propaganda campaign to shore up any lingering doubts about its commitment. With the help of the OIAA and the use of art as one form of dissemination, Mexico attempted to educate the masses on the dangers of the Nazis and fascist infiltration and the importance of supporting the war effort. The US propaganda campaign and Mexico's renewed enthusiasm increased anxiety for Japanese Mexicans as their future became uncertain. The level of US control in the hemisphere during the war meant that Japanese Mexicans and nationals were not going to be allowed to roam freely. Although Mexico complied with the hemispheric policy of rounding up its Japanese population, it did not have all the intended results the United States anticipated. The next chapter explores Mexico's response to the hemispheric directive to round up and intern the Japanese population and how the Japanese population in Mexico reacted to their forced removal and relocation to the interior of Mexico.

CHAPTER FIVE

Prisoners without Chains

The Forced Relocation of Japanese Mexicans, 1942–1945

During the war, our compatriots were locked inside an invisible iron wall, prisoners without chains, psychologically and physically overwhelmed.
—Atsuko Tanabe, *Huellas Japonesas en la Cultura Mexicana*

On December 26, 1941, the United States intercepted a message from Japanese minister Yoshiaki Miura in Mexico City to Tokyo that indicated the Japanese diplomatic corps remained free to wander the streets of Mexico undisturbed. This message provided one of the first hints of Mexico's position regarding the treatment of Japanese in Mexico in the aftermath of Pearl Harbor. It also sheds light on the friendly relations between Japan and Mexico and the quid pro quo treatment of their citizens in their respective countries. The Mexican Foreign minister, Ezequiel Padilla, informed his Japanese counterpart that the Mexican government had no intention of persecuting Japanese residents as long as they confined themselves to their habitual activities according to the laws of the country. Minister Miura wrote to his superiors, "The Mexican government was disposed to consider matters with liberality and in accordance with the treatment that the Japanese Government grants the Mexican Legation in Tokyo."[1]

When Mexico broke diplomatic ties with Japan on December 8, 1941, the Portuguese embassy became the official channel of communication for Japanese interests in Mexico.[2] It would take Mexico nearly six months and the sinking of Mexican vessels by Germany for a declaration of war. By early 1942 the Japanese diplomatic corps in Mexico were repatriated to Japan. However, thousands of Japanese Mexicans and nationals remained in Mexico who were not part of the diplomatic corps, and their treatment ranged from benevolence to intense interrogation and confinement, as described in this chapter.

The following case study of Japanese Mexican Ernesto Benito Naito Hirokichi illustrates the precarious position many Japanese in Mexico faced and the complex web of Axis penetration that took place in Mexico and elsewhere in Latin America. Hirokichi's "chance" encounter with Teresa Kohn, a suspected Nazi agent, exposed the suspicious attitude of the Mexican government toward its Japanese population. The evidence further indicates that Mexican and US authorities were under the belief that a vast network of Japanese and Nazi agents and assets were deployed throughout Mexico to destabilize its regime and neutralize hemispheric solidarity. In one particular case they may have been right. In July 1941 Japanese intelligence officers had developed a plan to create a rebellion in Guatemala in an effort to undermine the country and force the United States to militarily intervene, thereby "casting a shadow on the so-called 'Good Neighbor Policy.'"[3]

Although Japan's intelligence efforts in Mexico were multifaceted and ambitious and involved acquiring war materials and strategic information on the United States, the reality is that Japan accomplished very little in Mexico regardless of the long stream of exaggerated claims to the contrary. This is especially true by August 1941, when Japanese officials conceded Mexico was too entrenched with the United States and any attempt at persuading Mexico to turn on the Americans or remain neutral was pointless. The small number of Japanese who were apprehended and sent to the United States for confinement, or Mexico, for that matter, also indicates Japan's efforts shifted to areas other than Mexico as war approached in late 1941. In fact, when the Japanese diplomatic corps was removed from Mexico in early 1942, the Japanese intelligence apparatus left with it.[4]

Nonetheless, the case of Benito Hirokichi typifies the hunt for Japanese spies in Mexico, which was extensive but simultaneously futile, since the majority of the Japanese in Mexico were loyal Mexicans. Furthermore, this case study reveals a Mexican state apparatus with an overly zealous, and often times corrupt, investigative agency cooperating with US authorities in their effort to identify and destroy any Axis penetration into the region. Mexico's other aim was to counter detractors in the United States that it was not doing enough to fulfill its obligations under pacts to ensure hemispheric defense and solidarity. Lastly, the result of Mexico's efforts and US pressure was the round up and removal of Japanese Mexicans and nationals from strategic zones throughout Mexico. The forced removal of Japanese, their relocation to Guadalajara and Mexico City, and their eventual internment represents a paradoxical situation for Mexico and the Japanese population, where, on the one hand, the Japanese essentially remained free within the confines of the urban sectors of Guadalajara and Mexico City, but on the other hand, their forced relocation and subsequent self-internment were the result of war time measures exacted on the Japanese community. This was no different than the harsh reality of Japanese Americans in the United States. Mexico struggled to strike a balance between hemispheric defense, deflecting US imposition, and an appropriate response to the Japanese situation in Mexico. Based on the available evidence, it is highly unlikely Mexico would have removed the Japanese residing in the country to Guadalajara or Mexico City without pressure from the United States. The case study that follows sheds light on the conflicting strategies and treatment of the Japanese population, but it is also a tragic story of loneliness that cost Benito Hirokichi nearly four years of his life.

Ernesto Hirokichi: A Tale of Being Japanese

At the age of seventeen, Ernesto Benito Naito Hirokichi entered Mexico on December 8, 1929, through the Port of Manzanillo, Colima, with two Japanese associates and set out for Huixtla, in the state of Chiapas. According to Hirokichi, Huixtla offered employment opportunities. Hirokichi found employment in Huixtla with the Japanese Mexican Company, S.A., a company founded by members from the original Enomoto Colony of the late nineteenth century. With the Japanese Mexican Company, Hirokichi earned 120 pesos per month. According to his testimony, Hirokichi later moved to the estate of "La Esperanza" in Motozintla, Chiapas, where he worked as a small merchant earning approximately 300 to 400 pesos per month as he built up his business. When Mexico declared war against the Axis nations in July 1942 Hirokichi was ordered to relocate to Mexico City by federal authorities as part of the national relocation efforts that were under way. Hirokichi, prior to his departure from Chiapas, wrote to Mr. Luis T. Tsuji, president of the Japanese Mutual Aid Committee (Comité Japonés de Ayuda Mutua), to request that he be placed on a list for a future exchange of nationals between Mexico and Japan and was told he had been placed on that list. Hirokichi sold his business to Teresa Lopez, a Mexican national, for 1,200 pesos and with his savings arrived in Mexico City with 5,000 pesos.[5]

On October 4, 1942, the Dirección General de Investigaciones Políticas y Sociales (IPS) that included Agents Alejandro Ortega and José Lelo de Larrea, head of the department, interrogated Hirokichi, who had languished several months in the San Carlos Immigration Detention Center in Perоté, Veracruz, about his activities. After a series of questions about his actions in Chiapas and Mexico City, Mexican authorities released Hirokichi from detention. At the age of thirty-six and having resided in Chiapas for thirteen years, Hirokichi was under suspicion of espionage. Although released from custody, the Mexican secret police continued a pattern of interrogation, detention, and surveillance of Hirokichi that went on for several months. Then finally on January 16, 1943, Hirokichi was formally arrested in Mexico City by the police and charged with espionage against the state and ordered detained by immigration authorities at Perоté, Veracruz. Hirokichi had been suspected of espionage activities in and around the region of Soconusco in the state of Chiapas. He was also charged with collaborating with Teresa Deustch (Deutch) Kohn, a Czechoslovakian national and a suspected active agent of the Gestapo in Mexico. Mexican authorities also filed charges against Hirokichi for his solicitation to be exchanged in order to return to Japan and fight against the Allied nations.[6]

Hirokichi's experience with Mexican authorities demonstrates one of several ways in which Japanese in Mexico were affected by World War II. His case is well documented and provides insight into the experience of Japanese in Mexico, the Mexican State apparatus, anxiety over Axis penetration into Mexico, and the influence of the United States regarding the adjudication of Axis nationals such as Hirokichi. The "insidious penetration of Axis nationals in Mexico" was, like all things Japanese, exaggerated. The idea of the Mexican government about to fall from the infiltration of Japanese agents was hyperbolic but simultaneously effective in creating a state of uncertainty and fear in Mexico regarding its Japanese population. Overall, hundreds of Japanese in Mexico were suspected of espionage, with many arrested or detained, and a small number deported or interned in the United States. Simultaneously, Mexican authorities confiscated Japanese properties and businesses regardless of whether one was a national or Mexican citizen. Those Japanese that lost their livelihood through relocation and confiscation of property became the most vulnerable in the aftermath of Pearl Harbor. In fact, a large percentage of those falling under this category became some of the first residents of what became known in Mexico as Japanese concentration camps, Hacienda de Temixco and Hacienda Castro Urdiales, discussed in detail in chapter 6.

In the final adjudication that took place in 1944, the Mexican government dropped espionage charges against Hirokichi because definitive proof of such activity was never found. In fact, in his final interrogation in 1944 investigators stated Hirokichi was probably unaware that Teresa Kohn was a suspected Gestapo agent and was lured to her for companionship, but that it was plausible that Kohn was grooming Hirokichi as a possible asset. Hirokichi's only known suspicious activity was his sexual relationship with Kohn. In the end, Hirokichi's loneliness and attraction to Kohn cost him several years of life. The Mexican government continued to hold Hirokichi in confinement and eventually had him transferred to the Mexican penitentiary of Isla de Tres Marías in July 1945, which held dangerous enemy aliens. Hirokichi gained his freedom and was released from confinement on October 21, 1945.[7]

Overall, the case study of Japanese Mexican Ernesto Benito Naito Hirokichi demonstrates the unstable position of Japanese in Mexico, where a sexual tryst with the wrong individual could lead to intense interrogation and detention. Although Mexicans of Japanese ancestry appear to have been treated better than their counterparts in the United States, the Hirokichi case reveals that regardless of their location in the Americas, Japanese were vulnerable to overzealous officials who viewed all Japanese with suspicion. The remainder of this chapter explores how Japanese nationals were hunted, detained, interrogated, and sent to concentration camps either in Mexico or to the United States.

Mexican War Measures, Mexican Intelligence Apparatus, and the Japanese

In 1940 it was estimated that the population of Japanese nationals in Mexico was approximately 5,145 and Mexicans of Japanese ancestry (Mexican citizens) roughly 13,052 for a total Japanese population within Mexico of 18,197.[8] Most of the Japanese settled in the northwestern part of Mexico and on the Pacific Coast, where they engaged in cotton farming, fishing, and agriculture. Prior to World War II the Japanese Mexican population was primarily made up of males, with a significant number marrying Mexican women.[9] Even before the bombing of Pearl Harbor, US-Japanese relations began to deteriorate, with the Japanese populations in the United States and Mexico increasingly under surveillance and suspicion.

Furthermore, because of the strategic location of Mexico and occupations of Japanese Mexicans, US authorities believed that many of the Japanese were naval and military officers engaged in espionage and survey work. There is some evidence that Japan did infiltrate US and Mexican waters by disguising operatives as fisherman. This was a logical choice since so many Japanese Mexicans were either employed or were operators of fishing vessels that had the potential of providing cover for Japanese intelligence officers. Japan, like other countries, had a wide array of intelligence-gathering agencies throughout Latin America. On the eve of the bombing of Pearl Harbor, the Japanese Legation in Mexico consisted of twenty-nine officers and employees and was considered the focal point for all Japanese espionage and propaganda activities in Mexico prior to their detention and repatriation through the United States in February 1942. It is alleged that espionage efforts were concerned primarily with the collection of maritime information, US military strengths and weaknesses, and the general attitude of Latin American countries regarding the emerging global conflict. In this regard, Japan was most interested in knowing the position of Latin American countries in the event the United States entered the conflict. Japanese intelligence efforts also included the raising of funds to be used for bribing Mexican officials and for the protection of Japanese commercial interests by transferring their property to a "dummy" Mexican citizen who was deemed reliable by the Japanese. The distribution of Japanese propaganda was also believed to be an important part of the Legation's espionage work.[10]

Shortly after the bombing of Pearl Harbor, on December 9, 1941, Mexico froze millions of pesos that belonged to Japanese Mexicans and nationals. And President Manuel Ávila Camacho's military adviser and member of the general staff, General J. Salvador Sánchez, described and issued on behalf of the Mexican president, the following statement regarding the Mexican government's policy toward Japanese Mexicans and those considered Axis aliens,

> All Axis citizens have been urged to depart from the prohibitive Zone (150 kilometers or 93 miles) from the coasts and frontiers within ten days from December 31 [1941]. . . . There will be no concentration camps. We will make them move into the interior, but we will not imprison them unless they are charged under the Espionage Law.[11]

The brief statement above was Mexico's equivalent to President Franklin Roosevelt's Executive Order 9066, but with a decidedly Mexican intent. Although General Sánchez uses the word "urged," all Japanese in Mexico were forced to leave the security zones and resettled in the interior of the country. Mexico did not hastily create assembly centers to process the Japanese community, and more important, the Mexican state provided no basic assistance such as transportation or shelter. Most of the evidence indicates that Mexico never seriously considered interning its Japanese Mexicans or nationals, but it did have a concern regarding espionage. Yet, as I have already mentioned, so few Japanese were interned or arrested as spies that the number is insignificant.

A large number of Japanese were in close proximity to the centers of airplane production in California and valuable oil fields and refineries. Because of security concerns, it was deemed imperative that those Japanese be evacuated to the interior of Mexico. Accordingly, in January 1942, the Mexican government in cooperation with US authorities ordered that all Japanese be removed from Baja California, the rest of the West Coast, and from the US-Mexican border to a distance of at least ninety-three miles into the interior. The evacuation program was carried out over a period of three months with approximately 2,100 Japanese removed from the states of Baja California, Colima, Sonora, Chihuahua, Sinaloa, Veracruz, and Nayarit. The Japanese from these regions were evacuated to Mexico City and Guadalajara.

The evacuees came under the supervision of the Dirección General de Investigaciones Políticas y Sociales (IPS), a department of the secretaría de gobernación (secretary of the interior). After registering with the department and promising not to leave the designated area without permission, the Japanese were released on parole. The method of evacuation is one of the clearest differences between the removal of Japanese Americans and Japanese Mexicans. The informal removal of Japanese Mexicans and their release into either Mexico City or Guadalajara created additional hardship above and beyond their forced removal with no adequate assistance, provisions or transportation to their designated relocation.[12]

Prior to the 1940s Mexico had a fledgling intelligence service that struggled from inception. Scholarship on the modern Mexican intelligence service remains quite small, but most studies indicate that the founding of Servicios Confidenciales in 1918 is its genesis. In the following two decades the Servicios Confidenciales went through a number of name changes until it became known as the Dirección General de Investigaciones Políticas y Sociales (IPS) in the 1940s. The Japanese Mexicans and nationals are well documented within the IPS case files of the 1930s and 1940s. Within the IPS ranks, a cadre of Mexican agents fanned out across the country observing, interrogating, and arresting Japanese Mexicans and other Axis nationals. Additionally, and according to Aaron Navarro, by the time of World War II at least four intelligence services were in operation for the Mexican government with varying degrees of success and competence that included the Mexican Army's general staff; the Office of the Attorney General, the Secret Service of the Chief of Police for Mexico City, and the Special Services of the President.[13] Also, in February 1942 President Camacho appointed Demetrio Flores Fagoaga to act as chief of the newly formed espionage bureau of the Mexican government, as it was known to US officials, but known officially in Mexico as Jefatura de Servicios de Vigilancia Policía. Fagoaga was directed to coordinate the investigative activities of federal and state law enforcement agencies of Mexico in order to more efficiently combat the activities of Axis agents.

The IPS, under the leadership of the secretaría de gobernación, Miguel Alemán (1940–45), was put in charge of prevention and punishment of crimes involving subversive activity, espionage and other actions connected with the national defense of the country.[14] It is generally accepted that prior to World War II the Mexican intelligence apparatus lacked adequate training and an understanding of domestic and foreign intelligence gathering. And up until the late 1930s the intelligence service remained under the control of military officers. The professionalization of Mexican intelligence gathering is essentially a post-World War II development. This partially explains the hundreds of US FBI and Office of Strategic Services agents in Mexico during World War II conducting counter-espionage activities and training their Mexican counterparts.[15] Nevertheless, counterespionage became hampered by what many perceived as Mexico's reluctance to cooperate and trust US intelligence officials and agents. This apparent unwillingness to cooperate was often interpreted by the United States as Mexico, "vacillating between alliances with the United States and with the Axis."[16] I argue that World War II became the training ground for the professionalization of the Mexican intelligence apparatus and Mexico's contributions to counterespionage during the war suffered due to a lack of experience, training, and professionalism. An excellent example, Mexican agents remained susceptible to corruption, especially regarding the traditional Mexican *mordidad* or bribe. Germane to this study are the bribes attempted and exacted from Japanese by IPS agents. Some of these cases are detailed later in this chapter. The IPS and other Mexican intelligence organizations not only honed their skills during World War II but also received a much-needed shot in the arm from their US counterparts.

Other war measures enacted by Mexico were the result of "fifth column" fears, which raised the level of anxiety and fear for Japanese Mexicans during the war years. For example, on January 16, 1942, President Camacho announced he had signed a decree by which naturalization papers would be refused to German, Italian, and Japanese nationals. On July 26, 1942, in an effort to curtail operations of Axis agents who were considered hiding behind their Mexican naturalization, Mexico decreed that any naturalized native or any national of Germany, Japan, or Italy must forfeit his or her citizenship if suspected of working against Mexico. In its efforts to control the movement of immigrants, Mexico on May 5, 1942, gave instructions to the immigration department, advising it to prohibit European immigration into Mexico until further notice. This step was necessitated by the status of affairs in Europe and the Mexican government's international policy. Mexico also implemented a registration policy for all foreigners in the country. However, because it provided exceptions to tourists, transients, and local visitors, it was considered to have little value in controlling the activities of foreigners.

In collaboration with the United States and to further its own program of war against the Axis powers, the Mexican government took a number of steps to relieve possible dangers relative to the concentrations of Japanese Mexicans and nationals in Mexico. In addition to the evacuation program, the Mexican government interned a number of Japanese who were considered the most dangerous in the country. For example, on March 30, 1942, a group of Japanese that included Dr. Tsunesaburo Hasegawa (later to be the attending physician at the Temixco concentration camp), a naturalized Mexican citizen and suspected district leader, were arrested in Juarez, Chihuahua, and removed to Mexico City to be tried on espionage charges. On June 9, 1942, fifteen enemy aliens, including nine Japanese, were arrested in the state of Nayarit and sent to Perote and Isla de Tres Marías penal colony for internment. In the district of Tamaulipas, the Japanese leader, Dr. Ichinosuke Konishi, was among the group interned for the duration of the war.[17]

Further action by the Mexican government against Japanese nationals was taken on February 18, 1942, when in an agreement with the government of the United States, Mexico sent twenty-nine Japanese consular and diplomatic officials and their families, comprising a total of fifty-three individuals, to Hot Springs, West Virginia, to await repatriation. Mexico ordered all persons of Japanese ancestry to leave Lower California and canceled all permits for Japanese fishing along the western coast of Mexico.[18] The measures taken appeared to be in line with US policy and mirrored the actions taken against the Japanese Americans in the United States. However, US officials continued to remain skeptical of Mexico's efforts. US authorities complained that Mexican officials remained susceptible to corruption and many exhibited pro-Japanese tendencies. In fact, the US

FBI stated, "General Antonio Cardenas Rodriguez appears to be the chief protector of Japanese interests among the Mexican politicians. He [Rodriguez] made a trip to Japan sometime during 1934 or 1935 where the Japanese Government and high Japanese naval officers lavishly entertained him."[19] US officials also complained that Mexico's efforts at checking Axis penetration into the country continued to be thwarted by either corrupt Mexicans officials or the pro-Japanese sentiment that permeated the country. In the end, it was feared that the expulsion efforts of the Mexican government would not be 100 percent effective, due to Japanese influence in areas where the Japanese had colonized.

The Ambiguity of the Japanese in Mexico

The loss of freedom to reside where they wished during World War II demonstrated to the Japanese Mexican community that they were viewed with some suspicion and on many occasions the Mexican government acquiesced to US demands on internment, arrest, and repatriation. Yet, the Japanese experience in Mexico differed from other countries in the Americas, and in some cases, dramatically from the United States, Canada, and Peru, which rounded up and interned their Japanese populations in what were literally prisons. The actions of the Mexican government and comments from some Japanese Mexicans, suggest a treatment that was less coercive and a level of tolerance bestowed on the Japanese in Mexico. To illustrate, when Mexico issued the order that forced its Japanese population to move inland away from the coast, frontiers, and important military zones, the majority of the Japanese were required to reside in Guadalajara and Mexico City, thus taking a different approach from the systematic and deliberate round ups into assembly centers and eventual concentration camps created for the Japanese in the United States, Canada, Cuba, Peru, and elsewhere.[20] Furthermore, not all Japanese were forced into Guadalajara and Mexico City. José Martín Nomura, from Acacoyagua, Chiapas, recalled very little repression from the Mexican government during World War II and stated that Mexicans and Japanese coexisted peacefully during this period.[21]

Mexico's informal approach to the forced removal of Japanese was restrained by emergency war measures that suspended, for individuals residing in Mexico from Axis nations, their naturalization and infringed upon constitutional guarantees. Mexico's relocation policy, although different from the United States, achieved similar results without the necessity of prison-like camps.[22] This can be partially explained by the Japanese experience in Mexico prior to World War II that included a relatively high level of acculturation and integration, a small population that did not threaten the country, and unlike in the United States after Pearl Harbor, a general public in Mexico that did not react with nationalistic fervor against the Japanese population. Nonetheless, some Japanese Mexicans did experience trauma similar to the Japanese Americans in the United States. For example, Katsuji Tosha wrote of the bitter experience of some Japanese as they were forced to relocate and lost their property:

> During the war, our compatriots were locked inside an invisible iron wall, prisoners without chains, psychologically and physically overwhelmed. The United States declared war against Japan's military, forced Mexico, the only friendly people in the western world towards Japan, to make a cruel law [that] decreed that all Japanese residents in the border area and in other states of the Republic concentrate in Mexico City and Guadalajara. Thus they stripped us all of our properties, we had built with the sweat of the brow for nearly half a century, this was for us one of the most severe punishments in the history of immigration.[23]

When Mexico declared war on Germany, Japan, and Italy in May 1942 and in conjunction with Japan's earlier attack on Pearl Harbor, it gripped the Japanese population in Mexico with fear and many envisioned a similar fate that occurred to their countrymen in the United States. In many ways this never came to fruition, yet, the Japanese in Mexico did share some commonalities with their US counterparts.[24] A Mexican policy of relocation, rather than official confinement became the destiny for the majority of Japanese Mexicans. While the United States expected Mexico to confine its Japanese population and exerted pressure to do so, the fate of the Japanese in Mexico was sealed long before the outbreak of hostilities. And with the outbreak of World War II the federal directive for Japanese removal and internment in Mexico City or Guadalajara were favorably contested in such places as Chiapas and other locales. In many ways the colonial adage "obedezco pero no cumplo" ("I obey but do not carry out") remained alive and well in early twentieth-century Mexico.

Pressure placed on the republics of the Western hemisphere regarding their Japanese populations came in a variety of forms. Although no direct evidence or "smoking gun" exists to prove that the United States directly asked Mexico to round up its Japanese population and intern them either in the United States or in Mexico, documents laying out US involvement, plans, and policy to deal swiftly with the Japanese and other Axis populations throughout the Western hemisphere in the aftermath of Pearl Harbor are evident. Countermeasures to prevent Axis penetration began with the third meeting of ministers of foreign affairs held in Rio de Janeiro in January 1942. At this meeting it was agreed that all efforts needed to be made to prevent Axis nationals and agents the freedom of movement in the hemisphere (Resolution XVII). These documents created a hemispheric wide policy to intern or deport dangerous Axis nationals. In fact, a document created by the Emergency Advisory Committee for Political Defense at Montevideo laid out the program for internment:

> Those Axis nationals whose liberty threatens the security of the Hemisphere should be interned for the duration of the present conflict in detention camps established by the Government in interior regions of the country, which are removed from vital areas and, which offer special advantage for the ends sought. They may also be detained in custody pending expulsion to another American Republic for detention or internment.[25]

These recommendations were transmitted to the governments of Latin America on June 5, 1943, with the final recommendation that they immediately institute a comprehensive program for the continuous detention, for the duration of the emergency, of all dangerous Axis nationals and nationals of Axis-ruled states. In this manner, Mexico and other Latin American countries followed a hemispheric plan for roundups, detention, and eventual internment. Yet, Mexico's malleable post-revolutionary political apparatus allowed many Japanese to have a different experience.

There were often exceptions to this national relocation directive for a variety of reasons. As previously mentioned Mexico was not a monolithic state where everything fell neatly into place for implementing national policy. Indeed, Mexican history is riddled with recalcitrant state governors, officials, and military bosses eschewing national directives for ones that better fit the local and regional setting or their personal objectives. These were early signposts that Mexico's Japanese population would be addressed in a different manner than in the United States. This challenged the US policy of roundups and confinement of Japanese in the United States and elsewhere in the hemisphere. In fact, nearly all of the Western hemisphere complied with US policy on this matter. Mexico, by positioning itself as a vital ally in the war effort, used this leverage to maintain its independence and prevented the United States from forcing Mexico to intern its Japanese Mexican population either in-country or in the United States. The state apparatus of Mexico and its unique development during the post-revolutionary era contributed to the disparate treatment of Japanese Mexicans during World War II. Mexico's decentralized system was often incapable of implementing national policies without negotiating with powerful politicos in the individual states. This decentralization proved crucial and provided influential politicos and military personnel the ability to resist national directives and independently deal with its Japanese populations, which many did.

Caciques, Caudillos, and Jefes

As previously mentioned, Mexico, rather than create assembly centers and US type concentration camps for Japanese, used a decentralized approach to relocate Japanese Mexicans to the interior of the country. This approach created an uneven and chaotic period for Japanese Mexicans. Two important points need emphasis. First, the concentration of Japanese into Mexico City and Guadalajara were the direct result of US policies in response to the Japanese bombing of Pearl Harbor. However, instead of interning the Japanese into smaller and isolated locations, Mexican officials chose two urban cities as the most cost effective method to ensure Japanese Mexicans and nationals were removed from security zones that simultaneously allowed some flexibility for the Japanese to readjust. Unlike the US experience, which mounted a military operation to round up Japanese Americans, the Japanese in Mexico were not given any assistance by the Mexican government. Second, the experience of the Japanese that were uprooted is similar to the Japanese throughout the Americas who were evacuated, displaced, and interned, leaving long lasting trauma. In subsequent years Japanese Mexicans speak of loss, confusion, deprivation, psychological trauma, and a feeling of being betrayed and violated regarding civil liberties and human rights. Francisca Ono de Takemura, seventy-nine years of age in 2007, was fourteen and the eldest of seven children when her father was forced to sell his Mexican restaurant in Tepic, Nayarit, and move his family to Mexico City. According to Francisca, "All of us [Japanese] who lived in Tepic left; we were six families. Each one looked for a place to live. My mother was very sad, but she kept it to herself."[26] Although Mexico did not create barbed wire camps with guards pointing weapons in the direction of the Japanese internees, from the Japanese Mexican perspective there is little difference between those

Japanese forced to live in US internment camps and the Japanese Mexican self-internment caused by their forced relocation.

An argument can be made that the decision not to systemically organize the evacuation and forced relocation of the Japanese in Mexico went in their favor. As a result of the decentralized method of relocating the Japanese population away from the security zones, hundreds of Japanese were able to challenge the so-called national directive. A perfect example of this occurred in the state of Sinaloa. In late 1943 nearly seventy Japanese were concentrated in Mazatlán for evacuation to Mexico City. However, the governor of Sinaloa, General Rodolfo T. Loaiza, interceded on their behalf. Similar to other situations throughout Mexico, a deferment was initially reached, which eventually turned into a countermand of the relocation order based on Governor Loaiza's intervention with final permission granted by the secretaría de gobernación, Miguel Alemán. It should also be mentioned that the countermand came with a price tag in which the Japanese were required to pay a 25,000 peso bribe.[27] Post-revolutionary Mexico was beset with such situations that made this example in Sinaloa not unique, but typical. State governors from Sinaloa, Michoacán, and Chiapas held considerable leverage over national politics and the state. As a result national directives were met with a variety of outcomes depending on the state and region. I argue that the Japanese community in Mexico during World War II benefited from the decentralized political apparatus of post-revolutionary Mexico that allowed them to postpone or avert relocation, albeit by paying a bribe to officials.

In local and regional areas where a powerful *cacique*[28] or *politicos* existed the Japanese were either quickly rounded up or were spared from relocation. In early 1942 the secretary of the interior ordered the territorial governor of Baja California to remove five Japanese based on suspicious behavior, but the minister of work and social provisions intervened and argued that those Japanese involved with providing technical and managerial assistance to the fish packing industry be exempt from removal. The rationalization for this exception stated, "The removal of Japanese technical assistance would seriously hamper this industry and the national economy. We now have an obligation for continental defense."[29] Unlike the United States, Mexico was not willing to self-sabotage its economy by removing Japanese deemed vital to various sectors of the Mexican economy.

Another example from the same state provides the conflicting situation that arose during this period. When the national directive ordered all Mexican governors to remove their Japanese population to the designated zones of Mexico City and Guadalajara, the territorial governor of Baja

California, Rodolfo Sánchez Taboada, quickly and systematically rounded up the states's Japanese population and forced them onto trucks and trains bound for Guadalajara and Mexico City. In fact, Taboada gave the Japanese population under his jurisdiction twenty-four hours to relocate, but ex-president Lázaro Cárdenas, who during World War II, was appointed commander of the Pacific military zone, gave one week for the relocation, countermanding the unrealistic twenty-four-hour order.[30] Personal connections and affiliations played an important role for the Japanese in limiting the impact of the national relocation order. Carlos Kasuga Osaka whose parents migrated to Mexico in the 1930s explained that he and his family were given seventy-two hours to evacuate to Mexico City from Cardenas, San Luis Potosí: "Two soldiers came to our house to escort us and another Japanese family to the train station. The entire town came to see us off. It was 1942 and I was seven years old."[31]

In contrast to the territorial governor of Baja California, the governor of Chiapas, Dr. Rafael Pascacio Gamboa, petitioned the federal government to exempt the relocation of the Japanese, and was successful. Governor Gamboa negotiated with the federal government that state officers would oversee the Japanese residents in his state and that the state of Chiapas would be responsible for every individual of Japanese ancestry. There are a couple explanations for this treatment. First, there is evidence that Mexican officials, at all levels of government, demanded and accepted bribes from Axis nationals in order to delay or prevent their relocation and internment. These were the accusations from a number of Mexican secret police and US military officials. For example, in a report dated August 23, 1943, a Mexican secret police inspector (identified only as P.S. 100) investigated reports that another secret police inspector, Fortunato Barajas, had demanded and accepted 2,000 pesos from a Mr. Suzuki, Mr. Saito, and two brothers with the last name of Shimizu all from Mazatlán. In return, Inspector Fortunato Barajas agreed to delay the men's relocation order for ten days.

Inspector Barajas was also accused of demanding bribes from Mr. Eduardo H. Nakazona and Mr. Toyohara Fukutaro for a sum of 650 pesos, who were from Culiacán and Navolato respectively and told their relocation order would be delayed for ten days. However, after further interrogation by Inspector Barajas that included a warning that it was dangerous to accuse a Mexican official of a serious crime, the Japanese retracted their accusation saying simply that they had collected the money for the poor and indigent Japanese of their community to help defray cost incurred from the relocation order. The Japanese even went as far as to denounce the Comité de Ayuda Mutua Japonés stating that the organization does not do anything to help the poor and only helps the rich.[32]

There is also evidence to support the theory that Japanese and Germans in the state of Chiapas secured permission to remain in their state by paying fees of 200 to 250 pesos to the *presidente municipal*, who happened to be the brother-in-law of the governor, with an additional fee ranging from 1,500 to 3,500 pesos to Governor Rafael Gamboa. For the money paid to officials, payees received a document known as a "Responsiva," which was an acknowledgement of the responsibility of the governor of the state with regard to the alien and permission to remain in the state. Two Japanese of Escuintla, Chiapas named Sagiro Nagana and Eize Matuda were reported to have paid 2,000 pesos each. It was reported that another Japanese by the name of Gonzalo Nishirawa was unable to raise such a sum and therefore was sent to Mexico City. US officials were concerned that the governor of Chiapas, Rafael P. Gamboa, exercised his fiscal powers toward the control of Axis nationals in his state andcircumvented official Mexican policy and hemispheric defense.[33]

Resistance, Negotiation, and Internment

As the oldest Japanese colony in Mexico, Chiapas represented the origins of the Japanese diaspora not just in Mexico but also in the Western hemisphere. The landing of thirty-four Japanese who established the Enomoto Colony in Chiapas in 1897 is considered the official beginning of Japanese immigration to the Americas. The Mexican government recognized this unique position of the Japanese population in Chiapas and their contributions to its development, as did Governor Rafael Gamboa. The influence of the late nineteenth century Enomoto Colony and the subsequent Japan-Mexico Cooperative were responsible for the full integration of the Japanese immigrants in that state economically, politically, and socially. This was most visible with the intermarriages that occurred between Japanese men and Mexican women. Initially, the Mexican government wanted the Japanese in Chiapas to relocate and then offered them the opportunity to return to Chiapas. However, the Japanese community resisted this option by petitioning federal authorities.

The Japanese Mexicans of Chiapas were quick to respond to the Mexican government when the official decrees ordering their relocation were announced. For example, in March 1942 Refugio Seichi Fukuy and Kenji Hueda, partners in Fukuy y Hueda, a trade and brokerage company founded in 1911, wrote the federal government expressing their deep concern regarding their relocation out of Chiapas: "We, the only two partners, have more than ten years as naturalized Mexicans; although our origins is Japanese, we arrived in the Mexican Republic at a very young age, in the year 1907, when he was only 17 and me 18 years of age."[34]

When agents from the IPS arrived in 1943 in Chiapas, Japanese Mexican Eizi Matuda wrote the following:

> In July last month, the Governor of Chiapas, Dr. Rafael Pascacio Gamboa, considering our social standing, honesty and faithful loyalty has given us the cards to stay in our current residence and this last January, the military zone commander and General of Division, Adrian Catrejen, also gave us the letters proving our loyalties, which are attached.
>
> Because we have strong desire to continue our lives in this same place, always with due observance of the laws of the country, we beseech you to authorize us in definitively permanent residence. Escuintla, Chiapas, February 18, 1943. The Representative of the Colony, Eizi Matuda.[35]

Eizi Matuda and his wife, Miduho Kaneko de Matuda, were Mexican citizens through naturalization and marriage, respectively, and had been in Mexico for over twenty years. They had five children ranging from twelve to seventeen years of age, all native-born Mexicans. Unlike a handful of Japanese that were apprehended on suspicion of espionage, the Matudas are representative of the majority of Japanese residing in Chiapas and elsewhere during World War II. These examples indicate a Mexican state that was not all encompassing or monolithic in its treatment of the Japanese in Mexico during World War II but mirrored the decentralization of the Mexican state, where governors, military commanders, or regional *caciques* held considerable authority. Indeed, at some of the highest levels of the Mexican government individuals were intimately connected to the Japanese diaspora in Mexico. Cabinet members of the Camacho administration had relatives who had married Japanese individuals. American officials stationed in Tapachula, Chiapas, worked to prevent the special treatment of the Japanese, but only a handful were removed from the state.[36]

This unique apparatus made the Japanese situation in Mexico complex. However, it is also evident that even without traditional confinement, the forced relocations created a sense of uncertainty and anxiety among the Japanese Mexican community. As mentioned earlier, Mexico on June 1, 1942, suspended constitutional guarantees and empowered the Mexican president and Congress to legislate by decree.[37] One of those decrees, issued on July 26, 1942, empowered the government to suspend and revoke certificates of naturalization to persons of German, Italian, and Japanese origin.[38] Japanese who had become Mexican citizens could be denaturalized if suspected or engaged in subversive acts against the state.[39] Furthermore, those Japanese who met all the requirements for Mexican citizenship but failed to register and secure a certificate were designated "enemy aliens." In some cases individuals who were Mexicans by birth, but married or related by blood to enemy aliens, also had their certificates suspended or liable for annulment. Many of the people that fell into this category were native-born Mexican women or Mexican-born individuals whose parents were deemed aliens for failing to register and acquire certificates of nationality.[40] After Pearl Harbor the arrest and detention of Japanese nationals and Japanese Mexicans was widespread, but only as a precautionary measure. The majority of Japanese Mexicans detained were released, with only a small number of Japanese nationals imprisoned for the duration of the war.

Some Japanese were detained in Mexico based on suspicions by US officials. For example, on January 17, 1942, five months before Mexico declared war on the Axis powers, the president of the Mexican republic, Manuel Ávila Camacho, received a telegram from nine Japanese Mexicans who had been detained in Ensenada, Baja California. Mexican authorities arrested them for crossing into a restricted military zone with their fishing vessel. In their telegram they pleaded with the president to free them since they saw no justification for their detention.[41] US government attempted to use this incident as a pretext to station US military personnel in Baja California. However, former president Lázaro Cardenas, commander of the Pacific military zone during World War II, refused to allow Americans to enter the region. Cardenas had the nine Japanese immediately relocated to Mexico City and directed the remaining Japanese population in Baja California to relocate to the two designated cities within one week.[42]

To further illustrate the complexity of the Japanese in Mexico, President Camacho received another letter dated June 28, 1944, from Leticia Jimenez de Takahashi. Senora Takahashi was a Mexican national by birth but married to a naturalized Mexican citizen of Japanese ancestry, Enrique K. Takahashi. Mr. Takahashi, fifty-two years of age, had been living in Mexico for over thirty years and was a practicing physician, and together he and his wife were the parents of six children. In her letter to the president she appealed for the release of her husband from detention due to an illness, his patriotic fervor for Mexico, and that when their children were old enough, they, too, would sacrifice for the Mexican nation.[43] These two examples provide important insights into the Japanese Mexican situation. First, unlike in the United States, the naturalization of Japanese was permitted, but similar to the Japanese in the United States, holding Mexican citizenship did little to prevent the mass relocation of Japanese in Mexico. Second, a significant number of Japanese men married Mexican women, facilitating their integration into Mexican society but creating a moral and legal conundrum for the Mexican state when Mexican women wrote the state seeking the whereabouts or release of their husbands.

As the United States began rounding up Japanese in 1942 and placing them in concentration camps, it simultaneously pressured Latin American countries to follow a similar policy. As mentioned earlier, Canada, Peru, and sixteen other Latin American nations followed suit. Through a hemispheric wide policy the US pressured Mexico to round up its Japanese population and send them to Crystal City, Texas, or New Mexico, where concentration camps had already been created for Japanese from Latin America. Although Mexico agreed to the US policy in principal, it did so under the most severe cases; and only after each one had been thoroughly scrutinized did Mexico send Axis nationals for internment to the United States. Mexico, as an alternative to the US policy, developed a strategy that designated Guadalajara and Mexico City as locations where Japanese were required to reside for the duration of the war, but were not "imprisoned." From a physical and psychological perspective Guadalajara and Mexico City functioned in a similar vein as the concentration camps in the United States. If social, economic, and political displacement, racial profiling, and mass relocation to a designated area not of your choosing, was the measured experience of the Japanese in the United States, then the Japanese Mexicans had a similar experience. And, comparable to what occurred in the United States, the primary aim of relocating the Japanese was to remove them from coastal communities or areas designated military zones by the US and Mexican governments. The position developed by both countries revolved around the belief that the Japanese could not be trusted and their loyalties were suspect. If we view the US development of assembly centers, detention camps, concentration camps, and labor camps as the epitome of civil rights violations and contravention of constitutional guarantees by the Allied nations, then Mexico is also implicated.

Although Mexico did not have the vast network or infrastructure created by the United States to uproot and remove its Japanese population, it did designate two historical penal colonies to function in a similar fashion. As previously discussed Mexico designated two penal institutions: one in Perotė, Veracruz, and the other Isla de Tres Marías; the latter was located off the coast of Nayarit in northwest Mexico. These were for the most dangerous foreign nationals considered a security threat living in Mexico and who were from the Axis nations. All Axis nationals considered dangerous were first sent to the Mexican Penal Colony of Tres Marías. Those considered a nonthreat to national security were confined in the old fort of San Carlos at Perotė, which also served as an immigration detention center. As I will discuss later in more detail, the majority of Japanese Mexicans were concentrated in and around the Federal District of Mexico City and Guadalajara, Jalisco, and were required to report daily to proper officials and sign a register. Furthermore, as with Benito Hirokichi, there is evidence Mexico interned some Japanese Mexicans and nationals based on suspicious activity, but those numbers are small. Nevertheless, a handful of Japanese residing in Mexico were arrested and sent to high security prisons such as Isla de Tres Marías or interned in the United States. Most of the Japanese arrested were recent arrivals and not long established Japanese Mexicans who saw themselves as Mexican and loyal to the state.

However, the fact that the Japanese Mexicans were forced to relocate indicated their loyalty was suspect and their liberty and freedom diminished based only on their ethnic background. Individuals and families who had prospered and developed enterprises throughout the barred zones in Mexico were uprooted, such as those in Baja California where hundreds of Japanese had developed fishing industries and other enterprises. These people found themselves forced to give up those operations and relocate inland after the emergency decree issued by President Camacho in 1942. Almost universally the Japanese Mexicans complied with the government's decree. Once concentrated in Guadalajara and Mexico City some Japanese realized that survival depended on the ability to organize and work cooperatively.

By May 1944, Mexico had sent individuals from all three major Axis nations and their satellite countries to the United States for internment. Many others had been repatriated from Mexico to their native land.[44] For example, above and beyond the fifty-three diplomats and their families who were repatriated in early 1942, over 335 Japanese diplomats from throughout Latin America and their families were returned to Japan. These individuals were from Washington, DC, Havana, Cuba, and Mexico City. Before their repatriation, Japanese diplomats from other Latin American countries were initially housed in the Greenbrier Hotel in White Sulphur

Springs, West Virginia; Grove Park Inn in Asheville, North Carolina; and the Assembly Inn in Montreat, North Carolina. After the diplomatic corps was removed from Mexico what remained were long established Japanese nationals and Mexicans of Japanese ancestry. For the majority of Japanese Mexicans, survival during World War II depended on the Mexican state and a collective response to their relocation. The Japanese response to their forced relocation came in many forms, by groups, and individuals. Prior to World War II, Mexico had a number of Japanese Mexicans that were prominent and successful and carried out the task of insulating the Japanese population during the war.

Conclusion

This chapter highlighted the Japanese experience in Mexico after the bombing of Pearl Harbor and Mexico's severing of diplomatic ties with Japan. Unlike in many places through the Western hemisphere, the Japanese in Mexico had varied experiences. With the outbreak of World War II Japanese nationals who were in Mexico running legitimate business enterprises were quickly shut down. Some of these individuals were interned in the United States with Japanese diplomats, while others were relocated to Mexico City or Guadalajara and eventually into internment camps such as Hacienda de Temixco, or exchanged for Mexican personnel in Japan. Mexico also had a significant number of Japanese Mexicans who owned and operated a variety of different businesses such as mercantile stores, farms, medical practices, brokerage houses, and fishing companies that operated throughout the country. As mentioned in previous chapters, by 1935 Japanese in Mexico owned or were employed in over seventy different occupations. Nevertheless, this important shift in socioeconomic status came to a screeching halt on December 7, 1941. The forced relocation of Japanese Mexicans and nationals and how they reacted and coped with their removal sheds insight into the Japanese Mexican experience in Mexico.

For example, the history of Benito Hirokichi serves to illustrate that even under less formal conditions, like in Mexico, the Japanese population remained under constant suspicion and harassment. Mexico's war measures were not unlike those of the United States. Indeed, although the general Mexican population initially seemed reluctant to show enthusiasm for the war effort, the government seemed almost too eager. Not only were the emergency war measures adopted by Mexico such as the forced relocations, freezing of assets, suspension and forfeiture of naturalization, and confiscation of property in-line with US policy, but also Mexico imposed these measures before it even declared war on the axis nations.

When Mexico broke diplomatic ties with Japan shortly after December 7, 1941, a period of uncertainty and ambiguity set in for Japanese Mexicans and nationals. Although the Mexican government clearly indicated, "there would be no concentration camps," the forced relocation and loss of property and livelihood represented another form of oppression eerily similar to their counterparts in the United States. Added to this uncertainty were a significant number of Japanese who were not affected by the relocation order because of geographical location, the intercession of Mexican officials, or the ability of some Japanese to pay off corrupt officials. The Japanese Mexican experience during World War II was not monolithic, but rather, extremely diverse. This multiplicity of experiences was possible because of the unique Mexican political apparatus that had long characterized Mexico where *caciques*, *caudillos*, and *jefe politicos* often challenged the central government. Combined with the various recalcitrant state governors and military and civilian officials were those Japanese who simply resisted and negotiated their way out of relocation and internment.

In this manner, the Japanese experience during World War II included relocation, internment, and resistance and negotiations to maintain their freedom. Within a limited scope Mexico kept the United States at bay regarding its Japanese population. Mexico never created an internment infrastructure like the United States, but on a number of occasions Mexico succumbed to US pressure to intern specific individuals the United States deemed "dangerous" and "subversive." Benito Hirokichi, although exonerated by Mexicans officials, nevertheless, remained incarcerated until the end of World War II because the United States viewed him with suspicion. Also, as described in chapter 3, Dr. Tsuru Kiso, one of the most powerful Japanese Mexicans before the 1940s, lost everything and remained under constant surveillance for the duration for the war. Yet, many other Japanese remained unscathed from the World War II experience. Chapter 6 discusses how Japanese nationals and Japanese Mexicans reacted, survived, and resisted their relocation and internment during World War II.

CHAPTER SIX

El Comité Japonés de Ayuda Mutua

Hacienda Internment Camps and Japanese Resistance, 1942–1945

There will be no concentration camps. We will make them move into the interior, but we will not imprison them unless they are charged under the Espionage Law.

—Mexican General J. Salvador Sánchez, December 31, 1941

In September 2008 the Japanese Association of Mexico published one of its bimonthly bulletins that featured a cover image of the Hacienda de Temixco, located south of Mexico City in the state of Morelos near Cuernavaca (see figure 6.1).[1] Today, the Hacienda de Temixco is a resort and aquatic park and bares little resemblance to what it once was or housed, an internment camp for Japanese Mexicans and nationals (see figure 6.2). Another image is just as striking because it features a beautiful garden surrounded by an antiquated aqueduct with water majestically flowing into an enchanted illuminated crystal blue pool (see figure 6.3). This is not the image depicted by government reports from the 1940s or the ex-inhabitants of the hacienda: Japanese, who interned themselves as a form of self-preservation and resistance during World War II. The featured article included photographs that are more stunning than the cover, as if wanting to hide or forget that for nearly four years the Hacienda de Temixco, and others like it, were sanctuaries for thousands of Japanese during World War II.[2] In fact, throughout this study I have emphasized how Mexico treated and approached its Japanese population differently than the United States and other Latin American countries. Mexico, unlike the United States, Canada, and Peru, did not officially intern its Japanese population or create infamous concentration camps such as Tule

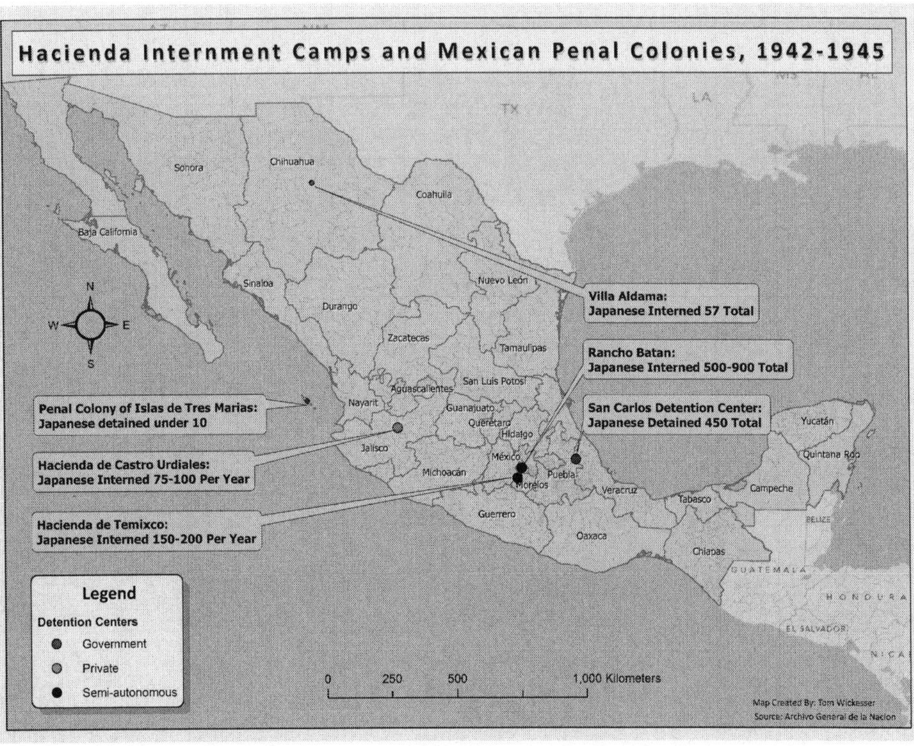

Figure 6.1. Hacienda internment camps and Mexican penal colonies, 1942–1945. Besides private residences, a variety of facilities were created to house Japanese Mexicans and Nationals. This map illustrates three types of detention that were utilized in Mexico during World War II: federal detention: Penal Colony of Islas de Tres Marías, San Carlos Detention Center; private: Hacienda Castro Urdiales, Villa Aldama; semi-autonomous: Hacienda de Temixco, Rancho Batán. Map created by author from a variety of sources from the Archivo General de la Nación, México.

Lake, Minidoka, Heart Mountain, and Manzanar in the United States, or Canadian internment camps such as Bay Farm, Bridge River, Minto City, and Kananaskis. Peru reached an agreement with the United States to round up and transport Japanese Peruvians to internment camps in the United States.[3] Nonetheless, in many ways the Japanese self-concentration into these haciendas resulted from Mexican war time policies, such as the directive that established Mexico City and Guadalajara as megacity relocation camps for Japanese residing in prohibitive zones. Similar to the US experience, not all the Japanese in Mexico were forced to relocate.

Figure 6.2. Japanese Mexicans at the Hacienda de Temixco, 1945. Image courtesy of the Archivo General de la Nación, México.

Figure 6.3. Hacienda de Temixco, 2008. The facility is now an aquatic center and resort. Image courtesy of Julia Taylor.

Only those Japanese living in security zones (coastlines and the border) were required to uproot, which resulted in the displacement of thousands of Japanese, loss of livelihood, and persecution based on their ethnicity.

This chapter is an attempt to illustrate the Japanese Mexican experience after their forced relocation and displacement to Guadalajara and Mexico City. Vital to this experience is an organization known as Bokuto Kyoeikai or Comité Japonés de Ayuda Mutua (CJAM, Japanese Mutual Aid Committee), which was directly responsible for the protection and welfare of the relocated Japanese, as well as the overall Japanese community residing in Mexico. This organization was also responsible for the purchase, development, and management of several haciendas that sustained the Japanese community during the bleak years of the war. By examining internment compounds such as the Hacienda de Temixco outside of Cuernavaca, Morelos; Hacienda Castro Urdiales, near Tala, Jalisco; and in a limited scope, Hacienda de Batán in the vicinity of Mexico City, we are able to understand the trials and tribulations of the Japanese diaspora in Mexico and contrast their treatment to other regions of the Americas, including the United States. These haciendas could not have been occupied, resurrected, and sustained without the leadership, financing, and creativity of the CJAM. Further, I address the self-internment of the Japanese community as a form of resistance to their condition in Mexico during World War II. In this manner the Japanese position and reaction are not unlike those of the indigenous communities of Mexico who often isolated themselves from Spanish and Mexican institutions to prevent direct contact as a form of protection. The Japanese Mexicans and nationals during this uncertain period of World War II chose a similar path. Their self-exile, after forced relocation to Mexico City and Guadalajara, in many ways, a subsequent internment, represented a concerted attempt by the Japanese to isolate themselves from the possible dangers that lurked around every corner during the war. The Mexican government had two additional locations in Mexico that were used exclusively for the detention of enemy aliens, Isla de Tres Marías, Nayarit, and San Carlos Detention Center, Peroté, Veracruz. The Mexican government interned those they considered the most dangerous Japanese Mexicans and nationals into these two facilities.

The haciendas that the Japanese occupied during World War II were haciendas in name only. Most of these ex-haciendas were dilapidated nonfunctioning structures, with any sense of opulence, luxury, or utility long ago swept away by decades of civil strife, revolution, and despair. The names of these hacienda camps obscure the fact that during World War II,

Japanese Mexicans, out of desperation, voluntarily interned themselves as a collective response to their displacement and resettlement. And since these haciendas went beyond their original utility and were not created by the Mexican government but were self-run semiautonomous camps, very little has been written about their history or the people located inside during the war. More important and as mentioned in chapter 5, Mexico only recently provided access to the files of its intelligence apparatus, the Dirección General de Investigaciones Políticas y Sociales (IPS), located within the national archives. This governmental agency was charged with overseeing all Japanese and Axis nationals in Mexico and conducted investigations of suspected espionage activities. These files, although institutional in nature, nonetheless provide the few opportunities to hear the voices of the Japanese community during this period. From the dusty pages of the IPS case files, a better understanding of the Japanese Mexican experience during World War II is revealed.

A Culture of Fear

Prior to the bombing of Pearl Harbor a sense of fear gripped the Japanese diaspora throughout the Americas. Much of this fear emanated from decades of animosity and distrust directed toward all things Japanese. Before the outbreak of hostilities, the Japanese community had been racialized due to constant harassment and repression based on an ideology that viewed Japanese as a danger culturally and economically. After December 7, 1941, the level of anxiety and racialism intensified. From the Japanese Mexican position alarm was fueled by the internment of Japanese Americans in the United States and the elaborate infrastructure created for their eventual isolation and imprisonment. And, from the perspective of the media, civilian and military officials, all Japanese were suspect, not for committing some act against the state, but by simply being Japanese. Once war broke out the racialism that gestated for decades had a profound impact on the Japanese at the hemispheric level. The launch of round ups and detentions of the Japanese diaspora throughout the Americas psychologically tormented the Japanese Mexicans who speculated if the US style of internment awaited their community. Consequently, for many Japanese the secluded haciendas scattered throughout Mexico represented a lifeline and a last means of defense and survival as they awaited their fate. In this manner, the Japanese experience in Mexico had much in common with the Japanese in the United States and elsewhere during World War II.

And, although it is useful to compare and contrast those experiences, it is also easy to succumb to temptation and base a comparison strictly on the question: which Japanese community suffered more—those at the hands of the US Government and its officials or at the hands of Mexican officials? As I have already discussed in previous chapters, the United States role in developing a hemispheric wide policy for the round up of the Japanese population without regard to due process, is an indictment unto itself. Indeed, the United States was so fearful of Japanese "fifth columns" in the hemisphere that it demanded of all Latin American countries that if they were unwilling or incapable of interning their Japanese populations, they were to be sent to the United States for final adjudication.[4]

Nevertheless, some differences in treatment did occur and are attributed to the general Japanese experience in Mexico and the development of the Mexican State during the post-revolutionary period. These differences tend to obscure the commonalities Japanese Mexicans and nationals shared with all Japanese in the Americas as they were hunted, arrested, detained, relocated, interned, or repatriated to other countries. For post-revolutionary Mexico a large array of historians have discussed how regional caudillos and local caciques resisted centralized control from the state and were able to maintain a sense of autonomy by finding either a middle ground through negotiations or by outright defiance. The relevance of these developments for the Japanese is that these caudillos and caciques often dictated, directly or indirectly, the Japanese experience before and during the war period. As a result some Japanese in Mexico were able to defy and negotiate the national directive that ordered their forced relocation to Mexico City and Guadalajara. Unlike in the United States, the Japanese Mexican community had direct dialogues with the highest echelons of the Mexican government that allowed them access to power to negotiate their position.

Documents from this period illustrate that the Japanese in Mexico were not passive victims of the forced relocations, but actively resisted their displacement and were determined to use their talents as a successful community to counter the effects of their forced relocation and subsequent internment. Along these same lines, the Japanese also used their unique relationship with the Japanese and Mexican governments to counter the hegemony of the United States. The result of this resistance was a mass Japanese community mobilization to protect and carve out a space in Mexico during a period of intense scrutiny. What is certain is the Japanese in Mexico refused to succumb to their victimization.

Comité Japonés de Ayuda Mutua

As discussed in chapter 3, the Japanese associations in Mexico had multiple roles within the Japanese community, but germane to this discussion is the continuity of mutual assistance that formed the basis of the CJAM, which became the only recognized Japanese organization in Mexico during World War II and a vital link to the survival of thousands of Japanese. When war broke out, decrees issued by the Mexican government made the Japanese associations illegal, and all were forced to disband. Nevertheless, the leadership of these associations remained intact. As would be expected, most were successful in their chosen profession or occupation and had a level of respect from their community. These community leaders were also useful to the Japanese government for gathering social-economic information and the status of Japanese subjects in the country. Because of this level of contact and collaboration a blanket of suspicion lingered regarding the actual intent of the relationship. Prior to World War II, many wondered if something more sinister had developed between Japanese Mexicans and the Japanese government. The convenient relationship that developed between the Japanese officials and Japanese Mexicans produced important consequences after Mexico forced thousands of Japanese to relocate.

Shortly after the bombing of Pearl Harbor on December 12, 1941, the Japanese ambassador to Mexico, Yoshiaki Miura, summoned Sanshiro Matsumoto, Heiji Kato, and Kiso Tsuru to his residence and advised them that Japan and Mexico had severed diplomatic relations. Miura also persuaded the three individuals to become the de facto leadership of the Japanese community in Mexico. Ambassador Miura chose Matsumoto, Kato, and Tsuru due to specific abilities each possessed that were crucial to protect the Japanese that remained in the country. Two other individuals were later selected to help direct the CJAM, Luis Tsuji Tadasu and George S. Makita.[5]

Sanshiro Matsumoto was a well-established businessman with many connections in Mexico City. Sanshiro's father was a skilled gardener who had been in charge of the presidential residence and succeeded in running a large-scale nursery-florist business. When the war started, the family owned large nurseries in ten different locations around Mexico City, with nearly 200 Mexican employees. Matsumoto had many high level connections within the Mexican government. Indeed, Maximino Avila Camacho, President Manuel Ávila Camacho's brother, became the godparent to one of Matsumoto's grandchildren.[6] Heiji Kato owned and operated the largest department store that catered to the Japanese population in Mexico City, El Nuevo Japón, and Tsuru was socially, economically, and politically the most astute Japanese Mexican in all of Mexico. What they all had in common was keen business acumen, firm leadership, and strong organizational skills. Minister Miura gave specific instructions to Matsumoto, Kato, and Tsuru that they were to protect the interest of the Japanese residing in Mexico. With the Mexican government's permission, assistance from the Japanese minister to Mexico, private Japanese donations, and the ex-members of the Mexico City, Mexicali, Tijuana, Ensenada Japanese associations, the relief society CJAM was founded in January 1942, with its original address located at Sor Juana Inez De La Cruz, no. 112, Mexico, DF, later changed to Calle de San Antonio Abad 327, Mexico, DF.[7]

After the Japanese Association of Mexico City was dissolved, it sold its property to provide seed money for the CJAM. With donations and the sale of property CJAM raised a total of 230,000 pesos.[8] CJAM officially announced its existence through the publication of a circular, dated March 4, 1942, outlining its aims and bylaws. The circular provided a general overview of the Japanese situation in Mexico and alerted the Japanese community of the government directive to relocate. In many ways, CJAM functioned as the previous Japanese associations that had been dissolved, but during the war period, the CJAM went well beyond the normal functions of the previous associations.[9] The resemblance to the previous associations was not superficial. In fact, much of the hierarchy for CJAM consisted of the former leadership of the Japanese associations from various states. In their circular and bylaws the founders outlined the objectives of the CJAM:

> In order to assist each other at present and to move forward, we have formed an association in this capital that will be called: Japanese Committee of Mutual Aid (Comité Japonés de Ayuda Mutua), which will have a branch in Guadalajara, as you can see by the attachments to this circular. Because of the legislation passed recently by the government, that requires all the Japanese residents within 150 kilometers [93 miles] along the coasts and borders, be relocated to the interior of the Republic, and the problem of providing assistance to compatriots in need, it has been challenging, given the large number that are required to relocate. Therefore, we urge you to support us by getting any occupation of whatever kind to fellow internees, advise us immediately that you have knowledge of any occupation.[10]

The relocation of the Japanese in Mexico began in January 1942. By the time the CJAM came into existence hundreds of Japanese had already arrived in Mexico City seeking help with a total Japanese population residing in the federal district estimated at 4,000. It is difficult to know for certain how many Japanese eventually ended up in Mexico City and Guadalajara since no effort was made to track such numbers. However, one Japanese source estimates that roughly 80 percent of the Japanese in Mexico were forcibly relocated to Mexico City with the largest coming from Baja California.[11] The relocation order and its implementation created chaos, fear, and deprivation. Because of their displacement many Japanese saw as their only hope the well-organized Japanese community in Mexico City. As I noted earlier and discuss later in this chapter, CJAM eventually opened a counterpart (sub-Comité Japonés de Ayuda Mutua) in Guadalajara as part of their overall efforts to ensure the welfare of the Japanese community throughout the country. CJAM and the principal leaders of the Japanese community in Mexico City put into action a plan to protect and ensure the welfare of the Japanese population in Mexico.

CJAM's statutes indicated, "Its objective will be of mutual help and protection to the Japanese residents in need by reason of the current situation and the committee will handle a variety of issues aimed at the migration of Japanese within the country; help in finding employment, and helping the indigent."[12] Besides operating an employment bureau, the CJAM furnished food, money, medicine, clothing, and sleeping accommodations. As will be noted below, the funding for the CJAM came from donations and all services were free to the Japanese community.[13] Numerous individuals signed the bylaws and the document itself provided an organizational chart as well as how the leaders of the various Japanese associations initially financed CJAM. Not all saw CJAM as a benevolent organization created to salvage the remnants of the Japanese community in Mexico.

When the US intelligence community became aware of CJAM's existence, the organization and its members were interpreted and perceived as subversive and a Japanese intelligence asset, not a mutual aid society. Although not completely certain, US intelligence officers viewed CJAM with great alarm because many of its members were prominent Japanese from various locales throughout Mexico who had been on a watch list before their relocation. One report stated, "Many of its important members are suspected of subversive activities or are known to be engaged in such activities."[14] This air of suspicion plagued CJAM for the duration of the war.

In many ways, not only did the structure of the CJAM resemble its predecessor, the Japanese associations, but also much of the leadership was picked from the various defunct associations from throughout Mexico as indicated from the organizational chart below (table 6.1). Indeed, when the CJAM is examined in detail it resembled the traditional Japanese Association. For example, the Japanese associations had a governing body made up of a board of directors, represented in CJAM by Kiso Tsuru, Sanshiro, and Kato. And similar to the Japanese associations, the board of directors then elected a president, vice president, and a committee of management of seven or more members. Thus, CJAM was modeled after the associations and had similar functions. The Japanese Mexicans chose this model because of its familiarity, but also because the model had proven to be efficient. I also argue that this model represented a form of resistance and as mentioned earlier, a form of continuity. It is unknown if the Mexican government recognized that Kiso, Sanshiro, and Kato had simply centralized all the associations into one group and renamed it. Obviously there was some functionality of the associations the CJAM could not duplicate because of wartime measures enacted by the Mexican government. For example, on December 10, 1941, the Mexican government froze all Japanese assets and bank accounts preventing the CJAM from accessing vital funds for its operations. Although individual Japanese who had bank accounts were eventually allowed to withdraw 500 pesos on a

Table 6.1. Comité Japonés de Ayuda Mutua: Branch officials

President	Seiro Nakagawa (Guadalajara)
Vice president	Yonezo Ichikawa (Mexicali)
Treasurer	Minoru Wakita (Guadalajara)
Subtreasurer	Yasuke Okamoto (Mexicali)
Secretary of minutes	Yukyo Shimizu (Guadalajara)
Secretary of information	Nakagawa
Secretary of relations	Jinkichi Kumazaw (Guadalajara)
Secretary of locales	Kingo Tozuka y Kasuke Nakawatase (Mexicali)
	Kosaburo Ishino y Tomoichi Kawakami (Tijuana)
	Tamanosuke Suzuki and K. Yokokawa (Ensenada)
Auxiliary members	Isao Nishizaki
	Hirozo Funakoshi
	Tatsunobu Minakata
	Katsudo Yoshida
Matters of agriculture	Umeichi Kobayashi

monthly basis, just enough for subsistence, the small amount made it difficult to make ends meet.[15]

The Mexican government, through the director of the IPS, approved the formation of this new organization on April 23, 1942.[16] Matsumoto, Kato, and Tsuru were the charter members and initially managed CJAM. The headquarters for this relief agency was initially in a former school building in Mexico City located on the street of Sor Juana Inez de la Cruz no. 112. It was from this location that the CJAM began to receive and process Japanese arriving from areas designated military or sensitive zones such as the Pacific and Atlantic coastlines and the border with the United States.

The Japanese populations of Mexico City and Guadalajara swelled with Japanese arriving from Baja California, Sonora, Chihuahua, Coahuila, Tamaulipas, Nayarit, Oaxaca, Guerrero, and Veracruz.[17] CJAM, as the only legal Japanese entity in Mexico during World War II, became a vital organization for the survival of thousands of Japanese during the war. Although its charter spelled out its mission, CJAM's role in Mexico went well beyond relief. Indeed, it became the de facto official representative of the majority of the Japanese residing in Mexico City, Guadalajara and beyond. The decentralized campaign to force all Japanese into two major Mexican cities created a chaotic atmosphere with numerous Mexican states creating their own plans without national control. This in turn created and placed Japanese Mexicans in a perilous position. As thousands of Japanese were uprooted from their livelihood and forced to relocate, they did so at their own expense and without any means of employment once they arrived at their final destination. Upon their arrival in Mexico City and Guadalajara the Japanese competed against other Japanese and Mexicans for scarce resources and employment. Those unable to find employment or a reliable source of subsistence suffered and eventually sought relief. Many Japanese also felt a sense of isolation and fear regarding their precarious status in Mexico as well as the rumors and stories that circulated about incarcerations and roundups that occurred to their counterparts in the United States. Those Japanese unable to secure employment and subsistence looked to CJAM for help.

Hacienda Internment Camps

Prior to their forced relocation the overwhelming number of Japanese took pride in the fact that they were independent and self-sufficient. With their forced removal the Japanese had their livelihoods stripped, bank accounts frozen, and they were left to fend for themselves. The self-sufficiency and ability of the Japanese community to mobilize, to some extent, explains why the Mexican government readily and in most cases, approved requests by the Japanese to create their own colonies for self-imposed internment. By doing so it relieved the Mexican government from responsibility in providing care and assistance to those it had forcibly removed, displaced, and rendered nearly destitute. When Mexico issued its relocation order for the Japanese it did not empower or create any agency to develop a plan for the resettlement of the Japanese community. In Mexico there was no counterpart to the War Relocation Authority that the United States created to facilitate the internment of Japanese Americans. The Mexican military's sole charge was to enforce the relocation order and not assist in the resettlement. On the other hand, Mexico did not collectively round up the leadership of the Japanese community, which is what the FBI did with the Japanese American community.[18]

By unifying against such indifference the Japanese community deployed direct action against the Mexican government and resisted their exploitation through the creation of a mutual aid organization that was essentially a centralized Japanese Association during the war period. The efforts and infrastructure created by CJAM for the relocated Japanese had reached its limits by late 1942, especially regarding accommodations and feeding the hundreds that had arrived. As a result CJAM began to purchase land in various rural and urban locations or found sympathetic individuals with surplus land for Japanese to reside. The Japanese Mexicans, without a systematic plan in place, were forced to relocate without any sense of due process, protection, or assistance, which amplified their fear and hardship.

In local areas Japanese resisted their removal with the help of Mexicans and politically connected Japanese. Concerned Mexicans petitioned the government on behalf of Japanese Mexicans and requested an exemption from the relocation order. Cosme A. Sánchez, from Uruapan, Michoacán, did exactly this in May 1943:

> On this date in May of the current year [1943] I am writing the Government of Michoacan, seeking permission to utilize the service of the Japanese Namisabuto Matsui, Motomu Tagawa, Tokuichi Matsushita, Shigeo Kawashima, Uhei Ueda and Carlos Nakamura on my property called Rancho "Moctezuma." My ranch is located in the municipality of Apatzingan, Mich.[19]

The Japanese community also took action to relieve the suffering of those displaced by the forced relocation. Before the major hacienda of Temixco was purchased, CJAM initially placed Japanese Mexicans at the Hacienda de Batán, near Mexico City, which was owned by Sanshiro Matsumoto.[20] Before the war, Matsumoto had a thriving floral business and originally purchased Batán for the production of flowers. At its height during the war, Batán housed nearly 900 Japanese.[21] Matsumoto and CJAM unwittingly created a quasi assembly center at Batán whose residents eventually were transferred to Temixco, Castro Urdiales, or Mexico City.

It is unknown how many Japanese survived the war period under conditions described above, where a small group petitioned the government for exemption from the relocation order. The majority of the Japanese listed above were eventually relocated to Guadalajara or ended up at the Hacienda Castro Urdiales near Tala, Jalisco, Hacienda de Temixco's counterpart. The process of resettlement occurred quickly with most Japanese losing their property, savings, and ability to recoup fair prices for crops or property. Throughout Mexico enforcement of the relocation order varied by region, community, and whether or not the local or regional politico or cacique decided to employ the long held custom of *la mordida*. Put another way, a significant number of Japanese either had their relocation orders delayed, retracted, or enforced based on a "fee" to local authorities. Abuse of this type was common and other illustrations of this are found later in this chapter. However, according to Daniel M. Masterson, one of the most egregious cases of abuse of the Japanese in Mexico occurred in the state of Chihuahua:

> The state treasurer, Tómas Valles, had fifty-seven of the Japanese who had been living in Ciudad Juárez transported to his ranch near Villa Adama, where they were forced to work virtually as slaves. . . . Finally, the sad state of these evacuees was brought to the attention of the Portuguese Legation by the Bukoto Kyoei-kai (Japanese Committee of Mutual Aid) and these "forced laborers" were allowed to leave the Valles ranch, after which most of them very likely migrated to Mexico City.[22]

Like Batán, shortly after the relocation order, other "haciendas" began to emerge as an alternative for Japanese forced to leave their homes. These mostly forgotten haciendas became de facto "internment" camps for Japanese Mexicans and nationals throughout Mexico during World War II. These camps (haciendas/ranchos) were a direct result of the forced relocation efforts. Some contained a handful of families and individuals, but others hundreds over the duration of the war with the Hacienda de Temixco the largest. The locations had names such as the Hacienda Batán (also referred to as Rancho Batán), Hacienda de Temixco, Hacienda Castro

Urdiales, Hacienda de Michoacán, Rancho Querendero Michoacán, Hacienda de San Miguel Villalobos, and Villa Adama. Rancho Querendero, in the state of Michoacán, also became a de facto assembly center after CJAM was given permission by President Camacho and the minister of the interior, Miguel Alemán, to buy it as a sanctuary for displaced Japanese. Even though the contemporary image of Temixco (see figure 6.3) gives the allure and illusion that these were quaint haciendas where individuals lived in luxury similar to the *hacendados* of the past in all their regalia, nothing could be further from the truth. With its sea of blue pools and sense of modernity, the present-day Temixco represents a simulacrum of the original, thus creating an escape for the Japanese once interned and their descendants from the reality that the inhabitants of these haciendas and ranches during World War II had been forced to leave their homes for an uncertain future in locations that were initially uninhabitable and unfamiliar.

When CJAM's central location in Mexico City became insufficient to process the thousands of new Japanese arrivals in the capital and Rancho Batán too small to house them, CJAM realized that they needed to find an alternative location that could accommodate the hundreds that were arriving into the city. CJAM eventually funded the purchase of a derelict seventeenth-century hacienda in the state of Morelos known as Temixco for approximately 85,000 pesos. This hacienda had been in disrepair for decades and its rightful ownership in dispute since at least 1923. By the early twentieth century Hacienda de Temixco was no longer a functioning hacienda, but contained buildings and land that could house the Japanese and allow them to cultivate crops for subsistence. After falling into disrepair the hacienda was sold to Mr. Alejandro Lacy. Lacy was the son of two British immigrants born in the state of Sonora. Lacy's daughter married one of the sons of General Plutarco Elias Calles in the 1920s. With the approval of Calles the state government of Morelos put Temixco up for auction with Lacy acquiring the property. Lacy then sold it to the CJAM.[23] The village of Temixco is located approximately 85 km from Mexico City and 6 km from the city of Cuernavaca. The hacienda was situated on 200 hectares that was primarily used for farming. The hacienda was surrounded by three major structures that housed a mill for harvesting rice, a power plant that generated 60 kilowatt hours, and an abandoned chapel.[24]

As mentioned earlier, farms such as Rancho Batán near Mexico City also housed Japanese during the war. In fact the Mexican government also used Batán as a temporary holding facility when in January 29, 1942, five

Japanese fishing ships were captured offshore in Mexican waters, but near the United States. Three of the ships were registered in Mexico, but all the individuals on board the ships were Japanese. Initially, all were sent to Mexico City with fourteen Japanese males and one female eventually sent to Batán.[25] Haciendas and farms such as Temixco became safe havens for the thousands of Japanese who had no means of employment or subsistence. During the war period Hacienda de Temixco and Hacienda Urdiales Castro became cooperatives where the Japanese individuals and families collectively farmed and harvested such staples as rice, sugar cane, tomatoes, onions and raised poultry and swine.[26] On July 1942 Luis Tsuji, manager of the CJAM in Mexico, requested permission from the Mexican government to begin transferring and housing Japanese Mexicans to the Hacienda de Temixco in the state of Morelos. On August 1942 permission was granted and the individuals listed in table 6.2 became the first inhabitants of the Hacienda de Temixco and Yoshiuda Shunji became the first director of Temixco Farm Center for displaced Japanese.[27]

CJAM also facilitated the movement of Japanese to Hacienda Castro Urdiales, located near the Municipio (Municipality) de Tala in the state of Jalisco, west of Guadalajara.[28] On December 7, 1942, Jesús Gonzalez Gallo, owner of Hacienda Castro Urdiales, sent a letter to the secretaría de gobernación giving his permission to the CJAM to establish a Japanese colony on his property. In this same correspondence he invited the CJAM

Table 6.2. First inhabitants of Hacienda de Temixco, August 1942

Kei Hito Misida	Tomekichi Yamaguchi	Alejandro Y. Nubo
Takesaburo Ouchi	Yonekichi Yamamoto	Saemon Yamamoto
Otokichi Takaki	José Matsumoto	Toichi Morishige
Shinsa Taba	Antonio Suzuki Suzuki	Kanichi M. Kabay
Juan Narabe Takaku	Otokichi Shiba Kishi Yama	Yaioniro Sakaguchi
Kashiro Urano	Shibata Seki Mineji	Fruno Tanaka Nazario
Julio Hashimoto	Luis R. Okuno Okuno	Santiago Kobayashi
Noboru Murakami	Ando Kaeade Kaneichi	Antonio O. Mori
Ogawa M. Tokutaro	Jorge Masudo	Yokoyama Watanabe
Juan Akimoto Sono	Juan Kakimoto	Shirato Shirato Josuke
Gunmatsu Yamamoto	Watanabe W. Shigemitsu	Kudo S. Hiroshi
Pedro Sabajara Kawakami	Tomomo Nashiki	Shibata Shuibata Noboru
Suda Sakamoto Muneo	Kazo Oura	Juan Yamasaki

to his property to inspect the land for its suitability for the cultivation of crops. A subcommittee of the CJAM was created for the Hacienda Castro Urdiales with membership comprised of individuals from that community. After being declared suitable for occupation, the Hacienda Castro Urdiales received its first occupants from Mexico City in December 1942. The first occupants included a cross section of the Japanese community. Of the initial occupants, twenty-nine were adult males, twelve were adult females, twenty-nine were minor males, and seven minor females. One female cousin and and one mother were listed as dependents for a total of 79 individuals constituting the initial occupants of Hacienda Castro Urdiales. Surprisingly, of the twenty-nine head of households and single males, only two were naturalized Mexican citizens.

By February 1943 this initial group of Japanese started the process of achieving self-sufficiency. According to a report by a state engineer commissioned to oversee the Hacienda Castro Urdiales, but also to survey the progress of the Japanese residents, the residents had purchased twenty-three tons of different varieties of potato seed and had placed them in a germinator in preparation for planting. The engineer, Raymundo del Bosque, also reported that the residents were preparing over twenty hectares for planting the potato seed and various grasses, all done by machinery.[29] The Japanese residents also completed the construction of several *acequias* (canals) by tapping into the Cuicillos River for the watering of their crops. In March 1943 the residents constructed additional houses for the arrival of additional Japanese into the hacienda.

During the month of May 1943 Japanese farmers began to cultivate the land in preparation to plant peanut seed. By late June 1943 it was determined that the potatoes planted in February failed to produce enough plants for a successful harvest. Reports attributed the failure of the potato crop to over-watering and lack of experience on part of the Japanese farmers.[30] However, the peanut seeds planted were successfully cultivated, weeded, and continued to progress at a normal rate. Both haciendas experienced similar problems with crops, which is why for the nearly four years of their existence the residents struggled to subsist. However, the CJAM became so concerned regarding the sustainability of the Japanese settlement at Hacienda Castro Urdiales that it requested, through the Mexican government, to send a representative from Hacienda de Temixco to observe and inspect the settlement to determine if assistance was needed.

Nearly a year later, Luis Tsuji sent Moises Onuki Kato to Hacienda Castro Urdiales. The situation at the sister hacienda had deteriorated dramatically. Based on another report Tsuji had sent to the secretary of the interior outlining the situation, he simultaneously requested that he and Isaburo Horiuchi be given permission to leave Mexico City to travel to Guadalajara and the Hacienda Castro Urdiales for ten days. The fact that the director and codirector of the CJAM wanted to intervene indicated the seriousness of Castro Urdiales' situation. Indeed, in his report to the government Tsuji stated that the hacienda in Jalisco faced multiple problems that included production and economic woes, as well as low morale. However, Tsuji was most concerned about the social degradation that had manifested due to production and economic issues.[31] In general, the protection afforded by the haciendas worked, even with the struggles previously mentioned; the majority of Japanese Mexicans and nationals found a sense of normalcy and either remained within the confines of the haciendas or eventually transitioned out to Mexico City or Guadalajara seeking employment. Nevertheless, the Japanese regardless of their location remained under a veil of suspicion. In 1944, the Mexican secret police conducted an investigation at the Hacienda de Temixco based on accusations that Japanese spies lived within the compound.

Spies, Land, and the Agrarian Code: Japanese Agency and Resistance

Regardless of the measures taken by Mexico to relocate its Japanese population into the interior, US officials remained skeptical of Mexico's attempt at securing the Japanese population. Even after their forced removal and self-exile to such places as Hacienda de Temixco, US military intelligence reports continued to view Japanese Mexicans as a hemispheric threat as described in the following quote:

> They [Japanese] seem to be keeping a low on orders from some central Japanese source here in Mexico or in Japan. However, they give every appearance of being ready for any action desired of them by their home government, and they could undoubtedly cause some sabotage or perform other acts quickly if so ordered. The Japanese in Mexico are just as fanatical as the Japanese on the fighting fronts.[32]

Close scrutiny of US intelligence reports, such as the one just quoted, that emanated from Mexico indicates that individuals, groups, or organizations with ulterior motives may have played a role in maintaining a suspicious atmosphere of the Japanese in Mexico. For example, the source for the naval intelligence report quoted above was the Chinese minister in Mexico.[33] Other groups with an "axe to grind" played a similar role throughout Mexico during the war period.

As early as 1942 rumors circulated that the Japanese residents of Temixco were spies. Mexican newspapers and propaganda headlined the existence of a so-called Japanese spy center. Governor Jesús Castillo of Morelos asked to confer with Japanese representatives regarding these rumors. At this meeting Governor Castillo indicated that he believed the rumors to be false, but advised the Japanese not to listen to nighttime radio broadcasts from Tokyo. As the rumors persisted, the Mexican secret police carried out an investigation of the Hacienda de Temixco. In the course of the investigation it was determined that the local villagers had started the rumors because of their resentment toward the Japanese and their ownership of the hacienda. The village leaders had raised the question of legality of Japanese ownership since they were considered enemy aliens and precluded from owning land. Between March and November 1944 a series of investigations, correspondences, meeting, and demands were exchanged by a variety of parties that included the Japanese residents of the hacienda de Temixco, *agraristas* (agrarians or farmers), and Mexican government officials.[34]

The initial investigation began on March 6, 1944, when the Mexican secret police visited the hacienda after hearing complaints that the local *ejido* (a communal land holding) committee demanded that the Japanese residing at the hacienda cease any and all preparation for the cultivation of new crops during early spring 1944. A follow-up visit and report on March 15, 1944, by the investigators concluded that by presidential decree the Japanese had been given authorization to purchase the land at Hacienda de Temixco. It was also determined that the *ejidatario* managed lands (village lands) adjacent to the hacienda. In an effort to extricate the land from the Japanese, members the *ejidatario* (communal land holders) attempted to stop and/or prevent the Japanese from cultivating and planting new crops to give the appearance that the land laid fallow. Furthermore, villagers attempted to persuade Japanese farmers not to plant until they received official permission from the state agricultural authorities of Morelos. If the villagers had succeeded with their ruse, it would have given the appearance that the Japanese were not utilizing the land, thus allowing the *ejidatario* of Temixco to petition the government for the land based on the 1934 Agrarian Law.[35] This is exactly what a letter from the president of the Comisariado Ejidal (Ejido Commission) to the secretary of the interior stated:

> In order that this community be recognized before the Agricultural Department and the idleness of the land, granted by the President of the Republic, is truthful we sincerely pray that you inform the Secretary of the Interior and Agricultural Department that this is in violation of the affected lands. This is not to mock the presidential order, which benefits our landless peasants, and even our enemies. No doubt you will grant us this favor.[36]

After receiving the ejidatario's letter, Inspector Donaciano Ceballos wrote to his superior, the head of the Mexican secret police, urging that some resolution be found or the difficulties between the villagers and the Japanese subjects under his care may escalate. Another correspondence in November from the inspectors to their superiors validated that the lands that belonged to the Japanese were purchased under a presidential decree. Additionally, the report reinforced the need for Japanese self-sufficiency. In fact, part of the rationale within the report from the IPS investigators mentioned the great savings to the government by supporting the endeavors of the Japanese in the hacienda:

> The only difficulty, which has been seen at Temixco regarding the interned Japanese, is their inability to cultivate new crops because the ejidatario of Temixco insists the lands belong to their ejido. The delay in planting a new crop has already cost the Japanese a great deal of money. On the other hand, these Japanese do not cost the nation one penny because their production is solely for personal consumption and their daily subsistence.[37]

A special investigator from the Mexican secret police, Inspector no. 11, Ricardo Trujillo Q., was assigned to determine whether or not the 1934 Agrarian Law applied to the Temixco case. The agrarian reforms passed in the 1930s accelerated the number of petitions by peasants seeking lands, especially communal landholdings. Furthermore, the land reforms implemented by Lázaro Cárdenas changed the rural landscape as he redistributed land at a phenomenal pace that saw ejidatarios grow from 15 to 47 percent of the total land cultivated.[38] Based on testimony gathered by Trujillo, the surrounding communities of the region that included Temixco and Palmira had petitioned the government since 1923 regarding rightful ownership of the lands that included Temixco. However, the case became quite complex because the previous owner, Alejandro Lacy, had broken up the land into various parcels and sold some initially to a

Mr. Olaez, which resulted in transfers of the land to different individuals. As discussed earlier in this chapter, Lacy sold the main compound plus over 200 hectares to several Japanese that included Romaro Tago Tomaro [*sic*], Teiji Zeiki Guche [*sic*], Vicente Kadiyama [*sic*], and Tanduzu Tzuji [*sic*]. Under the guidance of the CJAM, the group purchased four parcels that were combined with an additional eight parcels purchased by the founders of the CJAM for a total surface area of 205 hectares. The native population made the argument that much of the land remained uncultivated and therefore they had the right to claim it under agrarian law. However, the inspector noted that the Japanese owners and occupants had cultivated all of the arable land. Furthermore, it was determined that the sold parcels were confirmed by the agrarian department and publicly announced first in the national *Diario* on February 19, 1944, and again in the state *Diario de Morelos* on April 4, 1944. After the official announcement of the intent to sell, the agrarian department ordered the sale to move forward. The inspector's final comments are simply in reference to verification of information provided and stated that the villagers' complaints were without merit.[39]

The surviving documents indicate that the ex-hacienda de Temixco and Castro Urdiales became functioning cooperatives, albeit with some difficulties. As discussed earlier, evidence indicates that these two haciendas were often barely able to grow enough food for their inhabitants and provide basic care. The majority of the inhabitants of both of these haciendas were primarily children, women, and the elderly. In fact, the Mexican government in February 1943 reported that 110 Japanese were residing at the hacienda de Temixco and that eighty were working in agriculture. Further, of the thirty that remained all were either sick or too elderly to work in the fields.[40] A year later, January 1944, the population of the camp included twenty-five individuals who were granted permission to travel to Mexico City: men, 67; women, 14; children, 67; in Mexico City: men, 23; women, 2.[41]

Because of the demographics of the population inside the haciendas, one of the highest costs incurred by the CJAM was health care. Detailed financial reports provide some sense of the well-being of the inhabitants of the haciendas, but also the general Japanese population residing in Mexico City. The largest cost incurred was the fees or honorariums to the Japanese doctors, such as Dr. Tsunesaburo Hasegawa, who was paid 500 pesos per month. The reports for all of 1945 show a similar monthly salary for Hasegawa. The reports also reveal the majority of the Japanese receiving care were men. One of the two women listed on the February report, a Mrs. Satoshi Onodera, received medical help or attention. The other female, Fuku Tachika, was paid an honorarium as a midwife.[42]

The cooperatives were organized to the extent that they established schools on the premises. The schools established by CJAM during World War II are one of its lasting legacies. It is interesting to note that during an era when anything Japanese was seen with suspicion, Director Tsuru sought permission to establish Japanese language schools in Mexico City, Temixco, Guadalajara, and Castro Urdiales. Based on correspondence with the charge d'affaires of Portugal, Tsuru had attempted to import instructional materials for Japanese language lessons for Japanese Mexican students. Japanese Mexican students attended Mexican public schools wherever they resided but rarely learned a foreign language. In other regions of Latin America, Brazil, for example, Japanese language schools were shut down or went underground.

However, on July 10, 1944, Tsuru sent a letter to the secretary of education seeking permission not only to establish Japanese language schools for their Japanese children, but also to allow CJAM to utilize books from Japan that the charge d'affaires of Portugal had purchased on behalf of the CJAM. In his letter, Tsuru outlined that the children would learn the language after their regular school hours thereby not interfering with the regular curriculum. As precedent, Tsuru cited their Japanese counterparts in the United States by stating, "We cite as a precedent that in the United States of America are currently in operation exclusively Japanese schools despite the conflict between that nation and the Empire of Japan."[43] Tsuru's last comment to the secretary of the interior indicates he was aware of the sensitive nature of the request: "Moreover, we want to avoid with your authorization, any suspicion that might arise against us, because we have always abided and been obedient to the rules and laws of the country that has given us hospitality."[44] The charge d'affaires of Portugal, José dos Santos Silva Taveira, was able to acquire a significant number of books from Japan and had them sent to a variety of different schools throughout Mexico in order to provide Japanese language lessons to the sons and daughters of Japanese Mexicans. Below is a response from José dos Santos Silva Taveira to Tsuru Kiso regarding the importation of the books:

> With reference to number 3 of the kind letter dated November 10, 1943, the Japanese sent 55 groups of books to schools teaching Japanese in Mexico and whose entry into this country was subject to the approval of the competent authorities. I have the pleasure to inform you that the Mexican Government, according to a communication just received,

> authorizes the books come to Mexico and be delivered to Japanese schools, after review by the censors.[45]

The school at Temixco was organized to the extent that even Mexican parents in the local vicinity sent their children to the school.

Very little documentation exists to provide a first-hand account of the daily functions of the haciendas or the daily activities of the inhabitants outside of agricultural duties. Available are government reports and correspondences between CJAM and various government agencies. The voice of the Japanese Mexicans is filtered through the bureaucracy of the Mexican reports and those of CJAM. In rare cases a Japanese Mexican or national filed a complaint that provided some detail of their personal experience either at the haciendas or their contact with Mexican officials. The most common were complaints against Mexican officials seeking bribes for a multitude of reasons. There are also a handful of letters from various individuals requesting to be sent to the various haciendas or relocated to a new state or city for employment purposes. There were many individuals who were destitute and their survival often was in the hands of the CJAM. For example, one letter was sent to the Director of CJAM, Luis Tsuji, in April 1943 from the immigration detention center at Perote, Veracruz. Nine detained Japanese were pleading to Tsuji to have them relocated to the hacienda because of the deplorable conditions at the detention center. One of the individuals that signed the letter was Ernesto Benito Naito Hirokichi, discussed in chapter 5, who was suspected of espionage.[46]

As mentioned at the beginning of this chapter, the fact that the Japanese Mexicans had found a place to live and subsist, such as the haciendas, did not necessarily equate to a life removed from the emergency measures taking place in Mexico, nor did it mean that they had provisions. Indeed, in the early months of their establishment the haciendas struggled to provide the basic necessities for survival. Relief of a sort came when various Japanese and groups collectively pooled their resources as a means to jump-start the communal camp to life.

Kiso Tsuru, Sanshiro Matsumoto, and Heiji Kato provided over 60 percent of the initial funding for the CJAM. This seed money allowed the Japanese who resided at the Hacienda de Temixco to purchase equipment, seeds, and materials needed to begin planting subsistence crops and to refurbish the hacienda to a livable condition. By December 1942 nearly 200 Japanese were residing at the Hacienda de Temixco and conditions were crowded and unsanitary. Based on a report issued by Dr. Felipe García Sánchez, head of the health department for the state of Morelos, one of his main concerns was the overcrowded condition where children slept and played. García Sánchez's other main concern was the unsanitary and makeshift toilets created at the hacienda that drained raw sewage into the area. He urgently requested that the state government provide funds to construct septic tanks to treat the sewage. García Sánchez also recommended sanitary and updated bathing facilities for the proper hygiene of the residents at Temixco.[47]

Ultimately, the haciendas that became de facto internment camps provided a safe haven for the most destitute of Japanese Mexicans uprooted from their homes. The wartime measures enacted by the Mexican government also reinforced the importance of prewar organizations such as the Japanese associations that morphed into CJAM and became an important lifeline during the war.

Conclusion

Mexico's directive that all Japanese relocate to Guadalajara and Mexico City resulted in a substantial increase of Japanese in those cities. Furthermore, since the Mexican government did not directly round up the Japanese Mexicans for confinement, the Japanese bore the burden of their relocation and daily subsistence in their new communities. Since little to no financial assistance emerged from the federal government, the Japanese in Mexico City and Guadalajara each organized mutual aid societies to facilitate their relocation. The Mexico City Japanese created the Comité Japonés de Ayuda Mutua (Japanese Committee for Mutual Aide) and Guadalajara created a sister organization known as the sub-Comité Japonés de Ayuda Mutua. These organizations worked in tandem securing living arrangements for those Japanese that asked for their assistance. The uniqueness of these two organizations is that each procured the purchase of haciendas as self-sustaining communes for Japanese Mexicans who volunteered to reside at the haciendas. The only requirement was that each adult had to perform agriculture labor.

By early 1943 the residents at Temixco settled in and implemented the necessary changes to bring the hacienda up to date and to safe standards. Also, the population at the hacienda fluctuated due to new arrivals and departures to other regions of Mexico. It should be recalled that the Japanese Mexicans were allowed to move about in Mexico, with proper travel documentation, as long as they did not enter the prohibitive zones. Once the Japanese residents of the haciendas were able to find permanent employment in such places as Mexico City, many left the difficult confines of the cooperative. The Japanese at Temixco also transitioned to Guadalajara, and some even requested to move to the Hacienda Castro Urdiales in Jalisco. The population at the Hacienda de Temixco reached into the hundreds by February 1943 and had a transitory population for the duration of the war. The initial Japanese internees were given permission to reside at the hacienda in return for their labor on the hacienda. This was a common condition and agreement reached by the Japanese residents and CJAM.[48]

The primary function of CJAM was to facilitate the movement of the Japanese away from the coasts and into the federal district of Mexico City or Guadalajara. To be precise, the Mexican government ordered all Japanese in the country to move ninety-three miles from the coasts and borders.[49] The Comité Japonés de Ayuda Mutua received permission from the secretary of the interior, Miguel Aleman, to act as an intermediary between the Mexican government and the Japanese population. This organization also functioned as a clearing-house for the movement in and out of two camps created by the Japanese. CJAM attempted to ensure the peaceful transition into the city of the newly arrived Japanese and their protection. The organization also helped in finding employment for the approximately 3,500 new Japanese residents in the areas of Mexico City.[50]

The evacuation of Japanese from border areas and various parts of the interior to Mexico City and Guadalajara was carried out in great haste with many losing homes, possessions, property, and businesses. However, the leadership, the community, and sense of collectivity they shared allowed the Japanese Mexicans to survive the nearly four years of wartime uncertainty. The establishment of CJAM and the placement of Japanese into hacienda internment camps created a sense of community and the ability to persevere. The wartime policies of Mexico uprooted the Japanese, but at the same time, reinforced their interdependence, group solidarity, and cultural bonds. Moreover, except for security regulations already noted, the Mexican government refrained from imposing restrictions that would destroy the Japanese national and cultural identity. The creation of CJAM is an excellent example of the Mexican government's approach that differed widely from other governments in the Americas. Prohibitions against Japanese elementary schools were removed in 1944, and all wartime restrictions were lifted in late 1945.

Conclusion

I Am 60 Percent Mexican and 60 Percent Japanese

The experience of the Japanese in Mexico during World War II can be understood only by examining their arrival in Mexico nearly five decades earlier. The central focus of this book has been to illustrate a very different experience for Japanese in Mexico than that experienced by Japanese elsewhere. Some of those differences include no discernible pattern of marginalization within Mexico and a high degree of intermarriages and integration into Mexican society. Yet, a careful examination of this experience also demonstrates that Japanese Mexicans shared some commonalities with other Japanese diasporas in the Americas. Some of those similarities included economic struggles, discrimination, racism, and displacement. This book has also been about the Mexican state and how it treated its Japanese population during difficult periods of its history. Mexico's treatment of the Japanese was predicated on several factors that included a general acceptance of the Japanese diaspora, cordial relations with the Japanese empire, and a small Japanese population that did not threaten the native population, but rather integrated itself for survival. The triangular relations between Mexico, Japan, and the United States also affected the Japanese experience in Mexico. Furthermore, beyond simply telling an academic story, the aim of this book was to uncover the Japanese experience in Mexico that has not just been forgotten but, rather, largely unknown.

Mexicans of Japanese ancestry existed in Mexico since the colonial period and increasingly arrived during the nineteenth century as tourists, diplomats, or foreign exchange students. However, it was not until the late nineteenth century that a concerted effort was made to send permanent

Japanese immigrants to Mexico. More important, the Mexican and Japanese governments sponsored the first official movement of Japanese to Mexico. Although these first movements of Japanese to Chiapas met with mixed results, they it became the catalyst for Japanese immigration to other regions of Mexico. Initially, many Japanese came under contract to work in Mexico as unskilled labor. During the first decade of the twentieth century, Japanese settled in the northern regions of Mexico to take advantage of socioeconomic opportunities in agriculture, mining, and mercantile businesses, but also due to its close proximity to the United States. During the first decade of the twentieth century nearly 10,000 Japanese immigrated to Mexico, yet by 1910 many disappeared into regions of the United States using Mexico as a back door before and after the implementation of the Japanese Gentlemen's Agreement.

The first decade of the twentieth century also represented the ascendancy of the Japanese empire. The rise of Japan and its control of the eastern orbit had several consequences for the Japanese in the Americas. In general, countries such as the United States viewed Japanese immigrants with suspicion, as possible agents for Japan, and as a fifth column waiting to unleash havoc or at the very least gathering intelligence for the Japanese empire. Additionally, Japan and Japanese immigrants were viewed as inferior and not fit for citizenship. This was not unlike the views of the Chinese in the United States and the Americas in general. The Japanese were also enveloped in a similar orientalization schema that was pervasive in the United States, Mexico, and elsewhere. The United States, through legislation, public discourse, and hegemony pushed the Orientalism of all Asians, which reverberated throughout the Western hemisphere. However, in Mexico two competing images developed for the Japanese: one that was similar to the Japanese experience in the United States and another that was unique to Mexico. As the Japanese empire ascended and challenged Western powers a significant portion of the Mexican population viewed the Japanese with admiration. Additionally, many Mexicans respected the military prowess of Japan and assumed all Japanese inherited an innate ability to fight. As a consequence, Japanese immigrants in Mexico were seen in a different light, especially compared with the Chinese diaspora. This difference imbued them with elements of whiteness, due to a perception that Japan not only reached parity with Western military powers but also defeated them, thus placing the Japanese on par with the West. Seen from the perspective of military dominance Japan reached a level of parity with the West measured by conquest and colonialism. By the early twentieth century, Mexico and Japan established friendly relations.

By the time of the Mexican Revolution in 1910 Mexican-Japanese relations were cordial, but both countries were at odds with the United States, which complicated the Japanese experience in Mexico. Although Mexico denied any alliance with the Japanese empire, it nevertheless used the deteriorating Japanese-US relations as leverage to antagonize the United States as an early form of diplomatic weapons of the weak. Furthermore, by the time of the Mexican Revolution a significant number of Japanese had settled in Mexico and were drawn into the conflict as civilian casualties, combatants, mercenaries and spies. The United States viewed all things Japanese with suspicion and made no differentiation between Japanese nationals, military attaches, or Japanese Mexicans. Spilling over the US-Mexican borderlands was the so-called Yellow Peril that entangled Japanese-Mexicans as many were accused of being imperial soldiers in the guise of farmers, merchants, and fishermen. The Orientalization of the Japanese in the Americas continued unabated, which grew as Japan gained strength, territory, and the United States shifted its antagonism from the Chinese to the Japanese diaspora, which filtered into Mexico.

Leading up to the outbreak of the Mexican Revolution and compared with other foreign groups in Mexico, the Japanese diaspora remained relatively small. Much of the Japanese population in Mexico remained in unskilled positions with a small number as successful merchants in the northern regions of the country and as far south as Chiapas. Furthermore, the majority of the Japanese immigrants were men who married Mexican women, which facilitated their transition and integration into Mexican society. Because of this integration various revolutionary factions did not see the Japanese as a threat. However, this did not completely prevent atrocities committed against the Japanese. As Mexican nationalism grew in the early years of the revolution, groups such as the Chinese, Japanese, and Americans became victims of robbery, murder, and indiscriminate violence. The Japanese in Mexico filed numerous complaints with the Mexican and Japanese governments. In many cases Japanese were mistaken as Chinese and killed outright as in the massacre in Torreón. In this two-day frenzy, more than 300 Chinese and Japanese immigrants were murdered by Maderista soldiers. In a paradoxical twist, most of the revolutionary factions welcomed with open arms any Japanese male who wanted to fight within their ranks based on the belief that all Japanese had been trained as imperial soldiers. By the end of the violent period of the revolution the Japanese experience ranged from combatant to victim to mercenary.

As the violence subsided Mexico attempted to rebuild as a nation. Germane to the Japanese experience was a national debate on immigration, which eventually revolved around the ideas of race and which groups were best suited to meet the needs of Mexico. Mexico encouraged and preferred European immigrants, but when very few came to Mexico it opted for secondary groups such as Middle Easterners and Asians. During the 1920s and 1930s the Japanese population became more diverse regarding occupations, location, and integration within Mexican society. Japanese immigration to Mexico continued during the post-revolutionary period bringing a better educated segment compared with the previous decades. At the same time the Japanese population in Mexico was increasing, relations between Japan and the United States remained strained with Mexico and on the defensive regarding its Japanese population and cordial relations with the Japanese empire. There was also a resurgence of nativism and nationalism within Mexico that heavily targeted the Chinese, but for the first time Japanese Mexicans became targets of xenophobia. In general, the Mexican state faced many internal and external challenges during this period, especially from its northern neighbor.

Since the nineteenth century Mexican-US relations remained under strain due to large segments of Mexico having been invaded and conquered by the United States, but also due to US intervention in Mexico and Latin American during the early part of the twentieth century. The Mexican Revolution also resulted in a large number of land claims against the Mexican government by US citizens that remained unresolved well into the 1930s. The election of Mexican president Lázaro Cárdenas in 1934 signaled a new era in Mexico that pushed it left of the political spectrum. As Mexican nationalism grew President Cárdenas nationalized the railroad and oil industry, which added additional strain to US-Mexican relations. In this manner, Mexico used one of the few options it had regarding relations with the United States: it limited access to its natural resources and delayed negotiations on issues of land claims, thus deploying "diplomatic weapons of the weak." By using such tactics, Mexico was able to achieve some measure of success against a much stronger United States. Additionally, I have argued that such strategies also impacted the position of the Japanese in Mexico as the United States reconfigured all Japanese as enemies throughout the Americas. As World War II broke out this reconfiguration was coupled with a barrage of US propaganda directed toward the Japanese empire and all Japanese residing in the Western hemisphere.

Long before the outbreak of World War II, the Japanese residing in the United States had been demonized to the point that when war broke out the Japanese empire and Japanese Americans were viewed as the same entity. This unfortunate position for Japanese Americans made it a simple transition to shift their position from loyal US citizen to round ups to internment camps. In Mexico and some other regions of Latin America such a position was not as simple. In fact, when Pearl Harbor was bombed Mexico did not react in the same manner as the United States. By this I mean Japanese Mexicans were not seen as public enemy number one. Although Mexico broke diplomatic ties with Japan in December 1941, the Japanese residing in Mexico were not demonized in the same manner. This was problematic for the US government as it mobilized for war domestically and throughout the Western hemisphere.

To achieve complete hemispheric solidarity and defense the United States conducted a sweeping propaganda campaign that reached all levels of Mexican society, while simultaneously pushing negative images of Japan and of Japanese residing in Mexico as possible saboteurs, sleeper agents, or simply not trustworthy based on their ethnicity. To shore up any lingering doubts about the dangers of the Japanese empire and Japanese in Mexico, a sense of fear needed to be created. As part of this multifaceted campaign a process of racialism of the Japanese Mexicans became necessary, which was conducted by various propaganda agencies and news outlets utilized by the US government, the most important being the Office of Inter-American Affairs. This racialism had already been conducted successfully against many groups in the United States that included the Chinese, Japanese, and Mexicans. These aforementioned groups had been reconfigured as the other groups that were seen as different based on physical or socially defined characteristics that perpetuated racism. Racializing the Japanese in Mexico was simply a matter of propaganda and persistence. Unfortunately for the Japanese this process had already begun with the process of Western hemispheric Orientalism discussed earlier. Using hemispheric Orientalism as a launching pad the US government created popular magazines and hired US and Latin American based journalists to write stories that promoted the US agenda of the war effort at all levels including the suspicious nature of all Japanese in the hemisphere. Furthermore, military and civilian personnel and the FBI wrote and disseminated unsubstantiated claims of Japanese sleeper cells in Mexico and Japanese invasion plans of the United States through Mexico. This vast network of propaganda had its desired effect and Mexico let loose its own form of propaganda to aid in the war effort. However, Mexico directed its propaganda toward the Japanese empire instead of the Japanese residing in Mexico. Nevertheless, when Mexico declared war on Japan and joined the Allied effort it removed, displaced, and forcibly relocated thousands of Japanese Mexicans.

Although Mexico was pressured by the United States to curtail the movement of Japanese to Mexico, limit its diplomatic relations with the Japanese empire, and when World War II broke out round up and intern the Japanese in similar fashion to the United States, Mexico refused. Indeed, Mexico did not declare war on Mexico for nearly seven months after the bombing of Pearl Harbor. This declaration of war meant that the lives of Japanese in Mexico became tense as they waited to see if their lives would follow their counterparts in the United States. In the end, no amount of assimilation or integration into Mexican society prevented the forced removal of Japanese Mexicans from their homes and mandatory relocation to the interior of Mexico. When the Mexican government ordered the round up and evacuation of all Japanese along the Mexican coastlines and its northern border there was no War Relocation Authority to handle the forced relocation, detention, and internment of Japanese Mexicans, no army going house-to-house rounding up the Japanese, and no iconic images of Japanese Mexicans boarding trains at gunpoint. Instead, Mexico developed a helter-skelter program of self-removal to the interior of Mexico, specifically to the cities of Guadalajara and Mexico City. Japanese Mexicans forced to relocate lost their homes, livelihood, property, and life savings. And due to no government oversight many Japanese arrived in Guadalajara and Mexico City destitute and unemployed. Yet, the Japanese experience in Mexico during World War II was not monolithic. Many Japanese, such as those in Chiapas, were spared from relocation at the behest of the state government. Others were caught up in the hysteria of the period and interned for the duration of the war in either penal colonies in Mexico or sent to the United States for internment. Although the outbreak of World War II disrupted and changed the lives of Japanese Mexicans forever, they were not passive victims. The Japanese in Mexico defended their community and mobilized it during this time of crisis.

As the Japanese populations swelled in Mexico City and Guadalajara, resources were quickly depleted, unemployment was rampant, and housing was in short supply. The Japanese Mexican community approached the World War II crisis in two significant ways. First, long-standing Japanese community leaders in Mexico City allowed their farms to be used as temporary housing such as Rancho Batán. Simultaneously, community leaders pooled their resources and purchased the ex-hacienda Temixco in the state of Morelos and Mexican landowners allowed the Hacienda Castro Urdiales in Guadalajara to be used in a similar fashion as Temixco. These two haciendas became quasi-internment camps where the most destitute of the displaced Japanese interned themselves as a mode of survival and isolation from the harsh realities of the war. Second, and more important, from the remnants of the disbanded Japanese associations the community organized the Comité Japonés de Ayuda Mutua (Japanese Mutual Aid Committee). This organization became the de facto representative of the Japanese population during the war. The Comité Japonés de Ayuda Mutua also provided assistance and became a clearinghouse for the placement of Japanese who had been displaced and relocated. The Comité Japonés de Ayuda Mutua also managed the camps of Temixco and Castro Urdiales. Finally, the Comité Japonés de Ayuda Mutua represented a form of resistance to the harsh conditions of World War II. Mexico's inability or unwillingness to provide assistance to the displaced Japanese community allowed the Japanese to reconfigure the outlawed and disbanded Japanese associations under the guise of the Comité Japonés de Ayuda Mutua. Indeed, the leadership of this organization was comprised primarily of the heads of the individual associations from throughout Mexico. The Comité Japonés de Ayuda Mutua became an important link to the prewar Japanese community, provided the initial funding for the purchase and maintenance of the haciendas, and maintained high-level contact with the Mexican government to ensure the welfare of the Japanese community in Mexico.

The Hacienda de Temixco and the Hacienda Castro Urdiales were camps for Japanese during World War II. These were not internment or concentration camps in the vein of the US version, but rather locations where Japanese Mexicans voluntarily went to live, albeit as a result of suspicions on part of the US and Mexicans governments. These camps, unlike their counterparts in the United States, had no barbed wire fences, no guards with machine guns, and the Japanese Mexicans were free to move about, although with permission and restricted to the interior of the country. In official documentation the Japanese in these haciendas were described as *Japoneses concentrados* or *campo de concentración de Japoneses*, the latter literally "Japanese concentration camp." Hacienda de Temixco contained individuals who had been relocated to Mexico City and Castro Urdiales those Japanese resettled in Guadalajara. Based on the initial directive, Mexico City and Guadalajara were citywide relocation sites. These two cities were the designated areas for those Japanese uprooted and relocated from strategic military zones. The Comité Japonés de Ayuda Mutua, whose leadership was gleaned from the various Japanese associations that existed throughout the country before the war, became the nucleus that maintained a sense of community for the relocated

Japanese Mexicans who organized it for self-sufficiency. Most important, it was CJAM, through its own form of weapons of the weak that kept the United States from relocating the Japanese Mexicans to the United States and convincing the Mexican government to provide CJAM with a level of autonomy during the war. CJAM lasted until January 1950 when it was disbanded and reorganized in 1951 as the Japanese Association of Mexico City.[1] Overall, very little has been written about the Japanese Mexican experience in Mexico and the World War II period. Also absent from Mexico's World War II experience are the various camps that housed displaced Japanese Mexicans.

Mexican officials of the 1940s and today, along with the Japanese Mexicans called Temixco a "concentration camp." After reading thousands of pages of documents on the Japanese experience I believe it was the intent of Mexican officials and the Japanese Mexicans to convey that at Temixco hundreds of Japanese were concentrated in a camp, not imprisoned or incarcerated. However, in some manner making such a distinction is irrelevant since all of these Japanese would not have been within the confines of these haciendas had they not been displaced and forced to relocate. Official Mexican documents as well as letters from Japanese Mexicans to government officials all used the Spanish word for concentration, *concentración* or *concentrados*, to be concentrated in one location. For example, in a letter dated December 17, 1942, the head of the sanitation services for the state of Morelos, Dr. Felipe García Sánchez, wrote to the secretary of the interior,

> With the approval of this Ministry a Japanese concentration camp has been created at the ancient hacienda of Temixco and is headed by Mr. Shybayema Takugoro [*sic*]—The Japanese have proceeded to build wooden huts small houses of wood to shelter 200 people.[2]

Unlike their US counterparts, government officials did not shy away from using terms like "concentration camp" or "colony" when referring to Temixco. Others have deemed the use of the phrase "concentration camp" for the experience of the Japanese incarcerated during World War II controversial and by some acceptable. One of the preeminent scholars on the Japanese American experience during World War II, Roger Daniels, argues that the use of the term "concentration camp" is justified for those Japanese held by US authorities and writes, "The American camps were not death camps, but they were surrounded by barbed wire and by troops whose guns were pointed at the inmates."[3] Angelo N. Ancheta, in *Race,*

Rights, and the Asian American Experience, uses the terms "internment" and "concentration camps" without apology.[4] However, Greg Robinson, in *A Tragedy of Democracy*, is conflicted over the use of the term "concentration camp" to describe the Japanese experience during World War II and uses terms such as "removal," "confinement," "camp," and "inmate," but never "internment" or "concentration camp." Many seem to associate the term "concentration camp" only through the lens of the Nazis regime and the death camps that followed.[5] Using such a position limits our understanding of the overall Japanese experience in the camps erected to concentrate and confine Japanese in various places in the Americas. With few exceptions, most of the Japanese in Mexico were forced to relocate to Guadalajara and Mexico City and although not surrounded by barbed wire most felt violated on multiple levels. Furthermore, at each hacienda the Mexican government appointed Mexican officials to oversee the facility. Daniels has documented that nearly 2,000 Japanese died in the American concentration camps with some "accidentally" killed by their American guards.[6] Temixco and Urdiales also recorded deaths within the walls of their haciendas. If Mexico indeed had similar concentration camps they were likely located at the federal detention center in Peroté in the state of Veracruz or the federal penal colony of La Isla de Tres Marías (Madre)[7] west of Nayarit. Each of these facilities incarcerated enemy aliens during World War II that included Japanese.

Although we temper our excitement regarding the Mexican response to its Japanese residents during World War II, Mexico took a different approach. Yes, the Japanese Mexicans were uprooted and displaced from many locales, but as a whole they were not interned in prison camps. Further, there was an element of sympathy toward the Japanese population from the Mexican population, unlike in the United States. Also, the Japanese did not meet the same fate as the Chinese in the previous decades where hundreds of Chinese were massacred and forced to leave Mexico altogether because of strong nationalistic fervor, racial animosity, and hatred. Two possible explanations for this include a much higher rate of adaptation and acculturation on part of the Japanese and the intermarriages between Japanese men and Mexican women. Lastly, unlike the Chinese, the Japanese were not seen as a numerical threat and were not viewed as jeopardizing the national identity of Mexico premised on a European and indigenous background or the so-called *Mexicanidad* of the nation. Anti-Chinese movements in Mexico promoted the argument that the Chinese posed an economic threat, but in reality this was simply a guise for the racism directed toward the Chinese. In the final analysis, it is imperative that the contrast between the fate of Japanese in Mexico and other places like the United States be recognized, but also be placed into perspective, especially from the Japanese Mexicans that lived through this period. The documentation of the Japanese experience in Mexico during World War II clearly shows a higher level of empathy on part of Mexican officials; nevertheless, Japanese Mexicans experienced psychological trauma and displacement reminiscent of Japanese Americans in the United States.

The events of World War II and the relocation of the Japanese population in Mexico changed the entire demographic pattern of the Japanese community. It broke up the prewar distribution pattern, produced a larger concentration of Japanese in Mexico City and Guadalajara, and gave impetus to the reformation of the Japanese community with a reinforced ethnic identity. With the end of World War II, Japanese immigration to Mexico continued but nowhere near the level of the pre-1940 period. However, a survey by the Japanese government in 1954, located approximately 5,600 Japanese residing in Mexico with the majority in Guadalajara and Mexico City.[8] In 1957 the Mexican government paid 700,000 pesos as reparations to the Japanese community in Mexico for their suffering and loss during the war.[9] Japanese business interests matched the Mexican funds and the result was the purchase of land and the establishment of the Mexico Japanese Association located in the Colonia Las Águilas, Mexico City. This association's primary function is to preserve Japanese culture, history, and document the Japanese experience in Mexico. It took the United States forty-three years (1988) to issue an apology and reparations to Japanese Americans. By 1980 one source puts the Japanese descendant population in Mexico at over 12,000 individuals.[10] One contemporary source indicates there are approximately 35,000 Mexicans of Japanese ancestry residing in Mexico. Very little has been written regarding the Japanese population in Mexico during the post-World War II period. More important, many questions regarding Japanese reentry into the larger Mexican society after 1945 remain unanswered. In recent years many Japanese Mexicans who were either detainees as adults or children and their descendants have come forward providing personal accounts of their experiences or their relatives'.

"We Had the Best Concentration Camp in the World!": Understanding the Japanese Mexican Experience

In a recent interview a Mexican of Japanese ancestry responded, "I am sixty percent Mexican and sixty percent Japanese."[11] Carlos Kasuga Osaka, who provided that quote, was born in Mexico to Japanese parents who immigrated in the 1930s. Carlos is the founder and president of the Japanese Mexican School, director general of Yakult, which produces a probiotic health care product, and president of the Pan American Nikkei Association.[12] Like so many other Japanese who were rounded up and relocated his words convey a very different experience from other Japanese in the Americas during World War II, "In spite of the suffering, I have to give some thanks to the Mexican government. We had the best concentration camp in the world! In Mexico City, we had access to schools and the chance to get an education."[13] And seventy-nine-year-old Francisca Ono de Takemura echoes those sentiments even though she and her family were forcibly removed from their home during World War II. Like so many other Japanese Mexicans with identical experiences she holds no animosity toward Mexico. In fact, she is quick to praise the generosity of the Mexicans throughout the years:

> They say that in some countries in South America the Japanese were not treated well. In Mexico we are held in high esteem. I am Mexican by birth and it is an honor because Mexico is a very worthy country. We are happy our parents came to Mexico, because here we have lived contentedly.[14]

The interviews above are excellent illustrations of the complex Mexican Japanese experience, where, on the one hand, the Japanese in Mexico shared a similar dilemma to other Japanese populations in the Americas during World War II. Like so many others Japanese Mexicans, they were forced to uproot from long established homes and relocate into the interior of Mexico losing generations of investment, community development, and their homes. On the other hand, as mentioned by Kasuga and Takemura, these individuals did not feel the level of oppression that other Japanese felt, such as those Japanese in the United States, and express benevolent feelings toward the Mexican government or at the very least acknowledge their experience was different than others during the war. However, this is not to say all Japanese Mexicans who were uprooted during the war share the same attitudes as Kasuga and Takemura. Indeed, in many instances I have also illustrated that some Japanese in Mexico felt violated and bewildered as to why they were being forced from their homes, which resulted in displacement and destitution. What is certain is that this multifaceted experience left a lasting impact on Mexico and the Japanese. The descendants of the original Japanese settlers are thriving in many areas throughout Mexico and many are searching for roots long ago lost to the nearly complete integration into Mexican society by their ancestors.

One hundred and seventeen years have passed since the first official arrival of Japanese to Mexico and the Nikkei are well established in the contemporary period.[15] José Martín Normura Hernandez was the municipal president of the community of Acacoyagua, Chiapas, with a population of approximately 15,000 people, from 2005 to 2007. José followed a path of politics laid down before him by previous generations of Mexicans of Japanese ancestry residing in Acacoyagua. In fact, individuals of Japanese ancestry have been municipal presidents of this community dating back to the early 1950s when Juvencio Nishizama Cruz occupied the position from 1954 to 1955.[16] Acacoyagua, in the region of Soconusco, Chiapas is considered ground zero and the foundation of the Japanese immigrant community in Mexico. The original Enomoto colony landed off the coast of Soconusco at Puerto Madero (Puerto Benito in 1897). José Martin is a descendant of one of the earliest Japanese immigrants to Mexico. José's great-grandfather was José Nomura, who arrived in Mexico from Yamaguchi Prefecture in Japan during the Mexican Revolution.[17] With its long established Japanese community, the municipality of Acacoyagua is considered to have one of the largest concentrations of individuals of Japanese ancestry in Mexico and according to José Martín, "It is no doubt one of the few towns in Mexico where white rice is a dietary staple."[18] Far removed from World War II, the descendants of the earlier pioneers feel comfortable discussing their ethnic background and simultaneously exhibit a sense of pride regarding their Japanese ancestry.

Harumi Quezada Yamamoto traces her history to the original Japanese immigrants. Harumi's great-grandfather, Asahiro Yamamoto, is one of the original Enomoto colonists who arrived in Mexico in 1897. Harumi sees herself as not only Mexican but also Nikkei, and proudly proclaims, "I am Mexican, but I am proud of my Japanese heritage."[19] And like other Mexicans of Japanese ancestry from her generation she is attempting to rediscover her Japanese heritage by studying the Japanese language and other customs. However, Harumi is quick to point out that "my upbringing at home inculcated Japanese values, like discipline, honor and loyalty, but you must adapt to the country where you live and take the best from each culture. Mexican people are hardworking, warm, spontaneous. One can share these different approaches to life."[20]

And Patricia Murakami, forty-one years of age, shared the following story that parallels the experience of many immigrant groups. While on a trip to New York City she had her passport stolen. As a Mexican national she went to the Mexican consulate and was turned away. "They told me, 'this is not the place, you're Asian' . . . In Japan we are not Japanese, and in Mexico we are not Mexican."[21] Something in common that most Japanese Mexicans share is a love and attachment to Mexico. For some, like the fifth-generation Mexicans of Japanese ancestry, it is the only place they know as home. Yet, for those old enough to remember the hardships and trauma, they too, maintain an affinity for Mexico. [Yoshiya] Nishimura articulated this sentiment, "I was born in Mexico. I am 80 years old and the end is nearing. Yes I go to Japan to visit but where to live day to day where to die and be buried, it's Mexico."[22]

Notes

Introduction

1. Yukihiro Tsunoyama, *Enomoto Buyo to Mekishiko Shokumin Iju* (*Buyo Enomoto and Migration to Mexican Settlements*) (Tokyo: Dobunkan, 1986), 185–98.

2. Akemi Kikumura-Yano, ed., *Encyclopedia of Japanese Descendants in the Americas: An Illustrated History of the Nikkei* (New York: AltaMira Press, 2002). This encyclopedia has the most extensive bibliography on the Japanese experience in the Americas, but especially for the region of Latin America. In Latin America the countries with extensive literature on Japanese migration and history include Argentina, Bolivia, Brazil, Chile, Mexico, Paraguay, and Peru.

3. Rudy P. Guevarra, Jr., *Becoming Mexipino: Multiethnic Identities and Communities in San Diego* (New Brunswick, NJ: Rutgers University Press, 2012).

4. Lane Ryo Hirabayashi, Akemi Kikumura-Yano, and James Aikira Hirabayashi, eds., *New Worlds, New Lives: Globalization and the People of Japanese Descent in the Americas and from Latin America in Japan* (Stanford, CA: Stanford University Press, 2002). According to the Discover Nikkei website, the term *Nikkei* is defined in the following manner: "We are talking about Nikkei people—Japanese emigrants and their descendants who have created communities throughout the world. The term nikkei has multiple and diverse meanings depending on situations, places, and environments. Nikkei also include people of mixed racial descent who identify themselves as Nikkei. Native Japanese also use the term nikkei for the emigrants and their descendants who return to Japan. Many of these nikkei live in close communities and retain identities separate from the native Japanese." Visit http://www.discovernikkei.org/en/about/what-is-nikkei/ for a longer discussion.

5. Richard S. Nishimoto, *Inside an American Concentration Camp: Japanese American Resistance in Poston*, with an introduction and postscript by Lane Ryo Hirabayashi (Tucson: University of Arizona Press, 1995); Lane Ryo Hirabayashi, "Community Destroyed? Assessing the Impact of the Loss of Community on Japanese Americans during World War II," in *Re/Collecting Asian America*, Josephene Lee et al., eds. (Philadelphia: Temple University, 2002), 94–107; Hirabayashi, A. Kikumura-Yano, and J. Hirabayashi, "Preface," in *New Worlds, New Lives*; Hirabayashi and A. Kikumura-Yano, "Japanese Latin Americans during World War II: A Reconsideration," in *Japanese Diasporas: Unsung Pasts, Conflicting Presents, and Uncertain Futures*, ed. Nobuko Adachi et al. (New York: Routledge, 2006), 159–71.

6. Jeffrey Lesser, *Negotiating National Identity: Immigrants, Minorities, and the Struggle for Ethnicity in Brazil* (Durham, NC: Duke University Press, 1999); Hirabayashi et al., *New Worlds, New Lives*; Daniel M. Masterson and Sayaka Funada-Classen, *The Japanese in Latin America* (Urbana: University of Illinois Press, 2004).

7. María Elena Ota Mishima, *México y Japón en el Siglo XIX: La política exterior de México y la consolidación de la soberanía Japonesa* (México, DF: Secretaría de Relaciones Exteriores, 1976); Ota Mishima, *Siete Migraciones Japonesas en México, 1890–1978* (México, DF: Colegio de México, 1982); Ota Mishima, *Destino México: Un Estudio de las Migraciones Asiáticas a México, Siglos XIX y XX* (México, DF: Colegio de México, 1997); Enrique Cortés, *Relaciones entre México y Japón durante el Porfiriato* (México, DF: Secretaría de Relaciones Exteriores, 1990). Outside of Japan and the Japanese language, Maria Elena Ota Mishima's and Enrique Cortes's scholarship on the Japanese experience in Mexico comprises the only published material providing any historical information on the Japanese in Mexico.

8. Ramon Guerra, "Continuity and Change: Japanese Ethnicity in Guadalajara, Mexico" (Ph.D. diss., Southern Methodist University, 1989); Chizuko Watanabe, "The Japanese Immigrant Community in Mexico: Its History and Present" (M.A. thesis, California State University, Los Angeles, 1983); Iyo Imura Kunimoto, "Japan and Mexico, 1888–1917" (Ph.D. diss., University of Texas at Austin, 1975).

9. For excellent essays and coverage on Japanese in the Americas, as well as an extensive bibliography for sources on Japanese immigration to the Americas in English, Japanese, Spanish, and Portuguese, see Hirabayashi et al., *New Worlds, New Lives*; and Kikumura-Yano, *Encyclopedia of Japanese Descendants in the Americas*.

10. Informative sources in Japanese examining Japanese immigration and the movement to Mexico include Hisashi Ueno, *Mekishiko Enomoto Shokumin* (Tokyo: Chuo Koron-Sha, 1994); Masaaki Kodama, *Nihon Imin-Shi Kankyu Josetsu* (*Introduction to the Study of Japanese Immigration History*) (Hiroshima: Keisui-sha, 1992); Atsuko Yamamoto, *Mekishiko in Ikiru Nikkei Immintachi* (Tokyo: Kawaide Shobo Shinsha, 1988); Yukihiro Tsunoyama, *Enomoto Buyo to Mekishiko Shokumin Iju* (*Buyo Enomoto and Migration to Mexican Settlements*) (Tokyo: Dobunkan, 1986); Motohiro Takayama, *Mekishiko ni Kakeru Yume: Hagita Masanosuke to Nikkei Iminno Sekai* (Tokyo: Heibonsha, 1986); and Japanese Mexican Immigrant History Compilation Committee, *Nihon Mekishiko Imin* (Tokyo, 1971). Overall, approximately twenty-five book-length studies in Japanese examine the movement of Japanese to Mexico. Most are cited in Kikumura-Yano, *Encyclopedia of Japanese Descendants in the Americas*.

11. For Maria Elena Ota Mishima, see her *Destino México, Siete Migraciones Japonesas*, and *México y Japón en el Siglo XIX*.

12. These ideas are articulated by Erika Lee in a number of different publications. See Lee, "Hemispheric Orientalism and the 1907 Pacific Coast Race Riots," *Amerasia Journal* 33, no. 2 (2007), 19–47; "Orientalism in the Americas: A hemispheric Approach to Asian American History," *Journal of Asian American Studies* 8, no. 3 (October 2005), 235–58; Erika Lee and Naoko Shibusawa, "What Is Transnational Asian American History? Recent Trends and Challenges," *Journal of Asian American Studies* 8, no. 3 (October 2005), vii–xvii.

13. Edward W. Said, *Orientalism* (New York: Vintage Books, 1979), 2–4.

14. Erika Lee, "Orientalism in the Americas," 235–58.

15. Although there have been a significant number of articles on the Chinese in Mexico, most notably those by historian Evelyn Hu-Dehart, very few book-length studies exist on the Chinese in Mexico. Exceptions include Robert Romero, *The Chinese in Mexico, 1882–1940* (Tucson: University of Arizona Press, 2010); Grace Delgado, *Making the Chinese Mexican: Global Migration, Localism, and Exclusion in the US-Mexican Borderlands* (Palo Alto, CA: Stanford University Press, 2012); and Julia Schiavone Camacho, *Chinese Mexicans: Transpacific Migrations, and the Search for a Homeland, 1910–1960* (Chapel Hill: University of North Carolina Press, 2012). For articles, see Charles C. Cumberland, "The Sonoran Chinese and the Mexican Revolution," *Hispanic American Historical Review* 40, no. 2 (May 1960), 191–211; Evelyn Hu-Dehart, "Immigrants to a Developing Society: The Chinese in Northern Mexico, 1875–1932," *Journal of Arizona History* 21 (Autumn 1980), 274–312; Hu-Dehart, "Racism and Anti-Chinese Persecution in Sonora, Mexico, 1876–1932," *Amerasia Journal* 9. no. 2 (1982), 1–28; Leo M. Jacques, "The Anti-Chinese Legislative and Press Campaign in Sonora, Mexico, 1916–21," *Immigrants and Minorities* 5, no. 2 (July 1986), 167–80; Robert Duncan, "The Chinese and Economic Development of Northern Baja California, 1889–1929," *Hispanic American Historical Review* 74, no. 4 (November 1994), 615–47; Gerardo Rénique, "Race, Region, and Nation: Sonora's Anti-Chinese Racism and Mexico's Postrevolutionary Nationalism, 1920s-1930s," in *Race and Nation in Modern Latin America*, Nancy P. Appelbaum et al., eds. (Chapel Hill: University of North Carolina Press, 2003), 211–36.

16. James C. Scott, *Weapons of the Weak: Everyday Forms of Peasant Resistance*. (New Haven, CT: Yale University Press, 1985), 29–30.

17. Jeffrey W. Rubin, *Decentering the Regime: Ethnicity, Radicalism, and Democracy in Juchitan, Mexico* (Durham, NC: Duke University Press, 1997), 11–14.

Chapter One

1. Census data from Mexico in 1999 estimated the population of Japanese descendants living in Mexico at 15,650.

2. There is no consensus on the term *Nikkei*. One definition indicates that the word refers to individuals of Japanese ancestry living overseas as part of an ethnic identity based on a shared heritage. I use it to refer to the current generation of individuals of Japanese ancestry living in the Americas. For a fuller discussion. see Lane Ryo Hirabayashi, Akemi Kikumura-Yano, and James A, Hirabayashi, eds. *New Worlds, New Lives: Globalization and the People of Japanese Descent in the Americas and from Latin America to Japan* (Palo Alto, CA: Stanford University Press, 2002).

3. Associated Press, "Acacoyagua, Mexico," date unknown, available from America Online, accessed December 31, 1997.

4. Erika Lee, "Hemispheric Orientalism and the 1907 Pacific Coast Race Riots," *Amerasia Journal* 33, no. 2 (2007), 19–47.

5. Jose C. Moya, "A Continent of Immigrants: Postcolonial Shifts in the Western Hemisphere," *Hispanic American Historical Review* 86, no. 1 (February 2006), 3.

6. Jurgen Buchenau, "Small Numbers, Great Impact: Mexico and Its Immigrants, 1821–1973," *Journal of American Ethnic History* 20, no. 3 (Spring 2001), 23–49.

7. John Womack, Jr., "The Mexican Revolution, 1910–1920," in Leslie Bethell, ed., *Mexico since Independence* (Cambridge: Cambridge University Press, 1998), 50.

8. Ibid, 57.

9. Stephen H. Haber, "Assessing the Obstacles to Industrialisation: The Mexican Economy, 1830–1940," *Journal of Latin American Studies* 24, no. 1 (February 1992), 1–32. Haber indicates that many Mexican provinces acted independently from the national government and imposed state taxes or tariffs on goods, regardless of their effects on the national economy.

10. John Mason Hart, *Empire and Revolution: The Americans in Mexico since the Civil War* (Berkeley: University of California Press, 2002), 259.

11. *El Siglo XIX*, October 25, 1871, in Raymond B. Craib III, *Chinese Immigrants in Porfirian Mexico: A Preliminary Study of Settlement, Economic Activity and Anti-Chinese Sentiment*, Occasional Papers, Center for Latin American Studies. (Albuquerque: University of New Mexico, 1998).

12. Hart, *Empire and Revolution*, 259–261.

13. Ibid., 36.

14. Miguel Ramos Lanz, *Estudio sobre Inmigracíon y Colonizacíon*, Tipográfica. de *El Tiempo*, Cerca de Santo. Domingo, no. 4 (1897), 8–9.

15. "Tells Conditions in Mexico: Imperial Government Office of Interior Describes Situation and Needs of Southern Republic," *Chicago Daily Tribune*, July 21, 1901. The following is a quote from the report:

> The First lies in the narrow limits of the consumptive ability of the Mexican population, of whom more than two-thirds are of purely Indian race, who offer a resistance to civilizing influences and their resulting wants which will be difficult to remove . . . the more intelligent Mexicans, therefore, express themselves that with the existing native population it will never be possible to reach a higher economic development; that this can only be hoped for through a large immigration of the white race. For this reason it is the constant endeavor of the Mexican government to attract European immigrants, and ever recurring efforts are made to secure for Mexico, if possible, immigration of the Teutonic race. Even projects for inducing Boers to come here have recently been discussed. Some owners of plantations, especially Americans, have imported Chinamen for farm laborers. This immigration, however, can only be a temporary expedient, as the government as well as the people is not favorably inclined to open the doors to a yellow race mixture.

16. Jose Maria Romero, *Mexico y la Colonizacion* (México, DF: Imprenta de A. Carranza e Hijos, 1901). Other studies that shared similar views include Guillermo Wodon de Sorinne, *La Colonizacion de Mexico* (México, DF: Oficina Tipografica de la Secretaria de Fomento, 1902); Luis Hijar y Haro, *Influencia de la Migracion Europea en el Desarrollo de los Principales Paises de Sud America y La Colonizacion Rural e Mexico con Aquellos Factores Para Simplificar Su Poblema Indigena* (Tacubaya, México: Secretaria de Agricultura y Fomento, 1924).

17. During the French occupation of Mexico (1862–67) Maximilian approved a plan to import Asians to Mexico in an attempt by the French emperor to populate the northern regions of Mexico. The plan, published in 1866, contained the agreement for the formation of a colonization company to import Asians. However, before

it could be implemented Maximilian was removed and executed in 1867, thus ending the venture. See Richard H. Dillon, "Maximilian's Asiatic Colonization Scheme," *Mid-America: An Historical Review* 34 (n.s.) 23, no. 2 (April 1952), 148–52.

18. Alan Knight, "Racism, Revolution, and Indigenismo: Mexico, 1910–1940," in *The Idea of Race in Latin America, 1870–1940*, Richard Graham, ed. (Austin: University of Texas Press, 1990), 73.

19. Buchenau, "Small Numbers, Great Impact," 32.

20. Lamarckian evolution is the idea that an organism can pass on characteristics that it acquired during its lifetime to its offspring. See Alexandra Minna Stern, "Eugenics and Racial Classification in Modern Mexican America," in *Race and Classification: The Case of Mexican America*, Illona Katzew and Susan Deans-Smith, eds. (Palo Alto, CA: Stanford University Press, 2009), 151–73.

21. Knight, "Racism, Revolution, and Indigenismo," 73.

22. Ibid., 72–73.

23. David A. Brading, "Manuel Gamio and Official Indigenismo in Mexico," *Bulletin of Latin American Research* 7, no. 1 (1988), 75–89.

24. Alexandra Minna Stern, "From Mestizophilia to Biology: Racialization and Science of Mexico, 1920–1960," in *Race and Nation in Modern Latin America*, Nancy P. Applebaum, Anne S, Macpherson, and Karin Alejandra Rosemblatt, eds. (Chapel Hill: University of North Carolina Press, 2003), 187–210.

25. *Indigenismo* was the movement in postrevolutionary Mexico that attempted to resurrect the indigenous past as a form of nationalism and the incorporation of the Indian into Mexican society.

26. Buchenau, "Small Numbers, Great Impact."

27. Quoted in Iyo Iimura Kunimoto, "Japan and Mexico, 1888–1917" (Ph.D. diss., University of Texas at Austin, 1975), 92.

28. In Torreon, Coahuila, 300 Chinese were massacred in 1911. Evelyn Hu-Dehart argues, and I agree, that the Chinese suffered this massacre and other forms of violence throughout Mexico because of their success as an immigrant group. For fuller details, see Hu-Dehart, "Immigrants to a Developing Society: The Chinese in Northern Mexico, 1875–1932," *Journal of Arizona History* 21 (Autumn 1980), 275–312; "Racism and Anti-Chinese Persecution in Sonora, Mexico, 1876–1932," *Amerasia Journal* 9 no. 2 (1982), 1–28; Hu-Dehart "Coolies, Shopkeepers, Pioneers: The Chinese of Mexico and Peru, 1849–1930," *Amerasia Journal* 15, no. 2 (1989), 91–116; Robert H. Duncan, "The Chinese and Economic Development of Northern Baja California, 1889–1929," *Hispanic American Historical Review* 74, no. 4 (November 1994), 615–47.

29. "Aumenta el Sentimiento Anti-Chino en el Estado de Sonora," *Excelsior*, August 1, 1919.

30. Jeffrey Lesser, *Negotiating National Identity: Immigrants, Minorities, and the Struggle for Ethnicity in Brazil* (Durham, NC: Duke University Press, 1999), 86–87.

31. Hu-Dehart, "Immigrants to a Developing Society."

32. Mexico's largest immigrant population was from the United States, second were Spaniards, and third were the Chinese. Other groups that came in significant numbers during the 1890s and 1980s included the Guatemalans, French, Germans, British, Japanese, and Lebanese. For additional details, see Buchenau, "Small Numbers, Great Impact," 23–49. For a comparison, in 1910 Mexico had 117,000 foreign-born individuals; the United States, 13,500,000; Argentina, 2,360,000; and Brazil, 1,280,000.

For additional details, see *Dirección General de Estadisticas, 1877–1910* (México, DF: Talleres Graficos de la Nacion, 1956). For a thoughtful discussion on Middle Eastern immigrants to Mexico, see Theresa Alfaro-Velcamp, *So Far from Allah, So Close to Mexico: Middle Eastern Immigrants in Mexico* (Austin: University of Texas Press, 2007).

33. "Nothing would satisfy my desires so much as to see merchant vessels establishing frequent communication between my country and New Spain," said a letter from Minamoto Ieyasu, shogun of Japan, to Don Pedro Bravo de Acuna, governor of the Philippines, May 1602. In Zelia Nuttal, *The Earliest Historical Relations between Mexico and Japan* (Berkeley: University of California Press, 1906), 4. See also "Informes Diplomaticos y Consulares: Japón," *Boletin Oficial de la Secretaria de Relaciones Exteriores* 20 (May-October 1905), 1–15; William Lytle Schurz, "Acapulco and the Manila Galleon," *Southwestern Historical Quarterly* 22 (July 1918–April 1919), 18–37; Juan Posada Noriega, *Mexico y Estados Unidos (España y el Japón)* (México, DF: Imprenta M.L. Sanchez, 1939), 65–72; C. Harvey Gardiner, "Early Diplomatic Relations between Mexico and the Far East," *Americas: Quarterly Review of Inter-American Cultural History* 6, no. 4 (April 1950), 401–14; Francisco Santiago Cruz, *Relaciones Diplomáticas entre la Nueva España y el Japón* (México, DF: Editorial Jus, 1964); María Elena Ota Mishima, *México y Japón en el Siglo XIX: La politica exterior de Mexico y la consolidación de la soberanía Japonesa* (México, DF: Secretaria de Relaciones Exteriores, 1976), 13; and Hideo Furuya, *Memoria del Servicio Exterior Mexicano en Japón* (México, DF: Secretaria de Relaciones Exteriores, 1985).

34. From 1868 to 1900 Japan went through a rapid industrialization and westernization. Part of this process included an expansion of its military. By the late nineteenth century Japan had embarked on the invasion and conquest of various regions of East Asia. After Japan defeated China in the 1894–95 war, it occupied Korea and Taiwan. Japan also went to war with Russia in 1904–5 and defeated its imperialistic rival. With its victory over China and Russia, Japan became the dominant power in the East and began its military colonization of the region that included Manchuria.

35. Alan Takeo Moriyama, *Imingaisha: Japanese Immigration Companies and Hawaii, 1894–1908* (Honolulu: University of Hawaii Press, 1985), 2.

36. According to Mitziko Sawada, the term *imin* literally means "a citizen who moves or migrates." *Hi-imin* means someone who is not an immigrant and oftentimes implies a tourist. After 1908 Japan began to stamp passports with these designations. There was also another group called *jiyu-imin*, or free emigrants, to distinguish those with labor contracts. See Mitziko Sawada, "Culprits and Gentlemen: Meiji Japan's Restrictions of Emigrants to the United States, 1891–1909," *Pacific Historical Review* 60, no. 3 (August 1991), 339–59.

37. Eiichiro Azuma, "The Politics of Transnational History Making: Japanese Immigrants on the Western 'Frontier,' 1927–1941," *Journal of American History* 89, no. 4 (March 2003), 1401–1430. In this article Azuma argues that Issei (first generation immigrants) historians, writing primarily in Japanese, used a reverse racialization approach in discussing the movement of Japanese to the West. By doing so, according to Azuma, the Japanese pioneers were viewed as important as the white pioneers in forging a state of civilization in the Western frontier, thus challenging the traditional view of the American West by placing Japanese immigrants at the center along with Anglo pioneers. Azuma also indicates that these Issei historians wanted to counter the

prevailing views of *imin* by both Americans and Japanese back home, who were viewed as undesirable by Americans and as abandoning the nation by Japanese. These views were also attached to the term *dekasegi*, or an individual sojourning. From the perspective of these Japanese historians, the term *dekasegi* placed the Japanese pioneers in the crosshairs of Americans because it meant no commitment to the host nation. Also, since the Japanese immigrants were increasingly viewed in negative terms in the United States or other areas, Japan blamed the Issei for the growing tensions between Japan and the United States.

38. Kenneth B. Pyle, *The Making of Modern Japan* (Lexington: Heath, 1996), 97–98. See also Tsuchida Nobuya, "The Japanese in Brazil, 1908–1941" (PhD diss., University of California, Los Angeles, 1978), 24.

39. Akira Iriye, *Pacific Estrangement: Japanese and American Expansion, 1897–1911* (Cambridge, MA: Harvard University Press, 1972), 19.

40. Treaty of Amity, Commerce, and Navigation between Mexico and Japan, Washington DC, November 30, 1888. This treaty is the first that Japan signed with a country that offered equal status, unlike those imposed on Japan between 1854 and 1894 with such countries as the United States, Great Britain, Russia, and Holland. The signing of the treaty accelerated contact between the two countries and encouraged Japan to create the Department of Migration under Takeaki Enomoto in 1891.

41. Enomoto Takeaki held a number of high level posts during the latter part of his career: minister of navy, 1980; minister of communication, 1885–88; minister of agriculture and commerce, 1888, 1894–97; minister of education, 1889–90; foreign minister, 1891–92.

42. James L. Tigner, "Mexico and Japan: A Trans-Pacific Historical Survey" (undated, unpublished manuscript in the author's possession), 16.

43. Nobuko Krych, "The History of the Early Japanese Emigration and Colonization in Mexico" (MA thesis., California State University Long Beach, 1996), 61. Krych cites Minoru Izawa, *Nihonjin Mekishiko Ijushi* (*History of Japanese Emigration to Mexico*) (Tokyo: private printing, 1971).

44. Lieutenant Colonel T.W. Jones, "A Report Compiled from Reports and Other Data Showing the Activities of Japanese and Japanese Officials in Relation to the United States and Her Possessions," Second (Military Information) Division, General Staff, 1907, NARA, record group 165, box 530, Records of War Department General and Special Staffs, Military Intelligence Division Correspondence, 1917–41, 1766-1 to 1766-152.

45. This number is the official count of the Japanese Emigration Companies. The Mexican census and other sources have counts ranging from 8,000 to 10,000 Japanese arrivals. See Delia Salazar Anaya. *La Población Extranjera en México (1895–1990): Un Recuento con base en los Censos Generales de Población.* (México: Instituto Nacional de Antropología e Historia, 1996), 279–281.

46. Erika Lee, "Hemispheric Orientalism and the 1907 Pacific Coast Race Riots," *Amerasia Journal* 33, no. 2 (2007), 19–47, 20.

47. Erika Lee, "Orientalism in the Americas: A Hemispheric Approach to Asian American History," *Journal of Asian American Studies* 8, no. 3 (October 2005), 235–58.

48. R. D. McKenzie. *Oriental Exclusion—the Effect of American Immigration Laws, Regulations, and Judicial Decisions upon the Chinese and Japanese on the American Pacific Coast* (Chicago: University of Chicago Press, 1928), 15–16.

49. Angelo N. Ancheta, *Race, Rights, and the Asian American Experience* (New Brunswick, NJ: Rutgers University Press, 1998), 21.

50. Ibid., 26.

51. Delia Salazar Anaya, *La Población Extranjera en Mexico (1895–1990): Un Recuento con Base en los Censos Generales de Población* (México, DF: Instituto Nacional de Antropología e Historia, 1996), 279–81.

52. Kunimoto, "Japan and Mexico, 1888–1917," 69.

53. A number of Japanese files contain US visas showing their origins as Mexico.

54. María Elena Ota Mishima, *Siete Migraciones Japonesas en México, 1890–1978* (México, DF: Colegio de México, 1982), 52.

55. Japanese Compilation Committee on Immigration History, *Nihon Mekishiko Imin (Japanese Emigration to Mexico)* (Tokyo: 1971), 168–69.

56. Ibid.

57. *Pan American Bulletin* (1923–1927) 12, 627.

58. In 1908 Japan stopped issuing passports to Japanese laborers, which became known as the Gentlemen's Agreement. In 1924 the US passed the National Origins Quota or the Johnson-Reed Act, which prevented individuals from the Asia-Pacific Triangle such as Chinese, Japanese, and Koreans from entering the United States.

59. "Mexican Immigration Laws: New Regulations in Force Barring Undesirable Foreigners from Country," *New York Times*, March 5, 1909.

60. James C. Scott, *Weapons of the Weak: Everyday Forms of Peasant Resistance* (New Haven: Yale University Press, 1985).

61. John J. Dwyer, "Diplomatic Weapons of the Weak: Mexican Policy Making during the US Mexican Agrarian Dispute, 1934–1941." *Diplomatic History*, Vo. 26, No. 1 (Summer 2003): 375–395. See also John J. Dwyer, *The Agrarian Dispute: The Expropriation of American Owned Rural Land in Postrevolutionary Mexico*. (Durham, NC: Duke University Press, 2008).

62. "La Ola Amarilla: Por Que el Problema de la Inmigración Asiatica es Destino en Mexico a los Estado Unidos," *El Imparcial* October 5, 1907, 1.

63. Bernardo Mallén, *¿En dónde están nuestras riquezas.* (Mexico, D.F.: Muller Brothers Publishing, 1908), 53–54

64. L. Aubert, "The United States and Japanese Colonization," *Review of Paris* 16 (August 1907), 878–79.

65 Alan Knight, "US Imperialism/Hegemony and Latin American Resistance," in *Empire and Dissent: The United States and Latin America*, Fred Rosen, ed. (Durham, NC: Duke University Press, 2008), 47n24.

66. Luke E. Wright. Dispatch to Mr. Root, American Embassy, Tokyo, December 26, 1906, in *Japanese Emigration and Immigration*. (Woodbridge, CT: Research Publications, 1988), 30–31. Parentheses my emphasis.

67. Erika Lee, "Enforcing the Borders: Chinese Exclusion along the US Borders with Canada and Mexico, 1882–1924," *Journal of American History* 89, no. 1 (June 2002), 72.

68. "En Busca de Espias Japoneses," *El Imparcial*, February 1, 1907; "4,000 Operarios Japoneses Para Las Obras Ferrocarrileras," *El Imparcial*, July 15, 1907; "1200 Japoneses Para Coahuila-Ninguno Llego Enfermo," *El Imparcial*. June 28, 1907; "The Menace of the Japanese Conquest of Mexico: Japan Said to Be in Practical Control of Four of the Pacific Ports of Mexico, to Have Acquired 800,000 Acres of Land Along

That Coast and Quietly to Have Placed 60,000 Japanese Men in the Republic," *St. Louis Daily-Democrat*, May 14, 1913; "60,000 Japanese in Mexico: Why Are They There and What Do They Do Besides Fish? Herewith Are Presented Certain Significant Facts for American Consideration," *Cleveland Leader*, July 6, 1913.

69. NARA, "A Report Compiled From Reports and Other Data Showing the Activities of Japanese and Japanese Officials in Relation to the United States and her Possessions," 1908.

70. Scott Michaelsen, "Between Japanese American Internment and the USA Patriot Act: The Borderlands and the Permanent State of Racial Exception," *Aztlan* 30, no. 2 (Fall 2005), 87–111.

71. "Japanese Ignore Exclusion Treaty. Thousands of Coolies Sneaking Over the Frontiers of Canada and Mexico in Spite of Agreement. Hard to Keep them Out. Mikado's Envoy Complains of Americans Violating Law, but Silent as to His Own People," *Chicago Daily Tribune*, May 31, 1907.

72. Memorandum: Military Information regarding Mexico, Lieutenant Colonel D.A. Frederick, November 3, 1910, NARA, record group 165, box 530, Military Intelligence, Divisional Correspondence, War Department, Office of the Chief of Staff.

73. Japanese generational ancestry categories are *issei*, first generation; *nisei*, second generation; *sansei*, third generation; *yonsei*, fourth generation; *nikkei*, no consensus (see note 3).

74. Japanese Compilation Committee, *Nihon Mekishiko Imin*, 168–69.

75. US Secretary of Commerce and Labor, Bureau of Immigration and Naturalization, "Report of the Commissioner-General of Immigration, July 1, 1908," in *Reports of Commerce and Labor, 1908* (Washington, DC: Government Printing Office, 1908), 222. See also Teruko Teruko Okada Kachi, *The Treaty of 1911 and the Immigration and Alien Land Law Issue Between the United States and Japan, 1911–1913* (New York: Arno Press, 1978), 164.

76. Kachi, *Treaty of 1911*, 165.

Chapter Two

1. Colonia Dublán, for mission beginning June 26, 1916, NARA, record group 393, Records of the US Army Continental Commands, 1821–1920, Intelligence Service, File 114–118.

2. NARA, record group 393, Records of the US Army Continental Commands, 1821–1920, Southern Department, 1913–20, entry 4442, General Correspondence, 1916–20, 370.23.

3. Ibid.

4. Douglas W. Richmond, "Nationalism and Class Conflict in Mexico, 1910–1920," *Americas* 43, no. 3 (January 1987), 279–303.

5. The periodization of the Mexican Revolution varies; the periods 1910–17, 1910–10, 1910–40 are most often used. Some argue that the Mexican Revolution came to an end with the implementation of the Constitution of 1917. However, I use 1910–20, as many others have, since this is when the last factional revolt is said to have occurred. See John Womack, Jr., "The Mexican Revolution, 1910–1920," in *Mexico since Independence*, Leslie Bethell, ed. (Cambridge: Cambridge University Press,

1991), 125–200. See also Gilbert M. Joseph and Daniel Nugent, "Popular Culture and State Formation in Revolutionary Mexico," in *Everyday Forms of State Formation: Revolution and the Negotiation of Rule in Modern Mexico*, Gilbert M. Joseph and Daniel Nugent, eds. (Durham, NC: Duke University Press, 1994).

6. Joseph and Nugent, "Popular Culture and State Formation," 5.

7. Alan Knight, "The Working Class and the Mexican Revolution, 1900–1920," *Journal of Latin American Studies* 16, no. 1 (May 1984), 51–79.

8. John Mason Hart, *Empire and Revolution: The Americans in Mexico since the Civil War* (Berkeley: University of California Press, 2002).

9. Tanabe, Atsuko, *Huellas Japonesas en la Cultura Mexicana*, Juan Manuel Rivera y Yukako Yoshida, trans. (Tijuana, México: Colegio de la Frontera Norte, 1995), 19.

10. James L. Tigner, "Mexico and Japan: A Trans-Pacific Historical Survey" (undated, unpublished manuscript in the author's possession), 67.

11. Ibid.

12. Ibid.

13. "Japan is Preparing-Whom Will She Fight." *Boston Sunday Globe*, January 30, 1916.

14. Tigner, "Mexico and Japan," 131. Tigner cites the following sources: *New York Times*, January 30, 1914, September 27, 1916; Sigmund Henschen, "What Is Behind the Japanese Peril?," *Forum* 56 (July 1916), 72–73.

15. Ibid., 143.

16. Erika Lee, "Hemispheric Orientalism and the 1907 Pacific Coast Race Riots," *Amerasia Journal* 33, no. 2 (2007), 19–47. These race riots occurred in San Francisco, California; Bellingham, Washington; and Vancouver, Canada.

17. Tigner, "Mexico and Japan," 94.

18. American Consulate General to Secretary of State, Nogales, Sonora, Mexico, "Japanese and Americans Are Negotiating for Rich Lands in Sonora, Mexico," March 22, 1919, NARA, Records of the Department of State Relating to Internal Affairs of Japan, 1910–1929 (decimal 894.20212/178).

19. Ibid.

20. Ibid.

21. Friedrich Katz, *The Secret War in Mexico: Europe, The United States and the Mexican Revolution* (Chicago: University of Chicago Press, 1981), 76.

22. Ibid.

23. Ibid, 78–79.

24. Harry H. Dunn, "60,000 Japanese in Mexico: Why Are They There and What Do They Do Besides Fish? Herewith Are Presented Certain Significant Facts for American Consideration," *Cleveland Leader*, July 6, 1913. Dunn also published an earlier article on a similar topic: Harry H. Dunn, "The Menace of the Japanese Conquest of Mexico," *St. Louis Daily-Democrat*, May 4, 1913.

25. Letter to the Secretary, War College, Washington (through military channels) from Henry Barber, Major, USA. Retired, military attaché, Havana, Cuba, December 24, 1910, NARA, record group 165, Records of the War Department General and Special Staffs, Military Intelligence Division Correspondence, 1917–41, box 530, 1766-1 to 1766-152. See also letter to the Chief, War College Division, War Department General Staff from Wallis O. Clark, Major, USA., military attaché, American Legation Guatemala, December 27, 1910.

26. Confidential letter to War College Division, General Staff from Lieutenant C. Cordier, 4th Infantry, military attaché, Lima Peru, January 9, 1911, NARA, record group 165, Records of the WDGS, Military Intelligence Division Correspondence, 1917–41, box 530, 1766-1 to 1766-152.

27. Letter to the Chief, War College Division, General Staff, Washington, DC, from Military Attaché, American Embassy, Mexico, January 3, 1911, NARA, record group 165, Records of the WDGS, Military Intelligence Division Correspondence, 1917–41, 1766-1 to 1766-152, box 530.

28. Ibid.

29. Iyo Iimura Kunimoto, "Japan and Mexico, 1888–1917" (Ph.D. diss., University of Texas at Austin, 1975), 202.

30. Ibid., 203.

31. Tigner: "Mexico and Japan," 102–3. Tigner cites the following for this interview: Aoyama Masabumi, *Karerawa Kakunnogotoku Mekishiko ni funto seri* (*The Japanese Struggle in Mexico*) (México, DF, 1938), 68–71.

32. Tanabe, Atsuko, *Huellas Japonesas*.

33. Ibid.

34. Secretaria de la Defensa Nacional, "Se Reconozce oficialmente como Veterano de la Revolución en el Segundo Perido al C. José Kingo Nonanka," México DF, November 4, 1966, AGN, Mesa Cuarta, no. 42, expediente T-1585.

35. Se expide copia certificada de una manifestación del C. Luis Bojorquez, Captain 2/o.del 35/o Batallón de Linea, SRE, VII(N)112-13.

36. Hoja Servicios del Capitan 20 Luis Bojorquez, June 2, 1917, SRE, VII(N)112-13.

37. Ibid.

38. Tigner, "Mexico and Japan," 103–4. Tigner cites Masabumi, *Karerawa Kakunnogotoku*, 93–95.

39. Ibid., 127–29.

40. Evelyn Hu-Dehart, "Racism and Anti-Chinese Persecution in Sonora, Mexico, 1876–1932," *Amerasia Journal* 9. no. 2 (1982), 1–27.

41. Ibid.

42. Tigner, "Mexico and Japan," 114–16.

43. Robert Duncan, "The Chinese and Economic Development of Northern Baja California, 1889–1929," *Hispanic American Historical Review* 74, no. 4 (November 1994), 615–47.

44. Anaya, *La Población Extranjera en Mexico*, 105.

45. Hu-Dehart, "Racism and Anti-Chinese Persecution."

46. Kunimoto, "Japan and Mexico," 93.

47. Kumaichi Horigoutchi, Charge de Affairs Japanese Legation, Mexico, to Licenciado Don Manuel Calero, Secretary of Foreign Relations, Mexico, February 23, 1912, SRE, VII(N) 13-1-145 (13f).

48. Q. Moheno, Secretaria de Relaciónes Exteriores a Mineteiro Adatci (Adachi), Légation du Japón, October 21, 1923, SRE, VII(N) 13-1-149 (5f).

49. Kumaichi Horigoutchi, Charge de Affairs Japanese Legation, Mexico to Licenciado. Don Marcelino Dávalos, Director de Asuntos Internacionales de la Secretaria de Relaciones Exteriores, March 22, 1916, SRE, VII(N) 16-16-207 (12f).

50. Womack, "Mexican Revolution," 154–66.

51. Alan Knight, *The Mexican Revolution*, vol. 2 (Cambridge: Cambridge University Press, 1986), 344–45.

52. Womack, "The Mexican Revolution, 1910–1920," 167–90.

53. Knight, *The Mexican Revolution*, 351–52.

54. Tigner, "Mexico and Japan," 145.

55. Colonel F.W. Bibley, 14th Calvary to Commanding General, Southern Department, Fort Sam Houston, June 13, 1916. Subject: Report of Operations of Punitive Expedition. RG 395 Records of US Army Overseas Operations and Commands, 1898–1942, World War I and Organization Records Punitive Expedition to Mexico, Box No. 429.

56. Tigner, "Mexico and Japan," 145.

57. The two sources are Friedrich Katz, *The Life and Times of Pancho Villa* (Stanford, CA: Stanford University Press, 1998), 608–11; and Charles H. Harris and Louis R. Sadler, *The Border and the Revolution: Clandestine Activities of the Mexican Revolution, 1910–1920* (Silver City, NM: High-Lonesome Books, 1988).

58. M. E. Stone, *Judicial proceeding.* et al. should be lower case., September 10, 1916. RG 395 Records of US Army Overseas Operations and Commands, 1898–1942, World War I and Organization Records Punitive Expedition to Mexico, Box No. 429.

59. Ibid.

60. J. J. Pershing, Major General, USA, Commanding, El Paso, Texas, February 17, 1917. RG 395 Records of US Army Overseas Operations and Commands, 1898–1942, World War I and Organization Records Punitive Expedition to Mexico, Box No. 429.

61. *Japanese Weekly Mail*, November 29, 1913, 680.

62. The Mexican Constitution of 1917 also restricted foreigners from owning Mexican lands or its subsoil; curtailed the freedom of speech regarding politics; and provided for the expulsion of foreigners under presidential decree without judicial recourse. See Garcia y Greigo et al., 206.

63. *New York Times*, June 22, 1919, 6.

64. *New York Times*, January 28, 1920.

65. Ibid.

66. Hirabayashi et al., "Preface," in *New Worlds, New Lives*, xv. The authors state that approximately 1.6 million individuals of Japanese ancestry are living throughout North America and Latin America.

Chapter Three

1. "Japanese in Mexico," *Chicago Daily Tribune*, June 2, 1920, 8.

2. In the various Japanese, US, and Mexican sources I have used, I have been unable to determine if Kiso Tsuru's title is honorific or actually represents educational credentials. Throughout the hundreds of documents where Tsuru is mentioned he is referred to as "Kiso Tsuru or Dr. Kiso Tsuru."

3. Harry Bernstein, "Mexico's War with Japan," *Far Eastern Survey* 9, no. 24 (November 30, 1942), 245–50.

4. Alexandra Minna Stern, "From Mestizophilia to Biology: Racialization and Science in Mexico, 1920–1960," in *Race and Nation in Modern Latin America*, Nancy P.

Appelbaum, Anne S. Macpherson, and Karin Alejandra Rosemblatt, eds. (Chapel Hill: University of North Carolina Press, 2003), 189.

5. Jeffrey W. Rubin, *Decentering the Regime: Ethnicity, Radicalism, and Democracy in Juchitan, Mexico* (Durham, NC: Duke University Press, 1997), 13–14.

6. Alan Knight, "Racism, Revolution, and Indigenismo: Mexico, 1910–1940," in *The Idea of Race in Latin America, 1870–1940*, Richard Graham, ed. (Austin: University of Texas Press, 1990), 77.

7. Alexander S. Dawson, *Indian and Nation in Revolutionary Mexico* (Tucson: University of Arizona Press, 2004), xv–xvii.

8. Ibid., xxi.

9. The advocates of social Darwinism and eugenics used Gregor Mendel's laws of inheritance to further their cause of selective breeding and racial biology. Francis Galton published *Hereditary Talent and Character* in 1865, where he first discussed the concept of eugenics and later published *Heredity Genius* (1869), which elaborated and promoted the concept of selective breeding. Galton later coined the term "eugenics" in *Inquiries into Human Faculty and Its Development* (1883). The concept of eugenics coupled with the development of Herbert Spencer's social Darwinism and his coining of the term "survival of the fittest," a corruption of Darwin's theories, ushered in new theories on race in the late nineteenth century and first half of the twentieth century that had profound effects on the social and political fabric of the United States. The rationalization in countries such as the United States and Brazil for the infusion of white Europeans rested on the notion that good Western and European stock immigrants would help breed out genetic weaknesses in their population and whiten, in the case of Brazil, the miscegenated population. Many Latin American countries viewed the United States as the standard of how a predominantly European-based population propelled a country into the modern age. As the United States began to create immigration policies that favored the movement of a Western and Northern Eurocentric population, Latin America implemented a similar path with Mexico developing its own version that fit its national experience.

10. Rick López, "The India Bonita Contest of 1921 and the Ethnicization of Mexican National Culture," *Hispanic American Historical Review* 82, no. 2 (May 2002), 291–328.

11. Masanosuke Oguita and Taro Takano, *Cancion de Chontal: Canciones antiguas de aborigines Mexicanos* (Tokio, Japón: Candelaria, 1983). The name *Chontal* originates from the Nahuatl word *chontalli*, which means foreigner.

12. Resume of investigations made by war department secret agents in Lower California and the Mexican states of Sonora, Sinaloa, and Nayarit to determine the number and occupation of Japanese in these areas, E.R.W. McCabe, Colonel, General Staff, Assistant Chief of Staff, G-2, September 8, 1937, NARA, record group 165, Military Intelligence Division Correspondence, 1917–41, box 1584.

13. Ibid.

14. Axis Propaganda and Activities in Latin America, Military Intelligence Division, Special Study Group, January 14, 1942, Records of the War Department General and Special Staffs, Office of the Director of Intelligence G-2, Subordinate Offices, of the Latin American Branch, 1940–46, NARA, record group 165, entry 188, box 985.

15. Ibid.

16. Cable Message from the American Ambassador in Tokyo, February 25, 1920, Records of the Department of State Relating to Internal Affairs of Japan, 1910–29 (decimal number unknown), National Archives Microfilm Publication Roll 1, 14–16.

17. Ibid.

18. As part of the Immigration Act of 1924 (Johnson-Reed Act), the US Congress inserted a clause stating that aliens ineligible for naturalization in the United States were barred from entering the country. This effectively ended the immigration of Asians into the United States. The ban was lifted for the Chinese during World War II. However, the last vestige of discrimination against the Japanese was not lifted until 1952 with the passage of the 1952 Immigration and Nationality Act (McCarran-Walter Act).

19. James L. Tigner, "Mexico and Japan: A Trans-Pacific Historical Survey" (undated, unpublished manuscript in the author's possession), 251.

20. Japanese immigrants, whether recruited by public or private agencies, were usually "impersonally sponsored" or *kobo-imin* (a class name for officially nominated immigrants). The other major class, *yobiyose-imin*, corresponds to the general formulation "chain migration." This system was also used in some places of the Americas for Japanese parents to bring their children. See also Tigner, "Mexico and Japan," 251.

21. Chizuko Watanabe, "The Japanese Immigrant Community in Mexico: Its History and Present" (M.A. thesis, California State University, Los Angeles, 1983), 50.

22. Maria Elena Ota Mishima, *Siete migraciones Japonesas en* México, *1890–1978* (México, DF: Colegio de Mexico, 1985), 67.

23. Tigner, "Mexico and Japan," 205.

24. Ibid., 341.

25. Antonieta Kiyoko Nishikawa Aceves, "La inmigración Japonesa a ensenada durante la primera mitad del siglo xx," Revista del Instituto de Investigaciones Históricas de la Univesidad Autónoma de Baja California, vol 1, no 1-8 (2004): 24–34. 4. See also María Elena Ota Mishima, *Siete Migraciones Japonesas en México, 1890–1978. (México, DF: El Colegio de México, 1982)*.

26. Watanabe, "Japanese Immigrant Community in Mexico," 41–42.

27. Ibid., 42–43; see also Taki Yasutaro, *Mekishiko Kokujo Taikan-Mexico, Gran Amigo del Japón a través de los 70 años* (México, DF: Meshiko Shimpo, 1968), 61.

28. Resume of Investigations Made by War Department Secret Agents in Lower California, and the Mexican States of Sonora, Sinaloa, and Nayarit to determine the number and occupation of Japanese in these areas. E.R.W. McCabe, Colonel, General Staff, Assistant Chief of Staff, G-2, September 8, 1937, NARA, record group 165, Military Intelligence Division Correspondence, 1917–41, box 1584.

29. "Field Notes on the Japanese in Latin America—Mexico," NARA, record group 165, box 978, Records of War Department General and Special Staff, Office of the Director of Intelligence G-2, Subordinate Offices, Latin American Branch, Security—Classified General Correspondence, 1940–46, NARA, record group 165, box 978, Records of War Department General and Special Staff, Office of the Director of Intelligence G-2, Subordinate Offices, Latin American Branch, Security—Classified General Correspondence, 1940–46. The numbers included 1,499 males, 216 females (including 26 children), totaling 1,715.

30. Tigner, "Mexico and Japan," 285.

31. Watanabe, "Japanese Immigrant Community in Mexico," 46–47.

32. Ibid.

33. Ibid, 52.

34. FBI, US Department of Justice, "Totalitarian Activities: Mexico . . . Today," September 1942, NARA, record group 165, box 997, Records of War Department General and Special Staffs, Office of the Director of Intelligence G-2, Subordinate Offices Latin American Branch, Security—Classified General Correspondence, 1940–46.

35. "Japanese Population in Mexico (Lower California is Not Included). Up to 1940," NARA, Records of the War Department and Special Staffs, record group 165, box 978. See also "Progress Report on Japanese Activities in Lower California and the West Coast of Mexico," E.R.W. McCabe, Colonel, General Staff, Assistant Chief of Staff, G-2, August 7, 1937, NARA, record group 165, Military Intelligence Division Correspondence, 1917–41, box 1584.

36. "Japanese Population in Mexico," NARA.

37. Watanabe, "Japanese Immigrant Community in Mexico," 19; see also Yasutaro, *Mekishiko Kokujo Taikan-Mexico*. 61.

38. Emma Chrishuru Nakatani Sánchez, "Memorias de un inmigrante japonés," *Istor* 6 no 21 (Summer 2005), 143. The H. Kato mentioned by Yoshigei was Heiji Kato, the owner of the largest department store in Mexico City that catered to the Japanese community. Kato also became a charter member of the Comité Japonés de Ayuda Mutua.

39. Ibid, 144.

40. Ibid, 144–45.

41. The 16 states with the highest population of Japanese immigrants in 1925 were Baja California, 1,036; Federal District, 602; Coahuila, 360; Chihuahua, 300; Veracruz, 295; Sonora, 228; Sinaloa, 228; Tamaulipas, 155; Jalisco, 84; San Luis Potosí, 60; Oaxaca, 55; Nuevo León, 29; Colima, 18; Guerrero, 12; Durango, 12.

42. Delia Salazar Anaya, *La Población Extranjera en Mexico (1895–1990): Un Recuento con Base en los Censos Generales de Población* (México, DF: Instituto Nacional de Antropología e Historia, 1996), 115.

43. SRE, Departamento Consular, Pasaportes, Yokohama, Consulado en . . . visados durante el año, 1932, 1933; SRE, Asuntos comerciales y de protección, Pasaportes, Yokohama, Japón, Consulado en . . . visados durante el año, 1935.

44. SRE, 401 files on Japanese who requested and obtained naturalization, conserved at Archivo Histórico "Genaro Estrada" de la Secretaria de Relaciones Exteriores.

45. Daniel M. Masterson with Sayaka Funada-Classen, *The Japanese in Latin America* (Chicago: University of Illinois Press, 2004), 62.

46. Ibid.

47. "D-2278 Japanese—History of Relations between Japan and Mexico," based on a hand-written note on the last page of this document it indicates this is a translation of 178–86 of a Japanese publication titled "Situación Actual de Mexico y Centro America; published in Mexico and forwarded by M/A Mexico in report #4986-44, November 14, 1944, subject: Japanese Activities—Jap directory of Mexico and Central America," NARA, Records of the War Department, General and Special Staffs, record group 165, box 978; see also Tigner, "Mexico and Japan," 450–55.

48. Tigner, "Mexico and Japan," 450.

49. Ibid., 455.

50. "D-2278 Japanese—History and Relations," NARA.

51. "Japanese Population in Mexico," NARA.

52. Ibid.

53. Tigner, "Mexico and Japan," 281–82.

54. Toshio Yanaguida and Taeko Akagui, "Mexico y Los Emigrantes Japonesas," *Estudios Migratorios Latino Americano* 10, no. 30 (1995), 373–401.

55. "President Orders Distribution of General Cedillo's Hacienda and Disarmament of His Men," H. E. Marshburn, Lieutenant Colonel, Infantry, military attaché, G-2 Report, October 30, 1936, NARA, record group 165, Military Intelligence Division Correspondence, 1917–41, box 1583. See also Alan Knight, "The Rise and Fall of Cardenismo, c. 1930–c. 1946," *Mexico since Independence*, Leslie Bethell, ed. (Cambridge: Cambridge University Press, 1991), 256–57.

56. "Immigration and Colonization—Agrarians Seize Mormon Property in Chihuahua," H. E. Marshburn, Lieutenant Colonel, Infantry, military attaché, G-2 Report, October 23, 1936, NARA, record group 165, Military Intelligence Division Correspondence, 1917–41, box 1583.

57. "Degree of Agricultural Development, Governor of Puebla Orders Distribution of Jenkins' Estate," H. E. Marshburn, Lieutenant Colonel, Infantry, Military Attaché, G-2 Report, October 22, 1937, NARA, record group 165, Military Intelligence Division Correspondence, 1917–41, box 1583.

58. "Public Order and Safety. Agrarians Take Possession of Lands Illegally," H. E. Marshburn, Lieutenant Colonel, Infantry, military attaché, G-2 Report, February 2, 1937, NARA, record group 165, Military Intelligence Division Correspondence, 1917–41, box 1583.

59. Tigner, "Mexico and Japan," 290–91.

60. FBI, "Totalitarian Activities," 42.

61. Alan Knight, *US-Mexican Relations, 1910–1940: An Interpretation* (San Diego: University of California, Center for US-Mexican Studies, 1987), 1. See also Benjamin T. Smith, *Pistoleros and Popular Movements: The Politics of State Formation in Post-revolutionary Oaxaca* (Lincoln: University of Nebraska Press, 2009).

62. Stuart Chase, *Mexico: A Study of Two Americas* (New York: Macmillan, 1931), 252.

63. John J. Dwyer, *The Agrarian Dispute: The Expropriation of American-Owned Rural Land in Post-revolutionary Mexico* (Durham, NC: Duke University Press, 2008), 5. Although Dwyer borrows the term "weapons of the weak," he is explicit in explaining that Mexican diplomats did not deploy the weapons of the weak used by peasant groups as discussed by James Scott. Indeed, Dwyer is clear in indicating that Mexican diplomats, although sometimes concerned with the lower classes, are from a different cultural strata. See also James C. Scott, *Weapons of the Weak: Everyday Forms of Peasant Resistance* (New Haven, CT: Yale University Press), 1987.

64. Dwyer, *The Agrarian Dispute*, 5.

65. John Dwyer uses James Scott's phrase "weapons of the weak" but adds that Mexico's government officials employed diplomatic forms of maneuvers that are parallel to peasant foot dragging and using a position of weakness as strength.

66. Response of Michitaka Sugawara, Member of the Japanese Imperial Diet, when asked if Japan was about to make a loan to Mexico. American Consul Guaymas, Mexico, to Secretary of State, "Japanese Activities in Lower California," June 20, 1917, NARA, Department of State Relating to Internal Affairs of Japan, 1910–29 (decimal 894.20212/130).

67. Office of the Director of Intelligence G-2, Subordinate Offices, Latin American Branch, Security-Classified General Correspondence, 1940–46, G-2 Report Mexico—Economic, Subject, Petroleum—Japanese Purchase of Oil, March 5, 1938, NARA, record group 165, box 1583, Records of War Department General and Special Staffs.

68. Confidential correspondence from Josephus Daniels, Ambassador to Mexico to The Secretary of State, Subject: Transmitting Unofficial Statistical Data Covering Mexican Exportations of Petroleum, March 12, 1940, Mexico DF, Mexico, NARA, record group 59, box 4177, General Records of the Department of State, decimal file 1940–44.

69. John Mason Hart, *Empire and Revolution: The Americans in Mexico since the Civil War* (Berkeley: University of California Press, 2002), 260. See also Appendix 1: Partial List of American Landholdings and Ownership in Mexico, 100,000 Acres and More, 1910–13, in Hart, *Empire and Revolution*. The total amount of acreage owned by Americans in this list totaled 94,104,909 acres!

70. Dwyer, *The Agrarian Dispute*, 289n13. According to Dwyer, by 1911 US investment in Mexico in mining, railroad, oil, and other industries totaled $1.265 billon, or 38 percent of all foreign investments in Mexico. This increased to $1.325 billon by 1929.

71. "Esta Trajabando Japón por Mantener La Paz en Asia y No por Provocar la Guerra," *Excelsior*, August 1, 1941.

72. Axis Propaganda and Activities in Latin America (January 14, 1942), Division of Reports, Coordinator of Inter-American Affairs, NARA, record group 165, entry 188, box 980, Records of War Department General and Special Staffs, Office of the Director of Intelligence G-2, Subordinate Offices, Latin American Branch, Security-Classified General Correspondence, 1940–46.

73. In the various sources I have used, i.e., Japanese, United States, and Mexican, I have been unable to determine if Kiso Tsuru's title is honorific or actually educational credentials. Throughout the hundreds of documents where Tsuru is mentioned he is referred to as "Kiso Tsuru and Dr. Kiso Tsuru."

74. Tokyo (Foreign Minister) to Mexico City, July 12, 1941, NARA, record group 457, entry 9011, box 15, National Security Agency, Japanese Diplomatic Messages, 12,219–13,067.

75. Axis Propaganda and Activities in Latin America (January 14, 1942), Division of Reports, Coordinator of Inter-American Affairs, NARA, record group 165, entry 188, box 980, Records of War Department General and Special Staffs, Office of the Director of Intelligence G-2, Subordinate Offices, Latin American Branch, Security-Classified General Correspondence, 1940–46. See also Maria Emilia Paz, *Strategy, Security, and Spies: Mexico and the US as Allies in World War II* (University Park: Pennsylvania State University Press, 1997), 37.

76. Paz, *Strategy, Security, and Spies*.

77. FBI, US Department of Justice, "Totalitarian Activities, Mexico . . . Today," September 1942, NARA, record group 165, entry 188, box 997, Records of War Department General and Special Staffs, Office of the Director of Intelligence G-2, Subordinate Offices, Latin American Branch, Security-Classified General Correspondence, 1940–46.

78. MAGIC was an Allied cryptanalysis project during World War II. Its efforts were directed at breaking Japan's diplomatic ciphers, allowing Allied policy makers to read

that country's diplomatic messages. See Ronald Lewin, *The American Magic: Codes, Ciphers, and the Defeat of Japan* (New York: Pengion Books, 1983).

79. Mexico to Tokyo, August 12, 1941, NARA, record group 457, box 15, National Security Agency, Japanese Diplomatic Messages.

80. *Enomoto Buyo to Mekishiko Shokumin Iju* (*Buyo Enomoto and Migration to Mexican Settlements*) (Tokyo: Dobunkan, 1986), 76.

81. Relacionado con situación de fondos a elementos enemigos, Junta de Administración y Vigilancia de la Propiedad Extranjera, February 17, 1943, México, DF, AGN, caja 373, Dirección General de Investigaciones Políticas y Sociales, Comité Japaones De Ayuda Mutua, expediente 9. See also Emilio E. Fernandez, Auditor Fiscal, "Relacion de los Jefes y Empleados de Origen Japonés, que Prestan sus Servicios en Las Siguientes Negociaciones: Compañía Internacional de Comercio, S.A.; Cia. Petrolera Mexicana 'La Laguna,' S.A.; Cia. Petrolera 'Veracruzana,' S.A.; Eduardo Gutierrez y Cia. S. E C. P.A," Casa Intervenidas, México, DF, June 22, 1942, AGN, caja 110, Secretaria de Gobernación, Dirección General de Investigaciones Políticas y Sociales, expediente 2-1/260/81.

82. From Minister Yamagata to Tokyo, "The Question of Obtaining Military Materials," June 24, 1941, NARA, record group 457, National Security Agency, Japanese Diplomatic Messages, entry 9011, box 15, SRDJ (Diplomatic Messages of Japan) 12,219–13,067.

83. FBI, "Totalitarian Activities." 248, 260–262, 374.

84. Japanese Clandestine Radio in Mexico, December 2, 1943, NARA, record group 165, box 978, Records of the War Department General and Special Staff, Office of the Director of Intelligence G-2, Latin American Branch, 1940–46.

85. Military Intelligence Division: Activities of Japanese in Mexico, May 19, 1944, NARA, record group 165, box 978, Records of the War Department General and Special Staff, Office of the Director of Intelligence G-2, Latin American Branch, 1940–46.

86. FBI, "Totalitarian Activities." 123–124.

Chapter Four

1. Hubert Herring, "Our New Ally, Mexico,"*Inter-American Monthly* 1, no. 3 (July 1942), 8–15.

2. James L. Tigner, "Mexico and Japan: A Trans-Pacific Historical Survey" (undated, unpublished manuscript in the author's possession), 410. According to Tigner, the Japanese diplomats and their families, a total of fifty-four individuals were sent to the United States for internment. For his source, Tigner cites Izawa Minoru, *Nihon-jin mekishiko ijushi (The History of the Japanese Immigrants in Mexico*) (Tokyo: private printing, 1971), 285. María Emilia Paz states that a number of Japanese officials, after staging a public celebration of the Emperor's birthday in Mexico in February 1942, were promptly apprehended and sent to the United States for internment. See María Emilia Paz, *Strategy, Security, and Spies: Mexico and the US as Allies in World War II* (University Park: Pennsylvania State University Press, 1997), 133.

3. Delia Salazar Anaya, *La Población Extranjera en Mexico (1895–1990): Un Recuento con Base en los Censos Generales de Población* (México, DF: Instituto Nacional de Antropología e Historia, 1996), 66.

4. Ibid., 67.

5. Gisela Cramer and Ursula Prutsch, "Nelson A. Rockefeller's Office of Inter-American Affairs (1940–46) and Record Group 229," *Hispanic American Historical Review* 86, no. 4 (November 2006), 785–86.

6. "Axis Propaganda and Activities in Latin America," Military Intelligence Division, Special Study Group, January 14, 1942, NARA, record group 165, box 985, Records of the War Department, General and Special Staff, Office of the Director of Intelligence, G-2, Subordinate Offices—Latin American Branch; Anaya, *La Población Extranjera en México, 1895–1990*, 105. See also María Elena Ota Mishima, *Siete Migraciones Japónéses en México, 1890–1978* (México, DF: Colegio de México, 1982). An exact number of Japanese living in Mexico is difficult to ascertain. Various sources range from 2,500 to 12,000. And depending whether one is reading a Japanese, US, or Mexican source, the estimates fluctuate. I have attempted to use Japanese and Mexican official data and secondary sources based on figures from census data or official ministries. For example, the Japanese Minister of Foreign Relations office counted 5,824 Japanese residing in Mexico in 1932. For additional figures, see Toshio Yanaguida and Taeko Akagui, "Mexico y Los Emigrantes Japonesas," *Estudios Migratorios Latinoamericanos* 10, no. 30 (1995), 373–402; Paz, *Strategy, Security, and Spies*. Using US government documents, Paz states that approximately 6,000 Japanese resided in Mexico at the end of the 1930s.

7. Equador-German Activities Axis to Mexico-Germany, Harry M. Gwynn, Lt. Col., G.S.C., Chief, Sub-Section 2, "Secret Memorandum for the Chief, Latin American Section," June 2, 1941, NARA, record group 165, box 973, Records of the War Department, General and Special Staff, Office of the Director of Intelligence G-2, Subordinate Offices Latin American Branch, Security Classified General Correspondence, 1940–46.

8. Ibid.

9. Greg Grandin, *Empire's Workshop: Latin America, the United States, and the Rise of the New Imperialism—the American Empire Project* (New York: Henry Holt, 2006), 20.

10. Daniel M. Masterson and Sayaka Funada-Classen, *The Japanese in Latin America* (Chicago: University of Illinois Press, 2004), 63–73.

11. The following newspaper articles and military documents are a small sample of the reports of Japanese military designs in and around Mexico. Most are highly exaggerated, simplistic, or riddled with US propaganda: "En Busca de Espias Japoneses," *El Imparcial*, February 1, 1907; "Estación Naval Japonesa en México," *El Nacional*, February 23, 1911; "A donde Van los Japoneses?" *El Norte* (Chihuahua), March 11, 1911; "Japan's Military Activity," *New York Times*, March 16, 1907; "Mexico Encourages Japan's Overtures," *New York Times*, August 23, 1919.

12. FBI, US Department of Justice, "Totalitarian Activities: Mexico Today," September 1942, NARA, record group 165, box 997, Records of the War Department General and Special Staffs, Office of the Director of Intelligence, G-2, Subordinate Offices—Latin American Branch, 1940–46.

13. FBI, "Totalitarian Activities."

14. Betty Kirk, *Covering the Mexican Front: The Battle of Europe versus America* (Norman: University of Oklahoma Press, 1942), 293–94. For her source, Betty Kirk used observations and an interview with the Chinese Minister to Mexico, Mr. Ching Tien-Ku. According to Kirk, Ching Tien-Ku provided the fourfold objectives of the Japanese empire for Mexico: (1) invade the United States via Mexico, (2) encourage

all Japanese colonies in Latin America to cooperate with the Axis nations, (3) gain raw materials from Mexico, and (4) ensure the neutrality of Latin American countries.

15. Franklin Delano Roosevelt, "No. 53 The Good Neighbor Policy," reprinted in Robert H. Holden and Eric Zolov's *Latin America and the United States: A Documentary History* (New York: Oxford University Press, 2000), 141–42.

16. Monica A. Rankin, *Mexico, la Patria: Propaganda and Production during World War II* (Lincoln: University of Nebraska Press, 2009), 65.

17. Paz, *Strategy, Security, and Spies*, 17–19.

18. Rankin, *Mexico, La Patria*, 75.

19. Stephen R. Niblo, *War, Diplomacy, and Development: The United States and Mexico, 1938–1954* (Wilmington, DE: SR Books), 91.

20. Burton St. John III, "An Enduring Legacy of World War I: Propaganda, Journalism and the Domestic Struggle over the Commodification of Truth," in *War and the Media: Essays on News Reporting, Propaganda and Popular Culture*, Paul M. Haridakis et al., eds. (Jefferson, NC: McFarland, 2009), 149–51. According to St. John, the Official Bulleting was the first state-sponsored newspaper in the United States.

21. Ibid.

22. Ibid., 152.

23. Pan American Union, *Report on the Activities of the Pan American Union*, 1923–27 (Washington, DC: United States Government Printing Office, 1927). See also "What the Union Is," NARA, record group 229, Office of Inter-American Affairs, entry 1, box 367, Information, Science, and Education. The Pan American Union went through several name changes after its establishment. In 1890 it was named the International Union of American Republics, but at the Fourth International Conference its name was changed to the Pan American Union.

24. Ibid., 1, 32.

25. Ibid., 2.

26. Pan American Union, *Report on the Activities of the Pan American Union*, 1923–27 (Washington, DC: United States Government Printing Office, 1927), 3.

27. Ibid., 3. The Pan American Union Bulletin ran a total of four series: Agricultural; Educational; Public Hygiene and Social-Welfare; and Industry, Commerce, and Finance.

28. Ibid., 5–13.

29. Cramer and Prutsch, "Nelson A. Rockefeller's Office of Inter-American Affairs." The OIAA predecessor was the "Office for Coordination of Commercial and Cultural Relations between the American Republics," created in 1940.

30. Rankin, *Mexico, La Patria*, 79.

31. Ibid., 86.

32. "Axis Propaganda and Activities in Latin America," Military Intelligence Division, Special Study Group, January 14, 1942, NARA, record group 165, box 985, Records of the War Department General and Special Staff, Office of the Director of Intelligence G-2, Subordinate Offices—Latin American Branch.

33. Rankin, *Mexico, La Patria*, 87.

34. The first issue of *En Guardia: Para Defensa de las Américas*, in August 1941, was published in Portuguese. It ceased publication with vol. 4 in July 1945.

35. Nelson A. Rockefeller, "New Economic Frontier," *Inter-American Monthly* 1, no. 1 (May 1942), 18–20.

36. Betty Kirk, "Mexico's War on Hidden Japanese," *Inter-American Monthly* 2, no. 1 (January 1943), 14–16.

37. Ibid.

38. Willie Knapp Jones, "Sport in Spanish," *Inter-American Monthly* III, no. 2 (February 1944), 21–25.

39. Kirk, "Mexico's War on Hidden Japanese," 14–16. The "Island of Tres Marías" mentioned in this article is likely Isla Maria Madre, an island off the coast of Nayarit that was used as a penal colony. Isla Maria Madre Federal Prison was established in 1905 and is still in use.

40. Ibid, 15.

41. Gregory Mason, "The Hyphen in Mexico," *Outlook*, January 17, 1917, 105.

42. Betty Kirk's other major publication was *Covering the Mexican Front*. Generally, this book is sympathetic to Mexico and especially to the policies of Lázaro Cárdenas. However, Kirk's discussion on the Japanese is heavily biased toward the United States and the Allied effort in the war. This book does not contain a single citation and when discussing Japan and fifth column activities in Mexico she fails to provide to the reader where she received such information.

43. Josephus Daniels, "Introduction," in Betty Kirk's *Covering the Mexican Front*, xi–xvi. While based in Mexico, Betty Kirk wrote a significant number of articles for the *Christian Science Monitor*. Kirk's articles covered such topics as the administration of Cárdenas, land redistribution, labor issues, the expropriation of oil in Mexico, and Mexico's trade with Germany and Japan.

44. The cover of Naft's study only indicates that it was published in 1943. Since Naft used Kirk's article from January 1943, it is most likely Naft's study was published sometime after Kirk's.

45. NARA, record group 165, box 978, Records of the War Department General and Special Staffs, Office of the Director of Intelligence G-2, Subordinate Offices—Latin American Branch, 1940–46; John W. White, "The Japanese Pincers in Brazil," *Saturday Evening Post*, June 27, 1942, 26–27, 44, 46, 48. By 1940 there were approximately 300,000 Japanese in Brazil. However, Brazil did not create concentration camps for its Japanese population and did not round up Japanese for internment in the United States. According to Jeffrey Lesser this was the result of the logistics involved in rounding up such a large number of Japanese and fears of Japan retaliating. For a longer discussion on the Japanese in Brazil, see Jeffrey Lesser, *Negotiating National Identity: Immigrants, Minorities, and the Struggle for Ethnicity in Brazil* (Durham, NC: Duke University Press, 1999).

46. Lesser, *Negotiating National Identity*, 127–36.

47. Thomas E. Skidmore, "Racial Ideas and Social Policy in Brazil, 1870–1940," in *The Idea of Race in Latin America, 1870–1940*, Richard Graham, ed. (Austin: University of Texas Press), 23–25. In 1934 Brazil implemented a 2 percent quota based on the number of immigrants from that nationality already in the country. This restriction was primarily aimed at the Japanese in Brazil.

48. Greg Robinson, *A Tragedy of Democracy: Japanese Confinement in North America* (New York: Columbia University Press, 2009), 145–46.

49. Paz, *Strategy, Security, and Spies*, 190. See also Friedrich E. Schuler, *Mexico between Hitler and Roosevelt: Mexican Foreign Relations in the Age of Lázaro Cárdenas, 1934–1940* (Albuquerque: University of New Mexico Press, 1998), 74–75.

50. Letra a C. Jefe del Departamento de Investigaciones Políticas y Sociales, El Inspector, Javier J. Villegas, Asunto: Informe general sobre el Movimiento Sinarquista, México, DF, July 19, 1945, AGN, caja 98, Dirección General de Investigaciones Políticas y Sociales, expediente 2-1/131/908, folio series. 29–33.

51. Schuler, *Mexico between Hitler and Roosevelt*, 74–75.

52. Paz, *Strategy, Security, and Spies*, 190.

53. David Craven, *Art and Revolution in Latin America, 1910–1990* (New Haven, CT: Yale University Press, 2002), 26.

54. Rivera's Detroit mural was not without controversy. Many of his contemporaries saw him as selling out to capitalism, and Siqueiros attacked him directly in the artist periodical *New Masses* as an "agent of the government." For more on this, see Andrew Hemingway, *Artist on the Left: American Artist and the Communist Movement, 1926–1956* (New Haven, CT: Yale University Press, 2002), 27–28.

55. Dawn Ades, Guy Brett, Stanton L. Catlin, Rosemary O'Neil, and South Bank Centre, *Art in Latin America: The Modern Era, 1820–1980* (New Haven, CT: Yale University Press, 1989), 181.

56. Deborah Caplow, *Leopoldo Méndez: Revolutionary Art and the Mexican Print* (Austin: University of Texas Press, 2007), 94.

57. Craven, *Art and Revolution in Latin America*, 63–71. See also Caplow, *Leopoldo Méndez*. 123–124.

58. Craven, *Art and Revolution in Latin America*, 67. According to Craven, TGP created "the first-known image outside of Europe of the Holocaust."

59. Secretaria de Gobernación, Oficina de Información Politica y Social, 2-1/130-633 tomo V, Jesus Gonzalez Valencia, January 1941, Inspector de la Oficina, AGN, caja 78, expediente 5 folio series 514. The twelve points were the following: (1) achievement of complete victory and organization of security and peace, (2) unity of the nation, (3) improving people's living conditions, (4) industrialization and economic development in Mexico, (5) development of agriculture and livestock, (6) continuation and completion of land reform, (7) monetary and financial policy, (8) social security, (9) cultural development of the people, (10) support for the indigenous population, (11) national defense and security, and (12) improvement of our democratic life. *Un Programa para Unir Más a la Nación: Lo Primero Ante la Campana Presidencial*, edicion de "La Voz de México" (México, DF: Fondo de Cultura Popular, S.C., March 1945).

60. These included the Atlantic Charter (1941), the Dumbarton Oaks Conference (1944), and the Yalta Conference (1945).

61. Jesus Gonzalez Valencia, January 1941; *Un Programa*.

62. Ibid.

63. Grandin, *Empire's Workshop*, 19.

Chapter Five

1. Diplomatic message from Mexico (Miura) to Tokyo, December 26, 1941, Urgent, NARA, record group 457, National Security Agency, Japanese Diplomatic Messages 17,663–18,616, entry 9011, box 21.

2. Letra, Urgente, Dir. Gral. de Asuntos Políticos y del Servico Diplomáticos, Manuel Tello a C. secretario de Gobernación, Asunto: Concentración de Subditos

Japoneses, Gestion de la legación de Portugal, AGN, caja 317, Dirección General de Investigaciones Políticas y Sociales, 1939–45, expediente 75, Japonesas.

3. Mexico (Miura) to Tokyo, July 4, 1941, NARA, record group 457, entry 9011, box 15, National Security Agency, Japanese Diplomatic Messages, 12,219–13,067. In the intercepted Japanese cable Ambassador Miura advised his superiors in Tokyo that a rebellion in Guatemala designed by Japanese military attaché Nisi stood a good chance of success. Miura also advised the use of Marshall Urutaado [Hurtado] of Nicaragua to lead the rebellion since he was not only a very influential man but a greatly respected person. The cable also indicated that the rebellion did not need to go to its fullest extent to be considered a success as long as it was carried out to the point where US intervention occurred. In this manner, a "cleavage" would occur among the countries in Latin America. It would also endanger considerably the fundamental policy on which the United States attached the greatest importance, a policy, which envisaged placing within her influence the regions extending to Panama. If it succeeded to an extent, it would at least upset at once the political balance among the countries as far as Panama.

4. By 1944, a total of 84 Japanese from Mexico had been brought to the United States for internment. By comparison, Peru sent 1,799 Japanese for internment to the United States. See Correspondence from Edward J. Ennis, Department of Justice, Alien Enemy Control Unit to Lieutenant Colonel George D. Dorroh, Chief, Visa and Passport Control Branch, Military Intelligence Service, Washington, DC, May 18, 1944, NARA, record group 165 Records of the War Department General and Special Staffs, Office of the Director of Intelligence G-2, Subordinate Offices Latin American Branch, 1940–46, entry 188, box 990.

5. Secretaria de Gobernación, Departamento de Investigaciones Política y Social, Teresa Deutch de Kohn y Benito Naito Hirokichi, Investigación relacionada con el Japonés Benito Naito Hirokichi que remitío la 18a Compañía de esta Jefatura de Policía del DF, México, October 10, 1942, AGN, caja 123, Dirección General de Investigaciones Políticas y Sociales, 1942–51, expediente 265.5/16.

6. Secretaria de Gobernación, Departamento de Investigaciones Política y Social, Teresa Deutch de Kohn y Benito Naito Hirokichi, Investigación relacionada con el Japonés Benito Naito Hirokichi que remitío la 18a Compañía de esta Jefatura de Policía del DF, México, DF, October 10, 1942, AGN, caja 123, Dirección General de Investigaciones Políticas y Sociales, 1942–51, expediente 265.5/16.

7. Ernesto Benito Naito Hirokichi, Japonés, Secretaría de Gobernación, Oficial de Información Política y Social, 2-1/265.5/19, October 1942, Acusado de dedicarse a actividades de espionaje, AGN, caja 124, Dirección General de Investigaciones Políticas y Sociales, 1939–45, expediente 265.5/18 al 265.5/725.1.

8. Digest of Information on Axis Activities in Latin America, January 14, 1942, Division of Reports Coordinator of Inter-American Affairs, NARA, record group 165, entry 188, box 980, Records of the War Department General and Special Staffs, Office of the Director of Intelligence G-2, Subordinate Offices, of the Latin American Branch, 1940–46.

9. Maria Emilia Paz, *Strategy, Security, and Spies: Mexico and the US as Allies in World War II* (University Park: Pennsylvania State University Press, 1997), 172.

10. FBI, US Department of Justice, "Totalitarian Activities, Mexico . . . Today," September 1942, 246, NARA, record group 165, entry 188, box 997, Records of the

War Department General and Special Staffs, Office of the Director of Intelligence G-2 Subordinate Offices Latin American Branch, 1940–46.

11. James L. Tigner, "Mexico and Japan: A Trans-Pacific Historical Survey" (undated, unpublished manuscript in the author's possession), 412. Mexico ordered all Axis nationals to evacuate at least 200 km (124 miles) from the coastlines and 100 km (93 miles) from the US-Mexican border.

12. Ibid. Other measures taken by the Mexican authorities included canceling all permits for Japanese fishing in Lower California waters, ordering all persons of the Japanese race to leave Lower California, removing Japanese residents in Barra de Navidad and Cihuatlan and the Tampico region, putting into effect a program to remove all Japanese residing on the west coast of Mexico, closing all amateur and private experimental radio transmittal stations by presidential decree, authorizing the passage of United States troops through Mexican soil, and granting permission for American naval forces and military planes to use Mexican harbors and bases.

13. Aaron W. Navarro, *Political Intelligence and the Creation of Modern Mexico, 1938–1954* (University Park: Penn State University Press, 2010), 150–52.

14. FBI, "Totalitarian Activities." 436–437.

15. Paz, *Strategy, Security, and Spies*. 155, 203–205.

16. Navarro, *Political Intelligence*, 176.

17. FBI, "Totalitarian Activities." 245.

18. Tigner, "Mexico and Japan," 412.

19. FBI, "Totalitarian Activities," 440.

20. Chizuko Watanabe, "The Japanese Immigrant Community in Mexico: Its History and Present" (M.A. thesis, California State University, Los Angles, 1983), 78–80. According to Watanabe, all adult male Japanese in Cuba were incarcerated during the war. Watanabe cites Dennison Nash and Louis C. Schaw. "Achievement and Acculturation: A Japanese Example," in Melford Spiro, ed. *Context and Meaning in Cultural Anthropology* (New York: The Free Press, 1965), 206–24. Peru, in collaboration with the FBI, rounded up 1,771 Japanese who were sent to the United States for the duration of the war.

21. José Martin Nomura and Daniela Nomura Hernandez, interviewed by Lorraine Orlandi, Acacoyagua, Chiapas, 2007.

22. Mexico did have two internment camps, Perote and Santa Maria, for nationals from the Axis powers considered dangerous or suspected of espionage, which included a handful of Japanese.

23. Atsuko Tanabe, *Huellas Japonesas en la Cultura Mexicana* (Tijuana, México: Colegio de la Frontera, 1997), 27.

24. Manuel Ávila Camacho, "Decreto por el cual se declara a Mexico en estado de Guerra," AGN, caja 828, expediente 550/44-2.

25. Emergency Advisory Committee for Political Defense, Detention and Expulsion of Dangerous Axis Agents and Nationals, May 21, 1943, NARA, record group 165, Records of the War Department General and Special Staffs, Office of the Director of Intelligence G-2, Subordinate Offices Latin American Branch, 1940–46, entry 188, box 990.

26. Lorraine Orlandi, "The Little Known Story of Japanese Migration, Assimilation, Suffering and Identity in Mexico," *Inside Mexico*, July 2007, 13–20.

27. Naval Intelligence Report, from US Naval Attaché at Mazatlán, September 10, 1943, NARA, record group 165, box 978, Records of the War Department General and Special Staffs, Office of the Director of Intelligence G-2, Subordinate Offices—Latin American Branch, 1940–46.

28. The term *cacique* is Taino in origin and refers to a chief of a tribe. During the colonial era Spanish officials utilized the term to refer to local leaders of indigenous groups. In Mexico, during the nineteenth and twentieth centuries the label is in reference to a local or regional boss.

29. Secretario del Trabajo y Prevision Social, Ignacio García Téllez a Sr. Licenciado. Miguel Alemán, Secretario de Gobernación, January 15, 1942, AGN, caja 317, Dirección General de Investigaciones Políticas y Sociales, 1939–45, expediente 75, Japoneses.

30. Tigner, "Mexico and Japan," 414.

31. "I am 60% Japanese and 60% Mexican," *Inside Mexico*, July 2007, 7.

32. Inspector P.S. 100 a Sr. Licenciado. Eduardo Ampudia V., Jefe del Depto. de Investigaciones Políticas y Sociales, Denuncia de Unos Japoneses de Haber Sido Victimas de un Inspector de Este Departamento, México, DF, August 23, 1943, AGN, caja 317, Dirección General de Investigaciones Políticas y Sociales, 1939–45, expediente 2-1/360/1 al 2-1/360/75; Secretaria de Gobernación, Departamento de Investigación Política y Social, expediente 2-1/260/12, Japoneses, January 1942.

33. Cantwell C. Brown, Major, G.S.C., Assistant military attaché. Restrictions on Enemy Aliens in the State of Chiapas. Military Intelligence Division, Mexico City, December 1, 1943, NARA, record group 165, entry 188, box 993, Records of the War Department General and Special Staffs. Office of the Director of Intelligence G-2, Subordinate Offices Latin American Branch, 1940–46.

34. Fukuy y Hueda. Letter to C. Presidente de la República, México, D.F., Motozintla, Chiapas, March 24, 1942. AGN, Manuel Avila Camacho, Vol. 824, expediente 550/9-1.

35. Dirección General de Investigaciones Políticas y Sociales Letra, Eizi Matuda a C. Jefe del Departamento de Investigación Políticas y Social, Secretario de Gobernación, México, DF, Escuintla, Chis, February 18, 1943, AGN, caja 317, expediente 75, 1939–45.

36. Izawa Minoru, *Nihon-jin mekishiko ijushi* (*History of the Japanese Immigrants in Mexico*) (Tokyo: private printing, 1971), 288.

37. Presidente Miguel Ávila Camacho, Decreto-Ley: Suspención de Garantías Individuales, June 1, 1942, AGN, Miguel Ávila Camacho, caja 828, expediente 550/44-2.

38. Tigner, "Mexico and Japan," 414. See also Edward N. Barnhart, "Citizenship and Political Tests in Latin American Republics in World War II," *Hispanic American Historical Review* 42, no. 3 (August 1962), 297–332.

39. Tigner, "Mexico and Japan," 422–23.

40. Ibid.

41. Telegram from Colonia Japonésa de Mazatlan (Japanese colony of Mazatlan) 50 Sr. Presidente De La Republica, General De Division Manuel Ávila Camacho, México, DF January 17, 1942, AGN, Manuel Ávila Camacho, box 824 bis, folder 550/9-1.

42. Minoru, *Nihon-jin mekishiko ijushi*, 288.

43. Letter from Leticia Jimenez de Takahashi to Sr. President de la Republica Mexicana, June 28, 1944, AGN, Manuel Ávila Camacho, box 824 bis, folder 550/9-1.

44. Military Intelligence Division, War Department, *Axis Espionage and Propaganda in Latin America*, Washington, DC, May 15, 1946, NARA, record group 165, Records of the War Department General and Special Staffs, Office of the Director of Intelligence G-2 Subordinate Offices Latin American Branch, 1940–46, Entry, 188, box 982.

Chapter Six

1. Yuko Akachi, "Ex Hacienda de Temixco," Publicación Bimestral no. 33, *Boletin Informativo* 14 (Asociación México Japonesa, September 2008), 2–5.

2. Yuko Akachi, "Ex Hacienda de Temixco," 2–3.

3. The ten US internment camps and their locations are as follows: Tule Lake, CA; Manzanar, CA; Poston, AZ; Gila River, AZ; Heart Mountain, WY; Minidoka, ID; Topaz, UT; Granada, CO; Jerome, AK; and Rohwer, AK. Many more internment camps were run by the United States. For example, the Justice Department operated the Immigration and Naturalization Service internment camps at Kooskia, Idaho, and Crystal City, Texas, housed Japanese Mexicans and other Japanese from Latin America. Canada had twenty-two camps and relocation centers in the provinces of British Columbia, Ontario, Quebec, New Brunswick, and Nova Scotia. For details on the Japanese Canadian experience, see Forrest E. LaViolette, "Japanese Evacuation in Canada," *Far Eastern Survey* 11, no. 15 (July 1942), 163–167; Maryka Omatsu, *Bittersweet Passage and the Japanese Canadian Experience* (Toronto: Between the Lines, 1992); Carmela Patrias, "Race, Employment Discrimination, and State Complicity in Wartime Canada, 1939–1945," *Labour* 59 (April 1, 2007), 9–41; Ken Adachi, *The Enemy That Never Was: A History of the Japanese Canadians* (Toronto, Ontario: McClelland and Stewart, 1976); Iyko Day, "Alien Intimacies: The Coloniality of Japanese Internment in Australia, Canada, and the U.S," *Amerasia Journal* 36, no. 2 (2010), 107–24; Pamela Hickman and Masako Fukawa, *Righting Canada's Wrong: Japanese Canadian Internment in the Second World War* (Toronto, Ontario: James Lorimer & Company, Limited, 2012); Roy Miki, *Redress: Inside the Japanese Canadian Call for Justice* (Vancouver, BC: Raincoast Books, 2005). Peru sent its Japanese population initially to Crystal City, Texas, where a Japanese American internment camp already existed. Eventually most of the Japanese Peruvians were interned in Immigration and Naturalization Service Internment Camps located in Kennedy, Texas, and Santa Fe, New Mexico.

4. Emergency Advisory Committee for Political Defense, Detention and Expulsion of Dangerous Axis Agents and Nationals, May 21, 1943, NARA, record group 165, Records of the War Department General and Special Staffs, Office of the Director of Intelligence G-2, Subordinate Offices Latin American Branch, 1940–46, entry 188, box 990.

5. *Nihon Mekishiko Imin*. (Japanese Emigration to Mexico). (Tokyo: Japanese Compilation Committee on Immigration History, 1971), 286; See also Tigner, "Mexico and Japan," 450.

6. Chizuko Watanabe, "The Japanese Immigrant Community in Mexico: Its History and Present" (M.A. thesis, California State University, Los Angeles, 1983), 46, 86n10.

7. AGN, I.P.S., Caja 373, Expediente 2–1/362.4(52)/1149, Dirección General de Investigaciónes Políticas y Sociales, Expediente 9, f.16, 1942 a 1943. Luis T. Tsuji, Letter to Al C. Secretaría Secretaría de Gobernación, October 16, 1942, AGN, Dirección General de Investigaciones Políticas y Sociales, caja 373, expediente 2-1/362.4(52)/1149, Dirección General de Investigaciones Políticas y Sociales, expediente 9, folio 16, 1942–43. Most of the letters written by this committee contained the Spanish phrase *Comité Japonés de Ayuda Mutua* (Japanese Mutual Aid Committee), which is the Spanish translation of the Japanese phrase *Kyo Ei Kai* (mutual aid). The committee's original address was located at Sor Juana Inez de la Cruz, No. 112, Mexico, D.F. However, by October 1942 it changed location to Calle de San Antonio Abad #327, Mexico, D.F.

8. Watanabe, "Japanese Immigrant Community in Mexico," 68–69.

9. Izawa Minoru, *Nihon-jin mekishiko ijushi* (*The History of the Japanese Immigrants in Mexico*) (Tokyo: private printing, 1971), 286–87.

10. Circular y Estatutos de CJAM de Ayuda Mutua, March 4, 1942, AGN, caja 373, expediente 2-1/362.4(52)/1149, fol. 3-5, 1942–43, Dirección General de Investigaciones Políticas y Sociales.

11. Minoru, *Nihon-jin mekishiko ijushi*, 286–87.

12. Circular y Estatutos de Comité Japonés de Ayuda Mutua.

13. Tigner, "Mexico and Japan," 450–15.

14. Naval Intelligence Report, from US Naval Attaché at Mexico City, October 2, 1943, NARA, record group 165, box 978, Records of the War Department General and Special Staffs, Office of the Director of Intelligence G-2, Subordinate Offices—Latin American Branch, 1940–46.

15. Estatutos del Comité Japonés de Ayuda Mutua, March 4, 1942, AGN, caja 373, Dirección General de Investigaciones Políticas y Sociales, expediente 9, fol. 16, 1942–43.

16. Licenciado. Marco Antonio Nunez T. a C. Jefe del Departamento de Investigación Políticas y Social, México, DF, April 23, 1942, AGN, caja 373, Dirección General de Investigaciones Políticas y Sociales, expediente 9, fol. 16, 1942–43.

17. Izawa Minoru, *Nihon-jin mekishiko ijushi*, 288.

18. Bill Hosokawa, *JACL in quest for Justice: The History of the Japanese American Citizens League* (New York: Morrow, 1982), 134, 137–38.

19. Cosme A. Sanchez, letra a Al C. Secretario de Gobernación, Departamento de Investigación Política y Social. Uhei Ueda Taniaguchi, Japonés, 1942, AGN, caja 367, expediente 2-1/362.4(52)/203.

20. "Ex Hacienda de Temixco." 2–5.

21. Ibid.

22. Daniel M. Masterson and Sayaka Funada-Classen, *The Japanese in Latin America* (Chicago: University of Illinois Press, 2004), 127. As their source, Masterson and Funada-Classen cite "Archivo Historico, 'Genaro Estrada de la Secretaría de Relaciones Exteriores de Mexico. Ciudadanos de Eje Concentrados en Mexico, Japoneses, Informe,'" document III-917-6.

23. Asunto: Informe acerca de observaciones practicadas en la Hacienda de Temixco, Morelos, September 1942, Agente Eliseo Castro Reina, AGN, caja 70, Secretaría de Gobernación, Oficina de Información Política y Social, expediente 130-553, tomo VIII. The $85,000 pesos were approximately US$17,000 at a 1941 exchange rate of 4.85 pesos to the dollar.

24. Al C. Jefe del Dpto. de Investigaciones Políticas y Social, de Eliseo Castro Reina, Inspector, Asunto: Informe acerca de observaciones practicades en la Hacienda de Temixco, Morelos México, DF, September 1942, PS-1, AGN, caja 70, expediente 1, Dirección General de Investigaciones Políticas y Sociales.

25. Minoru, *Nihon-jin mekishiko ijushi*, 299.

26. Al C. Jefe del Dpto. de Investigaciones Políticas y Social, de Eliseo Castro Reina, Inspector, Asunto: Informe acerca de observaciones practicades en la Hacienda de Temixco, Morelos México, DF, September 1942, PS-1, AGN, caja 70, expediente 1, Dirección General de Investigaciones Políticas y Sociales.

27. Al C. Jefe del Dpto. de Investigaciones Políticas y Social. Adolfo Ruiz Cortines, a Sr. Luis Tsuji, Representante de CJAM de Auyuda Mutua de la Colonia Japonesa en Mexico, Sor Juana Inés de la Cruz, no. 112, México, DF, August 26, 1942, AGN, caja 70, expediente 1, Dirección General de Investigaciones Políticas y Sociales.

28. Ibid.

29. Ingeniero Raymundo del Bosque a C. Secretario de Gobernación, México, DF, February 10, 1943, AGN, caja 373, Dirección General de Investigaciones y Políticas y Sociales.

30. Ingeniero Raymundo del Bosque a C. Secretario de Gobernación, México, DF Asunto: Informe General que rinde el Comisionado en Gobernación en la Colonia Agrícola Japonesa de Castro Uridiales, July 1, 1943, AGN, caja 373, Dirección General de Investigaciones y Políticas y Sociales.

31. Luis T. Tsuji y Isaburo Horiuchi, a C. Secretario de Borenacion, México, DF, December 10, 1944, AGN, caja 373, expediente 2-1/362.4(52)/1149, Comité Japonés Ayuda de Mutua, Dirección General de Investigaciones y Políticas y Sociales.

32. Naval Intelligence Report, from US Naval Attaché at Mexico City, March 17, 1944, NARA, record group 165, box 978, Records of the War Department General and Special Staffs, Office of the Director of Intelligence G-2, Subordinate Offices—Latin American Branch, 1940–46.

33. Ibid.

34. Eliseo Castro Reina, Al C. Jefe del Departamento, Departamento de Investigaciones Políticas y Sociales. Inspector no. 11 (Ricardo Trujillo Q.) Asunto: Hacienda de Temixco, Mor., México, DF, November 6, 1944, AGN, caja 70, expediente 1, Fs 176, 130–553, tomo VIII, Secretaría de Gobernación, Oficina de Informes Políticas y Sociales.

35. Asunto: Informe relacionado con la Orden Verbal que se nos dío para investigar lo relativo a las dificultades originadas entre los agraristas y los japoneses concentrados en la Hacienda de Temixco, Mor. Donaciano Ceballos (Investigaciones Políticas y Sociales #57) and Oscar Olvera Villafana (ISP), Temixco, Mor., March 6, 1944, AGN, caja 373, expediente 2-1/362.4(52)1141, Secretaría de Gobernación, Oficina de Informes Políticas y Sociales, Hacienda de Temixco, Estado de Morelos.

36. Al C. Inspector de la Secretaría de Gobernación comisionado en esta Población, hacienda Temixco de El Presidente del Comisariado Ejidal, Pedro Chavarria

y El Secretario, Efren Domínguez, Temixco, Morelos, October 20, 1944, AGN, caja 373, expediente 2-1/362.4(52)1141, Secretaría de Gobernación, Oficina de Informes Políticas y Sociales.

37. Al C. Jefe del Departamento de Investigaciones Políticas y Sociales. Asunto: Informe relacionado con la comisión que en union del C. Inspector Oscar Olvera Villafana se me confirió en la ex-Hacienda de Temixco, Mor. México, DF, March 15, 1944, Dirección General de Investigaciones Políticas y Sociales Núm. 57, Donaciano Ceballos, AGN, caja 373, expediente 2-1/362.4(52)1141, Secretaría de Gobernación, Oficina de Informes Políticas y Sociales.

38. Hans Werner Tobler, "Peasants and the Shaping of the Revolutionary State, 1910–1940," in *Riot, Rebellion, and Revolution: Rural Social Conflict in Mexico*, Friedrich Katz, ed. (Princeton, NJ: Princeton University Press, 1988), 513–18.

39. Al C. Jefe del Departamento, Departamento de Investigaciones Políticas y Sociales, Inspector no. 11 (Ricardo Trujillo Q.) Asunto: Hacienda de Temixco, Mor., México, DF, November 6, 1944, AGN, caja 70, expediente 1, Folio Series 176, 130–553, tomo VIII. Secretaría de Gobernación, Oficina de Informes Políticas y Sociales, Eliseo Castro Reina.

40. Comité Japonés Ayuda de Mutua, February 8, 1943, AGN, caja 373, expediente 2-11362.4(52)/1141, Secretaría de Gobernación, Departamento de Investigaciones Políticas y Sociales.

41. Letter to Al C. Jefe Depto de Investigaciones Políticas y Sociales de Inspector 168 (Manuel M. Barrera); Inspector 35 (Rodolfo Candiania); Inspector 32 (Romualdo J. Chazaro), México, DF, January 4, 1944, AGN, caja 373, expediente 2-11362.4(52)/1141, Secretaría de Gobernación, Departamento de Investigaciones Políticas y Sociales.

42. Ibid.

43. Kiso Tsuru, Director, CJAM de Ayuda Mutua a C. Secretario de Gobernación: Ensenanza del idioma México, DF, July 10, 1944, AGN, caja 373, expediente 2-1/362.4(52)/1142, Dirección General de Investigaciones y Políticas y Sociales.

44. Ibid.

45. José dos Santos Silva Taveira, Charge d'Affaires of Portugal and Japanese Interest in Mexico to Kiso Tsuru, Director, Comité Japonés Ayuda de Mutua, México, DF, June 22, 1944, AGN, caja 373, expediente 21/362.4(52)/1142, Dirección General de Investigaciones y Políticas y Sociales.

46. Tomas Hayakawa, Estavión Migratoria Perote, Veracruz a Sr. Luis Tsuji, CJAM Japonés de Ayuda Mutua, San Antonio Abad #327, México, DF, April 10, 1943, AGN, caja 373, Dirección General de Investigaciones y Políticas y Sociales.

47. El Jefe de los Servicios Sanitarios, Coordinados en la Estado, Dr. Felipe García Sánchez a Secretaría de Gobernación, Bucareli 99, México, DF, Curnavaca, Morelos, December 17, 1942, AGN, caja 70, expediente 1, F. 176, Secretaría de Gobernación, Oficina de Información Política y Social, 130–553, tomo VIII.

48. Ricardo Herrera, Inspector P.S. 67 a C. Jefe del Departamento de Investigaciones Políticas y Sociales, México, DF, February 8, 1943, AGN, caja 70, expediente 1, Folio 176.

49. Alicia Celis Feria, "Amistad en Tiempos Deficiles entre México y Japón," *Archivo General de la Nacion* 6, no. 22 (October–December 2008), 85–101. Various sources place the distance from 62 to 100 miles from the coast.

50. Jesus K. Akachi, Carlos T. Kasuga, Manuel S. Murakami, María Elena Ota Mishima, Enrique Shibayama, and Rene Tanaka, "Japanese Mexican Historical Overview," in *Encyclopedia of Japanese Descendants in the Americas: An Illustrated History of the Nikkei*, Akemi Kikumura-Yano, ed. (New York: AltaMira Press, 2002), 204–28.

Conclusion

1. James L. Tigner, "Mexico and Japan: A Trans-Pacific Historical Survey" (undated, unpublished manuscript in the author's possession), 436–37.

2. Dr. Felipe García Sánchez a Jefe de los Servicios Sanitarios, to Secretaría de Gobernación, December 17, 1942, AGN, caja 373, expediente 1, folio 263, Departemento de Investigaciones Políticas y Sociales.

3. Roger Daniels, *Prisoners without Trial: Japanese Americans in World War II* (New York: Hill and Wang, 1993), 46–47.

4. Angelo N. Ancheta, *Race, Rights and the Asian American Experience*, Second Edition. (New Brunswick: Rutgers University Press, 2006), 30–32.

5. Robinson, A *Tragedy of Democracy: Japanese Confinement in North America* (New York: Columbia University Press, 2009). Robinson describes his use of the terms "removal," "confinement," "camp," and "inmate" at the beginning of his book ("A Note on Terminology," vii–viii).

6. Daniels, *Prisoners without Trial*, 46–47. Daniels states that 1,862 Japanese Americans died of natural causes in the camps and 5,918 American citizens were born within. He writes, "But the few Japanese Americans who were killed 'accidentally' by their American guards were just as dead as the millions of Jews and others who were killed deliberately by their German, Soviet, or Japanese guards," 47.

7. There are three major islands in these archipelagos: María Madre, María Magdalena, and María Cleopas. In 1905 Mexico established a penal colony on the island of María Madre that remains an active prison. During World War II some enemy aliens were housed in this facility.

8. Midori Nishi, "Some Aspects of Japanese Postwar Migration to Latin America," *Professional Geographer* 14, no. 1 (January 1962), 47–53.

9. A statistical analysis of Japanese property confiscated and businesses broken up due to their removal from coastal communities and military zones has not been fully completed. The 700,000 pesos paid by the Mexican government appeared to be a small sum even by 1950s standards.

10. Watanabe, "Japanese Immigrant Community in Mexico," 91.

11. "I am 60% Japanese and 60% Mexican," *Inside Mexico*, July 2007, 7.

12. Ibid.

13. Ibid.

14. Lorraine Orlandi, "The Little Known Story of Japanese Migration, Assimilation, Suffering and Identity in Mexico," *Inside Mexico*, July 2007, 18

15. Nikkei also include people of mixed racial descent who identify themselves as Nikkei. For a fuller explanation, see Introduction, endnote #5 and www.discovernikkei.org/en/about/what-is-nikkei/ (accessed December 3, 2011).

16. *Encyclopedia de los Municipios y Delagaciones de México: Estado de Chiapas Acacoyagua*, www.e-local.gob.mx/work/templates/enciclo/EMM07chiapas/municipios/07001a.html (accessed December 3, 2011).

17. Orlandi, "Little Known Story," 13–20.
18. Ibid., 16.
19. Ibid., 14.
20. Ibid., 16.
21. Ibid., 19.
22. Ibid.

Bibliography

Archives, Libraries, and Special Collections

México

Archivo General de la Nación, México City (AGN).
Departamento de Investigaciones Políticas y Sociales.
Dirección General de Información.
Registro Nacional de Extranjeros, Migración, México.
Documentación de Instituciones Coloniales.
Documentación de la Administración Pública (XIX).
Ramo de Presidentes.
Lázaro Cárdenas (1934–40).
Manuel Ávila Camacho (1940–46).
Secretaria Relaciones Exteriores (SRE).
Archivo Histórico "Genaro Estrada."
Colegio de México.
Centro de Información y Documentación sobre Japón.
Biblioteca Daniel Cosió Villegas, Centro de Estudios de Asia y África, México.
Centro de Estudios sobre la Universidad (Universidad Nacional Autónoma de México), México City.
Hemeroteca Nacional de México (Universidad Nacional Autónoma de México), México City.

United States

National Archives and Records Administration (NARA), College Park, MD
Records of the Department of State, record group 59.
Records of the Department of State Relating to Political Relations between the United States and Japan, 1910–29, National Archives Microfilm Publication Roll 4.
Records of the Department of State Relating to Internal Affairs of Japan, 1910–29, National Archives Microfilm Publication Roll 1, 14–16.
Records of the Federal Bureau of Investigation (FBI), record group 65.
Records of the War Department General and Special Staffs, record group 165.

Records of the Office of Inter-American Affairs, record group 229.
Records of the Office of Inter-American Affairs, record group 229R.
Contact Prints: Photographs of the Activities of the Office of Inter-American Affairs, Mexico, Nicaragua, Peru.
Records of the US Army Continental Commands, 1821–1920, record group 393.
Records of the National Security Agency/Central Security Service, record group 457.
Benson Latin American Collection, University of Texas at Austin.

Government Publications and Reports

Direccion General de Estadisticas, 1877–1910. México, DF: Talleres Gráficos de la Nación, 1956.
Estadisticas Sociales del Porfiriato, 1877–1910. México, DF: Secretaria de Economía.
Exposición Que Hace el Secretario de Fomento sobre la Colonización de la Baja California. México, DF: Oficina Tip. de la Secretaria de Fomento, 1887.
Furuya, Hideo. *Memoria del Servicio Exterior Mexicano en Japón.* México, DF: Secretaria de Relaciones Exteriores, 1985.
"Informes Diplomaticos y Consulares: Japon." *Boletin Oficial de la Secretaria de Relaciones Exteriores* 20 (May-October 1905).
Landa y Pina, Andres. *El Servico de Migracion en México.* México, DF: Secretaria de Gobernacion, Tallers Gráficos de la Nación, 1930.
Luis Hijar y Haro, *Influencia de la Migracion Europea en el Desarrollo de los Principales paises de Sud America y La Colonizacion Rural e Mexico con Aquellos Factores Para Simplificar Su Poblema Indigena.* Tacubaya, México: Secretaria de Agricultura y Fomento, 1924.
De La Maza, Francisco F. *Código de colonizacion y Terrenos Baldíos de la República Mexicana.* México, DF: Oficina Tip. de la Secretaria de Fomento, 1893.
Pan American Union. *Report on the Activities of the Pan American Union, 1923–1927. Submitted to the Governments, Members of the Pan American Union by the Director General in Accordance with a Resolution of the Fifth International Conference of American States.* Washington, DC: US Government Printing Office, 1927.
Reports of Commerce and Labor, 1908. Washington: Government Printing Office, 1908

Oral History

José Martin Nomura and Daniela Nomura Hernandez, interviewed by Lorraine Orlandi, Acacoyagua, Chiapas, 2007.

Newspapers and Magazines

Chicago Daily Tribune
Cleveland Leader
Excelsior

El Imparcial
Japanese Weekly Mail
El Nacional
New York Times
El Norte
Pan American Bulletin
St. Louis Daily-Democrat

Books and Articles

Aceves, Antonieta Kiyoko Nishikawa. "La inmigración Japónesa a ensenada durante la primera mitad del siglo xx." *Revista de Instituto de Investigaciones Históricas de la Universidad Autónoma de Baja California* 1, no. 1–8 (2004): 24–34.

Adachi, Ken. *The Enemy That Never Was: A History of the Japanese Canadians* (1976).

Ades, Dawn. *Art in Latin America: The Modern Era, 1820–1980.*

Akachi, Jesus K., Carlos T. Kasuga, Manuel S. Murakami, María Elena Ota Mishima, Enrique Shibayama, and Rene Tanaka. "Japanese Mexican Historical Overview." In *Encyclopedia of Japanese Descendants in the Americas: An Illustrated History of the Nikkei*, Akemi Kikumura-Yano, ed. New York: AltaMira Press, 2002, 204–28.

——. *So Far from Allah, So Close to Mexico: Middle Eastern Immigrants in Mexico.* Austin: University of Texas Press, 2007.

Anaya, Delia Salazar. *La Población Extranjera en Mexico (1895–1990): Un Recuento con Base en los Censos Generales de Población*. México, DF: Instituto Nacional de Antropología e Historia, 1996.

Ancheta, Angelo N. *Race, Rights, and the Asian American Experience*. New Brunswick, NJ: Rutgers University Press, 1998.

Associated Press. "Acacoyagua, Mexico." Date unknown. Available from American Online, accessed December 31, 1997.

Aubert, L. "The United States and Japanese Colonization." *Review of Paris* 16 (August 1907), 878–79.

Azuma, Eiichiro. "The Politics of Transnational History Making: Japanese Immigrants on the Western 'Frontier,' 1927–1941." *Journal of American History* 89, no. 4 (May 2007).

Barnhart, Edward N. "Citizenship and Political Tests in Latin American Republics in World War II." *Hispanic American Historical Review* 42, no. 3 (August 1962), 297–332.

Bernstein, Harry, "Mexico's War with Japan." *Far Eastern Survey* 9, no. 24 (November 30, 1942), 245–50.

Bethell, Leslie, ed. "Manuel Gamio and Official Indigenismo in Mexico." *Bulletin of Latin American Research* 7, no. 1 (1988), 75–89.

——. *Mexico since Independence*. Cambridge: Cambridge University Press, 1998.

Buchenau, Jurgen. "Small Numbers, Great Impact: Mexico and Its Immigrants, 1821–1973." *Journal of American Ethnic History* 20, no. 3 (Spring 2001), 23–49.

Camacho, Julia Schiavone, *Chinese Mexicans: Transpacific Migrations, and the Search for a Homeland, 1910–1960*. Chapel Hill: University of North Carolina Press, 2012.

Caplow, Deborah. *Leopoldo Méndez: Revolutionary Art and the Mexican Print*. Austin: University of Texas Press, 2007.

Chase, Stuart. *Mexico: A Study of Two Americas*. New York: Macmillan, 1931.

Cortés, Enrique. *Relaciones entre México y Japón durante el Porfiriato*. México, DF: Secretaria de Relaciones Exteriores, 1990.

Craib, Raymond B., III. *Chinese Immigrants in Porfirian Mexico: A Preliminary Study of Settlement, Economic Activity and Anti-Chinese Sentiment*. Occasional Papers, Center for Latin American Studies. Albuquerque: University of New Mexico, 1998.

Cramer, Gisela and Ursula Prutsch, "Nelson A. Rockefeller's Office of Inter-American Affairs (1940–1946) and Record Group 229." *Hispanic American Historical Review* 86, no. 4 (November 2006), 785–86.

Craven, David. *Art and Revolution in Latin America, 1910–1990*. New Haven, CT: Yale University Press, 2002.

Cruz, Francisco Santiago. *Relaciones Diplomáticas entre la Nueva España y el Japón*. México, DF: Editorial Jus, 1964.

Cumberland, Charles C. "The Sonoran Chinese and the Mexican Revolution." *Hispanic American Historical Review* 40, no. 2 (May 1960), 191–211.

Daniels, Roger. *Prisoners without Trial: Japanese Americans in World War II*. New York: Hill and Wang, 1993.

Dawson, Alexander S. *Indian and Nation in Revolutionary Mexico*. Tucson: University of Arizona Press, 2004.

Day, Iyko. "Alien Intimacies: The Coloniality of Japanese Internment in Australia, Canada, and the US" *Amerasia Journal* 36, no. 2 (2010), 107–24.

Delgado, Grace, *Making the Chinese Mexican: Global Migration, Localism, and Exclusion in the US-Mexican Borderlands*. Palo Alto, CA: Stanford University Press, 2012.

Dillon, Richard H. "Maximilian's Asiatic Colonization Scheme." *Mid-America: An Historical Review* 34 (n.s.) 23, no. 2 (April 1952), 148–52.

Duncan, Robert H. "The Chinese and Economic Development of Northern Baja California, 1889–1929." *Hispanic American Historical Review* 74, no. 4 (November 1994), 615–47.

Dwyer, John J. *The Agrarian Dispute: The Expropriation of American-Owned Rural Land in Postrevolutionary Mexico*. Durham, NC: Duke University Press, 2008.

Encyclopedia de los Municipios y Delagaciones de México: Estado de Chiapas Acacoyagua. www.elocal.gob.mx/work/templates/enciclo/EMM07chiapas/municipios/07001a.html (accessed December 3, 2011).

"Ex Hacienda de Temixco." Publicación Bimestral no. 33. *Boletin Informativo* 14 (Asociación México Japonesa, Septimbre 2008), 2–5.

Feria, Alicia Celis, "Amistad en Tiempos Deficiles entre México y Japón." *Archivo General de la Nación* 6, no. 22 (October–December 2008), 85–101.

Gardiner, C. Harvey. "Early Diplomatic Relations between Mexico and the Far East." *Americas: Quarterly Review of Inter-American Cultural History* 6, no. 4 (April 1950), 401–14.

Graham, Richard, ed., *The Idea of Race in Latin America, 1870–1940*. Austin: University of Texas Press, 1990.

Grandin, Greg. *Empire's Workshop: Latin America, the United States, and the Rise of the New Imperialism—the American Empire Project*. New York: Henry Holt, 2006.

Guerra, Ramon, "Continuity and Change: Japanese Ethnicity in Guadalajara, Mexico." Ph.D. diss., Southern Methodist University, 1989.

Guevarra, Rudy P., Jr. *Becoming Mexipino: Multiethnic Identities and Communities in San Diego*. New Brunswick, NJ: Rutgers University Press, 2012.

Haber, Stephen H. "Assessing the Obstacles to Industrialisation: The Mexican Economy, 1830–1940." *Journal of Latin American Studies* 24, no. 1 (February 1992), 1–32.

Harris, Charles H., and Louis R. Sadler, *The Border and the Revolution: Clandestine Activities of the Mexican Revolution, 1910–1920*. Silver City, NM: High-Lonesome Books, 1988.

Hart, John Mason. *Empire and Revolution: The Americans in Mexico since the Civil War*. Berkeley: University of California Press, 2002

Hemingway, Andrew. *Artist on the Left: American Artist and the Communist Movement, 1926–1956*. New Haven, CT: Yale University Press, 2002.

Herring, Hubert. "Our New Ally, Mexico." *Inter-American Monthly* 1, no. 3 (July 1942), 8–15.

Hickman, Pamela, and Masako Fukawa, *Righting Canada's Wrong: Japanese Canadian Internment in the Second World War*. Ontario, Canada: Lorimer, 2012.

Hirabayashi, Lane Ryo. "Community Destroyed? Assessing the Impact of the Loss of Community on Japanese Americans during World War II." In *Re/Collecting Asian America*, Josephene Lee et al., eds. Philadelphia: Temple University, 2002, 94–107.

Hirabayashi, Lane Ryo, and Akemi Kikumura-Yano, eds. *Encyclopedia of Japanese Descendants in the Americas: An Illustrated History of the Nikkei*. New York: AltiMira Press, 2002.

——. "Japanese Latin Americans during World War II: A Reconsideration." In *Japanese Diasporas: Unsung Pasts, Conflicting Presents, and Uncertain Futures*, Lane Ryo Hirabayashi et al., eds. New York: Routledge, 2006, 159–71.

Hirabayashi, Lane Ryo, Akemi Kikumura-Yano, and James A. Hirabayashi, eds. *New Worlds, New Lives: Globalization and the People of Japanese Descent in the Americas and from Latin America to Japan*. Palo Alto, CA: Stanford University Press, 2002.

Hosokawa, Bill. *JACL in quest for Justice: The History of the Japanese American Citizens League*. New York: Morrow, 1982.

Hu-Dehart, Evelyn. "Immigrants to a Developing Society: The Chinese in Northern Mexico, 1875–1932." *Journal of Arizona History* 21 (Autumn 1980), 275–312.

——. "Racism and Anti-Chinese Persecution in Sonora, Mexico, 1876–1932." *Amerasia Journal* 9, no. 2 (1982), 1–28.

——. "Coolies, Shopkeepers, Pioneers: The Chinese of Mexico and Peru, 1849–1930." *Amerasia Journal* 15, no. 2 (1989), 91–116.

"I am 60% Japanese and 60% Mexican." *Inside Mexico*, July 2007, 7.

Iriye, Akira. *Pacific Estrangement: Japanese and American Expansion, 1897–1911*. Cambridge, MA: Harvard University Press, 1972.

Jacques, Leo M. "The Anti-Chinese Legislative and Press Campaign in Sonora, Mexico, 1916–21." *Immigrants and Minorities* 5, no. 2 (July 1986), 167–80.

Japanese Compilation Committee on Immigration History. *Nihon Mekishiko Imin* (*Japanese Emigration to Mexico*). Tokyo: 1971.

Jones, Willie Knapp. "Sport in Spanish." *Inter-American Monthly* 3, no. 2 (February 1944), 21–25.

Joseph, Gilbert M. and Daniel Nugent. "Popular Culture and State Formation in Revolutionary Mexico." In *Everyday Forms of State Formation: Revolution and the Negotiation of Rule in Modern Mexico*, Gilbert M. Joseph and Daniel Nugent, eds. Durham, NC: Duke University Press, 1994.

Kachi, Teruko Okada. *The Treaty of 1911 and the Immigration and Alien Land Law Issue Between the United States and Japan, 1911–1913*. New York: Arno Press, 1978.

Katz, Fredrich. *The Secret War in Mexico: Europe, the United States and the Mexican Revolution*. Chicago: University of Chicago press, 1981.

——. *The Life and Times of Pancho Villa*. Stanford, CA: Stanford University Press, 1998.

Kirk, Betty, *Covering the Mexican Front: The Battle of Europe versus America*. Norman: University of Oklahoma Press, 1942.

——. "Mexico's War on Hidden Japanese." *Inter-American* 2, no. 1 (January 1943), 14–16.

Knight, Alan. "The Working Class and the Mexican Revolution, 1900–1920." *Journal of Latin American Studies* 16, no. 1 (May 1984), 51–79.

——. *The Mexican Revolution*, vol. 2. Cambridge: Cambridge University Press, 1986.

——. *US-Mexican Relations, 1910–1940: An Interpretation*. San Diego: University of California, Center for US-Mexican Studies, 1987.

——. "Racism, Revolution, and Indigenismo: Mexico, 1910–1940." In *The Idea of Race in Latin America, 1870–1940*, Richard Graham, ed. Austin: University of Texas Press, 1990.

——. "The Rise and Fall of Cardenismo, c. 1930–c. 1946." In *Mexico since Independence*, Leslie Bethell, ed. Cambridge: Cambridge University Press, 1991, 256–57.

——. "US Imperialism/Hegemony and Latin American Resistance." In *Empire and Dissent: The United States and Latin America*, Fred Rosen, ed. Durham, NC: Duke University Press, 2008.

Kodama, Masaaki. *Nihon Imin-Shi Kankyu Josetsu* (*Introduction to the Study of Japanese Immigration History*). Hiroshima: Keisui-sha, 1992.

Krych, Nobuko. "The History of the Early Japanese Emigration and Colonization in Mexico." Ph.D. thesis, California State University Long Beach, 1996.

Kunimoto, Iyo Iimura. "Japan and Mexico, 1888–1917." Ph.D. diss., University of Texas at Austin, 1975.

LaViolette, Forrest E., "Japanese Evacuation in Canada." *Far Eastern Survey* 11, no. 15 (1942).

Lee, Erika. "Enforcing the Borders: Chinese Exclusion along the US Borders with Canada and Mexico, 1882–1924." *The Journal of American History* 89, no. 1 (June 2002).

——. "Orientalism in the Americas: A Hemispheric Approach to Asian American History." *Journal of Asian American Studies* 8, no. 3 (October 2005), 235–58.

——. "Hemispheric Orientalism and the 1907 Pacific Coast Race Riots." *Amerasia Journal* 33, no. 2 (2007), 19–47.

Lee, Erika, and Naoko Shibusawa, "What Is Transnational Asian American History? Recent Trends and Challenges." *Journal of Asian American Studies* 8, no. 3 (October 2005), vii–xvii.

Lesser, Jeffrey. *Negotiating National Identity: Immigrants, Minorities, and the Struggle for Ethnicity in Brazil*. Durham, NC: Duke University Press, 1999.

López, Rick. "The India Bonita Contest of 1921 and the Ethnicization of Mexican National Culture." *Hispanic American Historical Review* 82, no. 2 (May 2002), 291–328.

Mallén, Bernardo. *¿En dónde están nuestras riquezas*. Mexico, D.F.: Muller Brothers Publishing, 1908.

Masabumi, Aoyama. *Karerawa Kakunnogotoku Mekishiko ni funto seri* (*The Japanese Struggle in Mexico*). Mexico, DF, 1938.

Mason, Gregory. "The Hyphen in Mexico." *Outlook*, January 17, 1917, 105.

Masterson, Daniel M., and Sayaka Funada-Classen, *The Japanese in Latin America*. Urbana: University of Illinois Press, 2004.

McKenzie, R.D. *Oriental Exclusion—the Effect of American Immigration Laws, Regulations, and Judicial Decisions upon the Chinese and Japanese on the American Pacific Coast*. Chicago: University of Chicago Press, 1928.

Michaelson, Scott. "Between Japanese American Internment and the USA Patriot Act: The Borderlands and the Permanent State of Racial Exception." *Aztlan* 30, no. 2 (Fall 2005).

Miki, Roy. *Redress: Inside the Japanese Canadian Call for Justice*. Vancouver, BC: Raincoast Books, 2005.

Minoru, Izawa, *Nihon-jin mekishiko ijushi* (*The History of the Japanese Immigrants in Mexico*). Tokyo: 1971.

Moriyama, Alan Takeo. *Imingaisha: Japanese Emigration Companies and Hawaii, 1894–1908*. Honolulu: University of Hawaii Press, 1985.

Motohiro, Takayama. *Mekishiko ni Kakeru Yume: Hagita Masanosuke to Nikkei Iminno Sekai*. (*A Dream over Mexico: Masanosuke Hagita and the World of the Japanese Immigrants*). Tokyo: Heibonsha, 1986.

Moya, Jose C. "A Continent of Immigrants: Postcolonial Shifts in the Western Hemisphere." *Hispanic American Historical Review* 86, no. 1 (February 2006), 1–28.

Navarro, Aaron W. *Political Intelligence and the Creation of Modern Mexico, 1938–1954*. University Park: Penn State University Press, 2010.

Navarro, Moises González. *Los Extranjeros en México y los Mexicanos en el Extranjero*, vol. 2, *1821–1970*. México, DF: El Colegio de México, 1993.

Niblo, Stephen R. *War, Diplomacy, and Development: The United States and Mexico, 1938–1954*. Wilmington, DE: SR Books, 1995.

Nihon Mekishiko Imin. (Japanese Emigration to Mexico). Tokyo: Japanese Compilation Committee on Immigration History,1971.

Nishi, Midori. "Some Aspects of Japanese Postwar Migration to Latin America." *Professional Geographer* 14, no. 1 (January 1962), 47–53.

Nobuya, Tsuchida. "The Japanese in Brazil, 1908–1941." PhD diss., University of California, Los Angeles, 1978.

Noriega, Juan Posada. *Mexico y Estados Unidos (Espana y el Japón)*. México, DF: 14 de Abril de 1939.

Nuttal, Zeila. *The Earliest Historical Relations between Mexico and Japan*. Berkeley: University of California Press, 1906.

Ogita, Masanosuke, and Taro Takano, *Cancion de Chontal: Canciones antiguas de aborigines Mexicanos*. Tokyo, Japon: Candelaria, 1983.

Omatsu, Maryka. *Bittersweet Passage and the Japanese Canadian Experience*. Toronto: Between the Lines, 1992.

Orlandi, Lorraine. "The Little Known Story of Japanese Migration, Assimilation, Suffering and Identity in Mexico." *Inside Mexico*, July 2007, 13–20.

Ota Mishima, María Elena. *México y Japón en el Siglo XIX: La política exterior de México y la consolidación de la soberanía Japonesa*. México, DF: Secretária de Relaciones Exteriores, 1976.

———. *Siete Migraciones Japonesas en México, 1890–1978*. México, DF: El Colegio de México, 1982.

———, ed. *Destino México. Un Estudio de las Migraciones Asiáticas a México, Siglos XIX y XX*. México, DF: El Colegio de México, 1997.

Patrias, Carmela. "Race, Employment Discrimination, and State Complicity in Wartime Canada, 1939–1945." *Labour* 59 (April 1, 2007).

Paz, Maria Emilia. *Strategy, Security, and Spies: Mexico and the US as Allies in World War II*. University Park: Pennsylvania State University Press, 1997.

Phillips, Hart R. "Propaganda Free_For_All." The Inter-American Monthly, Volume III, No. 9, (September 1944), 17–19, 47.

Pyle, Kenneth B. *The Making of Modern Japan*. Lexington: Heath, 1996.

Ramos Lanz, Miguel. *Estudio sobre Inmigración y Colonización*. Tip. de *El Tiempo*, Cerca de Sto. Domingo, no. 4 (1897), 8–9.

Rankin, Monica A. *Mexico, la Patria: Propaganda and Production during World War II*. Lincoln: University of Nebraska Press, 2009.

Rénique, Gerardo. "Race, Region, and Nation: Sonora's Anti-Chinese Racism and Mexico's Postrevolutionary Nationalism, 1920s–1930s." In *Race and Nation in Modern Latin America*, Nancy P. Appelbaum et al., eds. Chapel Hill: University of North Carolina Press, 2003.

Richmond, Douglas W. "Nationalism and Class Conflict in Mexico, 1910–1920." *Americas* 43, no. 3 (January 1987), 279–303.

Rippy, Fred J. "The Japanese in Latin America." *Inter-American Economic Affairs* 3, no. 1 (Summer 1949), 50–65.

Robinson, Greg. A *Tragedy of Democracy: Japanese Confinement in North America*. New York: Columbia University Press, 2009.

Rockefeller, Nelson A. "New Economic Frontier." *Inter-American Monthly* 1, no. 1 (May 1942), 18–20.

Romero, Jose Maria. *Mexico y la Colonizacion*. México, DF: 1901.

Romero, Robert. *The Chinese in Mexico, 1882–1940*. Tucson: University of Arizona Press, 2010.

Roosevelt, Franklin Delano. "No. 53 The Good Neighbor Policy." Reprinted in *Latin America and the United States: A Documentary History*, by Robert H. Holden and Eric Zolov. New York: Oxford University Press, 2000, 141–42.

Rubin, Jeffrey W. *Decentering the Regime: Ethnicity, Radicalism, and Democracy in Juchitan, Mexico*. Durham, NC: Duke University Press, 1997.

Said, Edward W. *Orientalism*. New York: Vintage Books, 1979.

Salazar Anaya, Delia. *La Población Extranera en México (1895–1990): Un Recuentro con Base en Los Generales de Población*. México, DF: Instituto Nacional de Antropología e Historia, 1996.

Sánchez, Emma Chrishuru Nakatani. "Memorias de un inmigrante japonés." *Istor* 6, no. 21 (Summer 2005), 142–48.

Sawada, Mitziko. "Culprits and Gentlemen: Meiji Japan's Restrictions of Emigrants to the United States, 1891–1909." *Pacific Historical Review* 60, no. 3 (August 1991), 339–59.

Schuler, Friedrich E. *Mexico between Hitler and Roosevelt: Mexican Foreign Relations in the Age of Lázaro Cárdenas, 1934–1940*. Albuquerque: University of New Mexico Press, 1998.

Schurz, William Lytle. "Acapulco and the Manila Galleon." *Southwestern Historical Quarterly* 22 (July 1918–April 1919), 18–37.

Scott, James C. *Weapons of the Weak: Everyday Forms of Peasant Resistance*. New Haven, CT: Yale University Press, 1985.

Skidmore, Thomas E. "Racial Ideas and Social Policy in Brazil, 1870–1940." In *The Idea of Race in Latin America, 1870–1940*, Richard Graham, ed. Austin: University of Texas Press, 1990.

Smith, Benjamin. *Pistoleros and Popular Movements: The Politics of State Formation in Postrevolutionary Oaxaca*. Lincoln: University of Nebraska Press, 2009.

St. John, Burton, III, "An Enduring Legacy of World War I: Propaganda, Journalism and the Domestic Struggle over the Commodification of Truth." In *War and the Media: Essays on News Reporting, Propaganda and Popular Culture*, Paul M. Haridakis et al., eds. Jefferson, NC: McFarland, 2009, 149–51.

Stern, Alexandra Minna. "From Mestizophilia to Biology: Racialization and Science of Mexico, 1920–1960." In *Race and Nation in Modern Latin America*, Nancy P. Applebaum, Anne S, Macpherson, and Karin Alejandra Rosemblatt, eds. Chapel Hill: University of North Carolina Press, 2003, 187–210.

———. "Eugenics and Racial Classification in Modern Mexican America." In *Race and Classification: The Case of Mexican America*, Illona Katzew and Susan Deans-Smith, eds. Palo Alto, CA: Stanford University Press, 2009.

Tanabe, Atsuko. *Huellas Japonesas en la Cultura Mexicana*. Juan Manuel Rivera y Yukako Yoshida, trans. México, DF: Programa de Estudio Japoneses El Colegio De La Frontera, 1997.

Tigner, James Lawrence. "Mexico and Japan: A Trans-Pacific Historical Survey." Undated, unpublished manuscript in the author's possession.

Tobler, Hans Werner. "Peasants and the Shaping of the Revolutionary State, 1910–1940." In *Riot, Rebellion, and Revolution: Rural Social Conflict in Mexico*, Friedrich Katz, ed. Princeton, NJ: Princeton University Press, 1988.

Tsunoyama, Yukihiro. *Enomoto Buyo (Takeaki) to Mekishiko Shokumin Iju*. (*Takeaki Enomoto and Migration to Mexican Settlements*). Tokyo: Dobunken, 1986.

Ueno, Hisashi. *Mekishiko Enomoto Shokumin* (*Enomoto Settlement in Mexico*). Tokyo: Chuo Koron-Sha, 1994.

Watanabe, Chizuko. "The Japanese Immigrant Community in Mexico: Its History and Present." M.A. thesis, California State University, Los Angeles, 1983.

Wodon de Sorinne, Guillermo. *La Colonizacion de Mexico*. México, DF: Oficina Tipografica de la Secretaria de Fomento, 1902.

Womack, John, Jr. "The Mexican Revolution, 1910–1920." In *Mexico since Independence*, Leslie Bethell, ed. Cambridge: Cambridge University Press, 1991.

Wright, Luke E. Dispatch to Mr. Root, American Embassy, Tokyo, December 26, 1906. In Japanese Emigration and Immigration. Woodbridge, CT: Research Publications, 1988.

Yamamoto, Atsuko. *Mekishiko in Ikiru Nikkei Immintachi* (*Japanese Immigrants Living in Mexico*). Tokyo: Kawaide Shobo Shinsha, 1988.

Yanaguida, Toshio, and Taeko Akagui, "Mexico y Los Emigrantes Japonesas." *Estudios Migratorios Latinoamericanos* 10, no. 30 (1995), 373–402.

Yasutaro, Taki. *Mekishiko Kokujo Taikan-Mexico, Gran Amigo del Japón a través de los 70 años*. México, DF: Meshiko Shimpo, 1968.

Yukihiro, Tsunoyama. *Enomoto Buyo to Mekishiko Shokumin Iju* (Buyo Enomoto and Migration to Mexican Settlements). Tokyo: Dobunkan, 1986.

Index

Page numbers in italics indicate illustrations.

About the Author

Jerry García is the former director of the Chicano Education Program (CEP) and the College Assistance Migrant Program at Eastern Washington University (EWU) and is currently on the faculty with CEP and the Department of History at EWU. He received his PhD from Washington State University. Prior to his appointment at EWU, he was an assistant professor at Michigan State University and Iowa State University.

García's research examines Japanese immigration to Mexico and the Japanese experience in the United States. In addition to his present book, he has published several books and articles on the Chicano and Mexican experience in the United States, including *Mexicanos in North Central Washington* (2007); the collection *Memory, Community, and Activism: Mexican Migration and Labor in the Pacific Northwest*, coedited with Gilberto García (2005); "The Measure of a Cock: Mexican Cockfighting, Culture, and Masculinity," in Chon Noriega and Wendy Belcher, editors, *I am Aztlán: The Personal Essay in Chicano Studies* (2004); "Mexicanos, *Teamsters* y granjeros en el estado de Washington: inmigracion y raza en la industria de la manzana," in *Economía, política y cultura transfronteriza: 5 ensayos* (2011), edited by Roberto Sanchez Benitez; and "Becoming Latino: Empires, Hierarchies, and Immigrants," in the online database *The American Mosaic: The Latino American Experience* (2010). He is currently working on two manuscripts that examine Mexican cockfighting and the Chicano movement in the Pacific Northwest, respectively.